C000185826

THE AUDI FILE

AN ERIC DYMOCK MOTOR BOOK

THE AUDI FILE

ALL MODELS SINCE 1888

AN ERIC DYMOCK MOTOR BOOK

DOVE PUBLISHING

First published in Great Britain in 1997 by
DOVE PUBLISHING
Old Chapel House, Sutton Veny, Wiltshire BA12 7AY

Revised and updated 1998

Designed by Ruth Dymock
Consultant designers
Andrew Barron & Collis Clements Associates

British Library Cataloguing-in-Publication Data A catalogue record
for this book is available from the British Library

ISBN 0 9534142 0 5

Colour separation by
Fotographics Ltd, London and Hong Kong

Printed & bound in Slovenia by Printing House Mladinska knjiga
by arrangement with Korotan Ljubljana

Publisher's Foreword

The Audi File was the first in Dove Publishing's series of one-make books which have come to be regarded as definitive car-by-car histories. It has also been the first to be updated and, in response to some criticisms of the first edition, thoroughly revised to ensure it meets the standards of accuracy and comprehensiveness that the other books in the series have achieved. The research involved in compiling detailed specifications of cars built up to a hundred years ago is often a daunting task. Its magnitude makes it almost impossible to produce a book like this without access to a manufacturer's archives as well as an undertaking to buy a large portion of the book's print run. It was through Audi's pioneering tradition and with Audi UK's former managing director Len Hunt's encouragement that The Audi File was first in the field. Updating it with the latest models not only brings the book up to date but shows, we think, the virtue of an ingenious format that will make the "File" series of continuing value through the years.

Eric and Ruth Dymock

1937
AUDI

The key to the history of the four-ringed symbol that came to symbolise Audi, was the amalgamation in 1932 of the leading companies in the motor industry of Saxony, the German state south of Berlin on the borders of Bavaria and Bohemia. To the north lay the featureless farmlands of Magdeburg, and the industrial triangle of Dessau, Halle, and Leipzig. To the south in Upper Saxony, a necklace of commercial and cultural cities stretched from Görlitz on the Polish border, right across to Eisenach on the very threshold of Rhenish Prussia in the east.

Left: **Audi Front, 1937. Audi's commitment to front wheel drive began in the Auto Union era. Ferdinand Porsche himself drew up the prototype.**

These cities lay along the Erzgebirge, from which the Elbe, the Oder, and the Spree flow to the North Sea and the Baltic. They included Dresden, Chemnitz (Karl-Marx-Stadt in East German times), Zwickau, Jena, Weimar, and Erfurt. Here the peaks of Saxon Switzerland and the beautiful Thuringer Wald, a crescent of imposing, wooded uplands, cradled much of the German motor industry.

The four-ringed symbol, based shamelessly on the Olympic one, represented the four makes of car that came together to form the Auto Union. They joined together in an effort to weather the financial storms that followed the Great Depression, and the threat of what their leaders saw as state interventionism on a gigantic scale. The firms were Audi, DKW, Horch, and Wanderer. The midwife at the birth of Auto Union was the State Bank of Saxony, but the four parents already had long and distinguished careers behind them.

By rights the Audi symbol of the 1930s should have gained a fifth ring in the 1970s, for in 1969 the four parents, reconstituted as Auto Union GmbH, were joined by NSU whose roots went back farther than any of them, to the fledgling bicycle industry of 1873. Skill in bending and joining tubes went a long way towards creating the first cars that wheezed on to Germany's dusty roads.

Two Swabians, Christian Schmidt and Heinrich Stoll, set out to capitalise on the economic boom that followed the Franco-Prussian war of 1870, and set up business in Riedlingen on the Danube to make knitting machines. Customs unions between European states are not new and, although the German one of the 1870s was largely protectionist, they hoped to benefit from it. In 1879 the partnership broke up, Schmidt started making bicycles, and named the product from the initials of his Neckarsulmer Strickmaschinen Union, NSU.

The business prospered and NSU made its first car using the same wheel-making, bearing and steering technology that it used for two-wheelers. Technical director L Zeidler was appointed to draw up plans for Daimler's first four-wheeler in December 1888, and among the pioneering features the company developed were oil seals to keep dust out of pedals, and a ball-bearing bottom bracket. It was a major step forward in bicycle design.

So when it began to build motorcycles, NSU was already something of an innovator. Contracts to design cars came from Peugeot among others, but when it came to making them, NSU chose a well-

tried design from Pipe in Belgium. It was only a year before the Original Neckarsulmer Motorwagen went into production, and in 1911 the car appeared that would form the company's main product line until 1925, the NSU 8/24 2.1-litre 4-cylinder.

Motorcycles remained the mainstay although NSU cars received wide publicity through success in motoring sport, particularly the 1909 Prince Henry Trial. It repeated the accomplishment in 1923 when three NSUs finished first, second, and third in the small-car class at the Berlin Avus races on a track which incorporated the world's first motorway, and again in 1924 with the supercharged 5/15. NSU crowned further wins in 1925 by taking the first four places in the 1926 German Grand Prix with supercharged 1.5-litre 6-cylinder cars, the winner Klöble averaging 80mph (128.8kph) for almost 250 miles (400 kms).

NSU made cars until the end of the decade, but the cold winds of economic change were blowing through Germany and it was forced to sell its car interests to Fiat. By the time it regained its independence in 1932, motorcycling was once again in the ascendant, and after briefly examining Dr Ferdinand Porsche's ideas for a 'peoples' car, turned once more to motorcycles until 1957 when it brought out the NSU Prinz.

Ten years later it created one of the most ground-breaking designs in the history of motoring. The twin-rotor Wankel-engined NSU Ro80, elected Car of the Year in 1968, held out such promise that the following year the shareholders voted for a merger with Auto Union GmbH Ingolstadt, creating Audi-NSU Auto Union AG, in which Volkswagenwerk AG held a major interest.

The oldest of the four four-ring pioneers, Wanderer, was established in 1885 in Chemnitz, Saxony. Like NSU it was essentially a product of the flourishing bicycle industry of the 1880s. There was a lust for travel. The railways were making tracks to the corners of the Continent and road machines soon followed them. Wanderer started making motorcycles in 1902 but it was 1911 before serious car production got under way.

When it did, it was a winner. The Püppchen was an instant hit, with its 4-cylinder 1.5-litre engine and modest 43mph (70kph) top speed. By virtue of its military service between 1914 and 1918 it brought motoring to a new generation, and by the time the soldiers returned, the world they wanted to live in was to be furnished with cars.

Below: Wanderer Sport, 1931. Rakish lines, twin spare wheels, luggage trunk were essential on touring cars of the 1930s. Elegant Gläser bodywork typifies new-age motoring on new-age autobahns.

Above: Audi 1922 Type K 4 cylinder 3.5 litre 14/50. Aluminium cylinder block with pressed-in liners, ball-action gearshift, four wheel brakes. Vorsprung durch Technik.

August Horch set up in business in 1899 at Cologne-Ehrenfeld in the west of Germany, moved in 1902 to Plauen in the Vogtland, then in 1904 as a public company eastwards to Zwickau in Saxony. Horch Automobile made an impression on the sporting world when its enthusiastic founder entered an 18/22 model in the 1906 second Herkomer Rally. It was driven by Dr Stöss, and he won the event outright.

Alas like many gifted entrepreneurs Dr Horch did not get on with his fellow directors and he left in 1909. Under the conditions of his severance agreement he was forbidden to make cars under his own name. His old Horch company got on with the job of producing some of the best cars in Germany, while its founder promptly confounded his erstwhile colleagues and set up business making cars again.

Forced to find a new name for August Horch Automobilwerke GmbH, he Latinised his own German Horch (Hark!) into Audi (Listen!), and in 1910 Audi GmbH was accepted by the registrar of companies.

In August 1911, still an enthusiastic sporting motorist, Horch won the Austrian Alpine Rally at the wheel of one of his own Audis. His range of cars included a small 8/22, 10/28, and 14/35, as well as a large 18/45 and 22/55 with distinctive narrow pointed radiators.

The History of the Four Rings

Left: Enterprising Dane Jörgen Skafte Rasmussen came as student, and remained in Saxony when he gained engineering degree. Only 25, he co-founded Rasmussen & Ernst, boilermakers, Zwickau, in 1903.

Below: "The greatest motorcycle factory in the world", runs the 1930 caption to the DKW works in Zschopau. J S Rasmussen had come a long way since he stopped making boilers.

DKW also put down roots in Chemnitz. In 1904 a Danish entrepreneur, Jörgen Skafte Rasmussen, and a friend started Rasmussen & Ernst GmbH, buying an empty textile works at Zschopau in the Erzgebirge to make metal products. In 1914 the Zschopauer Maschinenfabrik J S Rasmussen engaged in military work and experimented with a large and, as it turned out, unwieldy, steam vehicle the Dampf Kraft Wagen (DKW – Steam-Power-Vehicle).

The 1920s were hard for small car companies. The four made headway only slowly. Wanderer got car production under way in 1923 with its 6/24 and in 1925 put Germany's first continuous assembly line for motorcycles into operation. The following year the first Wanderer car, with left hand drive and four wheel brakes, became the company's principal product and a new factory was erected at Siegmar near Chemnitz to make cheap cars bearing Wanderer's double-wing emblem.

Above: The original Dampf Kraft Wagen (DKW) of 1916. Heavy, clumsy, and soon discarded.

Horch aimed for the high ground, and its 1926 303 was the first German production car with an 8-cylinder engine. Professor Hadank designed a winged arrow motif for the bonnet emblem and in 1930 the Type 500, an 8-cylinder partly designed by the notable Fritz Fiedler, was introduced. The following year the 12-cylinder 670 was displayed at the Paris motor show.

DKW persevered with motorcycles until its first primitive car in 1928, but at the 1931 Berlin motor show made a notable breakthrough with the world's first production car with front wheel drive. Audi introduced four wheel brakes in 1923, introduced the memorable 8-cylinder Imperator in 1928, installed licence-built American Rickenbacker engines in the Zwickau and an in-line 6-cylinder in the Dresden.

Yet innovation and enterprise did not bring prosperity. DKW had to acquire a major shareholding in Audi, and Rasmussen became chairman of the supervisory board. Horch cars were too

Below: DKW cyclecar. Bicycle technology pressed into service for primitive single-seat runabout.

expensive for the post-Depression era and the company fell into debt.

By 1932 car sales in Germany had halved from 90,000 to 45,000. DKW began to suffer from Rasmussen's expansionism and, to make things worse, the new Hitler regime announced plans for a state-sponsored car at a seemingly impossible price, to be designed by Professor Ferdinand Porsche. The industry protested in alarm but was unable to change the course of events.

An amalgamation was proposed and after nine months of negotiation to agree terms and acquire funds from the state and the banks, Horch, Audi, and DKW merged to form a new company. With headquarters based by 1936 at Chemnitz, the Zschopauer Motorenwerke raised its share capital from 4.5 million Reichsmarks to 14.5 million and the new Auto Union AG bought Wanderer and leased its factories to add the fourth ring to the badge. DKW's contribution of share capital was RM10 million, Horch brought RM500,000, Audi RM2,500,000, and Wanderer RM15,730,000. The new combine had

a staff of 4,500 and factories at Zschopau making motorcycles and two-stroke engines, Zwickau (cars), Berlin-Spandau (wooden body frames) and Siegmar (cars and steel bodies).

Auto Union was now a major player in the German motor industry alongside Adler, BMW, Opel, Daimler-Benz, and Ford. The Volkswagen had not yet appeared.

Motor racing provided an opportunity for the group to forge an identity, and it took up a German state subsidy to build a 16-cylinder car designed by Professor Porsche, inaugurating a momentous period of grand prix motor racing. It was the 1930s equivalent of the space race, with Mercedes-Benz and Auto Union struggling for supremacy in a contest that overwhelmed all opposition. As a demonstration of German technical pre-eminence it was a triumph.

Auto Union's production cars were carefully positioned. DKW, with a workforce of 13,500, was making 27,200 cars a year and 23,700 motorcycles, mostly for the cheaper end of the market. Its two-stroke engines were successful and it exploited technical innovations such as front wheel drive. Wanderer put out a fine range of eleven models, middle-class, worthy, and well-made. Audi then, as now, occupied the technical high ground with its famous Audi Front. It was priced then as now in the upper-middle segment. Horch kept its strong luxury-market character, making some of the most dramatic and expensive cars in the world.

The war years took Auto Union into armament production along with the rest of German industry, the group workforce reaching 48,000. The factories emerged badly damaged, some beyond repair, and mostly in Soviet-controlled East Germany. The bulk of the equipment and machinery in the Horch plant at Zwickau, the DKW works at Zschopau and the

Wanderer factory at Chemnitz was dismantled and sent to the Soviet Union. Avtovelo, a state organisation, took over the former BMW plant at Eisenach as well as the old Auto Union, and built a modified DKW F-8 called the IFA (Industrial Collective for Automobiles). This was later superseded by a 1939 prototype 3-cylinder F-9, but it never prospered.

Left: DKW 1950 F-89 Meisterklasse. Slippery shape, stylish lines of two door coupe provided German motorists with a touch of class as the economic miracle took shape. Düsseldorf factory well equipped for monocoque structure to replace old-style chassis.

Opposite: Audi works at Zwickau, 1932.

25140

The History of the Four Rings

Accordingly in 1945 there were contenders in both East and West Germany claiming rights to the old company. The entire country's economy lay in ruins, along with much of its infrastructure, but by 1948 with the arrival of Marshall Aid and the currency reform by the federal finance minister Ludwig Erhardt which introduced the Deutsche Mark, West Germany turned the corner and the economic miracle was under way.

There was a demand for spare parts for DKWs, of which some 60,000 of the quarter-million two-strokes made pre-war survived in West Germany alone. The former president, Dr Richard Bruhn, and the sales director, Carl Hahn, found themselves in the west when the new German frontiers were drawn up, and began business in Ingolstadt with a DKW spare parts centre, claiming the rights to the old titles.

Left: Dr Richard Bruhn. Prime mover, state bank of Saxony nominee and first chairman of Auto Union AG, 1932.

Below: Four rings reborn. DKW Junior made at Ingolstadt imported to UK 1964.

The History of the Four Rings

In September 1949, ten years after the start of the second world war, the new Auto Union GmbH was officially inaugurated under the old name and four-ringed emblem, with loans from the state of North-Rhine Westphalia, reconstruction credits, and a local authority grant which paid for rebuilding the bomb-damaged Rheinmetall-Borsig plant in Düsseldorf.

It made a car based on pre-war designs with the 688cc transverse two-stroke twin-cylinder engine from the F-8, and a body intended for a 1940 F-9. The engine was little changed, and the fuel feed was by a mechanical pump instead of a scuttle-mounted gravity tank. The old backbone frame was discarded in favour of a sturdy box section chassis, and the rear suspension was by a transverse spring and dead axle beam. DKW wanted to reduce the heavy fuel consumption of the two-stroke and invoked the help of smooth aerodynamics. Flush headlights, full-width bodywork, and a long tail enclosing the luggage boot gave it a fashionable appearance and a smooth profile. The car was only eight inches (20.3cm) from

ground to floor, and 57 inches (144.7cm) tall.

Introduced at the 1950 Frankfurt motor show, the DKW looked well-engineered, stylish and carefully detailed in a frugal world where cheap engines mattered more than clever ones. Two-stroke rival manufacturers included Saab in Sweden, Champion, Goliath, Gutbrod, Hanomag, IFA, and Lloyd.

In a bold move, Auto Union made the DKW dearer than a Volkswagen. Production began in 1950 and in the first 12 months the rebuilt DKW factory made 1,380 cars, 6,873 vans and 24,606 motorcycles. By 1954 it was making nearly 60,000 cars and about to introduce a new model. It had made its high price stick, it was in a prospering market, and began to generate useful profits for Auto Union. Ingolstadt grew from being a spare parts depot to a major centre of car production.

In 1958 Daimler-Benz took 88% of Auto Union shares, acquired the Düsseldorf plant in 1962, and began a major expansion at Ingolstadt. Two years later the share capital was increased from

DM80 million to DM160 million. This was purchased by Volkswagen along with the Daimler-Benz shares, the cars were known as Auto Union DKWs, and in 1965 a 72bhp Audi, with a four-stroke engine developed from the DKW F-102, signified the end of the two-stroke. Audi was re-born under the Auto Union colours as a separate make in its own right.

The 1969 merger with NSU created a major force in the world motor industry, passing a significant milestone in 1973 with the millionth Audi to be made since its 1965 resurrection.

Audi's development was swift. Its position in 1970, with a workforce of 26,000 and 6,000 dealers in Germany and abroad, provided it with a platform to launch a range of cars commencing with the Audi 100, revealed at the 1969 Frankfurt motor show, and its companion 100 Coupe S. Their success was based on front wheel drive, superior handling and roadholding, a keen sense of style, and high levels of domestic demand. Soon Audi was producing cars to the limits of its capacity, and launched the Super

90 and the two-door 100 in North America. A design and development centre was inaugurated at Ingolstadt, and in 1973 the new Audi 80 created under Dipl Ing Ludwig Kraus received the accolade of Car of the Year from an international jury of motoring writers. The workforce expanded to 31,174 in Ingolstadt, Neckarsulm, Heilbronn, and Neuenstein. Awards proliferated, with the Audi 100LS voted Automobile of the Year by the American magazine Motor Trend.

The second fuel crisis of the 1970s was at its height when work began on a new Audi 100. In an effort to make it as economical as possible, it was designed as one of the most aerodynamic production cars ever. Its wind resistance was the lowest for the class, and its curved side windows and smooth detailing set a pattern which the industry soon followed.

It was one of the best envelopes for carrying five people at speed ever devised. The steep slope of the side windows had to be reduced later because Audi said it made the inside of the car like a greenhouse, needing as much energy to cool with air-conditioning as was saved through low fuel consumption.

The Audi 50 appeared in 1974, Porsche contracted out production of its 924 model to Audi at Neckarsulm, and in 1976 the new Audi 100 demonstrated Audi's radical approach to technical innovation with the world's first production 5-cylinder engine. Vorsprung durch Technik was given a further boost with the construction of the VW Iltis at Ingolstadt, leading in 1980 to the introduction of road-going quattro four wheel drive passenger cars at the 1980 Geneva motor show.

Right: Rump of 1971 Audi. Original caption says, "...rear part of Audi models redesigned so that it appears broader and appeals more to public. It can radiate charm and grace."

Audi's pioneering work in miniaturising four wheel drive to make it practical for cars was little short of revolutionary. The development contract from the West German Wehrmacht for the cross-country Iltis, provided the cash to design and develop a lightweight, strong four wheel drive system.

The engineers at Audi hit on the idea of running one shaft within another inside the complicated gearbox needed to take the drive to both sets of wheels, and made four wheel drive sufficiently small and light to work in a car. It was so efficient it hardly used up any extra power, unlike the heavy patterns used in conventional cross-country vehicles and trucks.

With the possible exceptions of skiers or mountain guides Audi was still unsure who would buy a four wheel drive car. It seemed unwise to go to the expense of a new body, so the Audi Coupe was pressed into service, the wheel arches flared to make space for wider wheels and tyres, and the 5-cylinder engine was turbocharged, another example of Audi's bold, innovative, radical approach to engineering.

The Quattro's potential as a rally car was clear, but it needed more power to exploit the astonishing grip that came from putting the drive through four, not just two wheels. Good traction on loose surfaces enabled the driver to accelerate hard out of corners without wasting power spinning the wheels.

The first cars were less than perfect. The 5-cylinder engine producing large amounts of power was rough and noisy. Turbo lag, the pause between opening the throttle and the turbocharger spinning up to speed, made it difficult

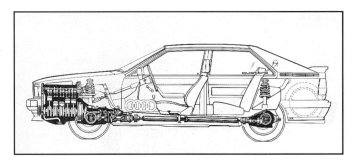

to drive without progressing in a series of sudden leaps and bounds. Yet the Quattro changed the course of rallying. By the 1980s it was winning more or less as it pleased, and rivals quickly converted to four wheel drive in order to keep up. It became almost obligatory for fast road cars such as the Porsche 959. Four wheel drive provided such a margin of safety and grip, that powerful all-weather road cars came to need it just as much as anti-lock brakes and limited-slip differentials.

In the way of these things, the pioneering Quattro had to deal with cleverer adversaries. It suffered from understeer, the tendency to plough straight on at corners, and when anti-lock braking was developed, it proved difficult to incorporate.

Left: Stroke of genius. Four-ring quattro, with permanent four wheel drive and inter-axle and rear differentials that could be locked on the move.

Right: Stirling Moss (on right) drives 140mph Audi Sport in 1981 British saloon car championship with youthful Martin Brundle.

Yet once its initial difficulties were overcome, the Quattro's handling and roadholding were almost beyond reproach. Its road grip was secure; its anti-lock brakes worked in conjunction with four wheel drive in all conditions.

The Quattro was only the first in a series of Audi innovations that marked it out for technical leadership. In 1989 a new low-emission engine was

announced for the Audi 80 turbo-diesel. The 1.8-litre exceeded the exhaust control laws introduced in the United States in 1983, which were to form the basis of European standards due in 1990, and were acknowledged to be the world's strictest.

Audi reduced pollutants by injecting the fuel precisely according to engine load so that less of it remained unburnt, and adjusting the temperature of the ingoing charge so that it used more efficiently. The engine gulped in extra air to clean the gases coming out. A side-effect of the improved efficiency was that it was more economical than the car it replaced, while performance was unaffected.

Audi's introduction of fully galvanised bodies provoked a change in automotive culture round the world. Its competitors improved their rust-resistance to a point where by the 1990s it was

no longer a major issue. Audi's engineering was a match for BMW or Mercedes-Benz while remaining less ostentatious than either. Its comfort and equipment levels were just as classy down to the shiny, wood trim without being copyist or imitative.

Its technical mettle was tested in the hybrid car of 1990, an alternative to all-electric cars which suffered from a limited range and could not keep up with urban traffic. Audi revealed a hybrid vehicle which could do shopping trips on electricity and use an ordinary engine on the motorway.

It never forgot that electricity was a means of transmitting power, not a source of power, and the electric car had not come very far since 1899, when Camille Jenatzy set the record for the flying kilometre with one at 65.79 mph. It had to have its batteries charged before it could do the return kilometre, and ninety years of development had not seen much real progress in terms of speed, range, or the weight and space needed to carry electricity. Even with sodium-sulphur or nickel-cadmium technology, a four-ton battery the size of a 550 gallon petrol tank was needed to provide a family car's 500 mile range and 100 mph performance. California had called for 1.7 million electric cars by

Left: Vorsprung durch aluminium.

Below: Hannu Mikkola won the 1983 world rally championship in Audi quattro. With Arne Hertz co-driving he won 1981 Lombard RAC Rally by ten clear minutes, here finishing second in 1983 to clinch title.

the year 2000 and seven cars in every ten to be electrically powered by 2010, but there seemed little hope of a pollution-free vehicle with anything better than the performance of a milk-float. Electric vehicles were able to go a long way slowly, or a short way quickly, but not both.

The Audi hybrid represented a practical response, using an Avant quattro, and installing an electric motor to drive the rear wheels, leaving the combustion engine (petrol or diesel) to drive the front ones. The advantage of the quattro was that the drive to the rear wheels was already in place, and the electric motor could be installed neatly in the transmission tunnel, driving through an electrically operated clutch.

Audi's new generation of racing cars, the dramatic quattro Spyder, Avus, and TT of the 1990s, and the striking aluminium body of the A8, created a reputation for technical and sporting achievement from the spindly beginnings before the end of the 19th century to the threshold of the 21st. This book is a portrait of the cars that made their contribution.

Daimler commissioned NSU at Neckarsulm to build what was in effect its very first production car. Just ten were made, using the expertise it had built up making bicycles.

The simple tubular steel chassis carried the vee-twin cylinder engine beneath the seat, with the drive being taken to the rear wheel through bevel gearing; braking was by a simple external contracting system operating on the right-hand rear wheel alone. The front wheels were carried in bicycle-type forks, with a link between the heads running to the steering tiller. At the front the wire-spoked wheels were 900mm diameter, while at the rear they were 1000mm.

The name Stahlradwagen translates as the steel – or wire – wheel car. The public got its first chance to see it at the Paris World Fair in 1889. Picture shows surface carburettor and Zahnrad four speed gearbox.

BODY
Open 2 seater.
ENGINE
2 cylinders in 45deg vee; mid; 60.0x100.0.0mm, 566cc;

1.1 kW(1.5bhp); 1.9 kW/l (2.7bhp/l).
ENGINE STRUCTURE
Automatic inlet, side exhaust; 2 valves per cylinder; 1 gear driven side camshaft; cast iron cylinder head and block; 2 bearing crankshaft; single carburettor; water cooled.
TRANSMISSION
Rear wheel drive; separate 4 speed gearbox; bevel final drive.
CHASSIS DETAILS
Tubular steel chassis; no suspension front or rear; single external contracting drum brake on one rear wheel.
DIMENSIONS
Wheelbase 140.0cm (55.1in), front track 115.0cm (45.3in), rear track 115.0cm (45.3in).
PERFORMANCE
Maximum speed 11-12mph (18-22km/h).

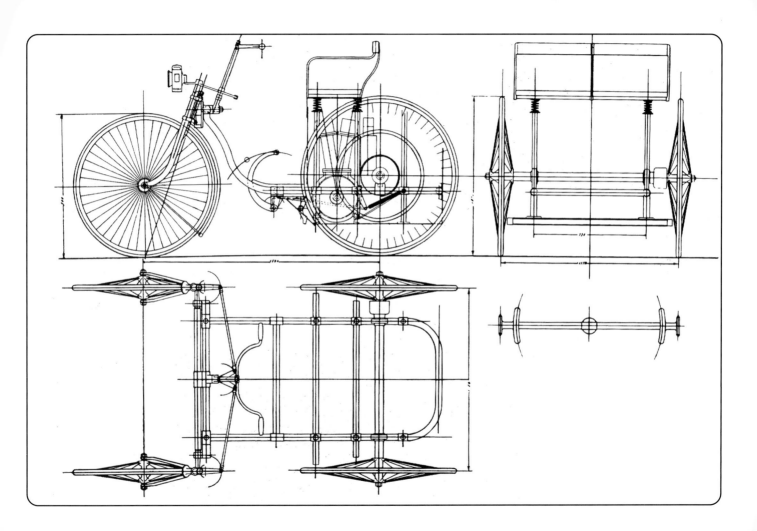

August Horch produced two prototypes before he started series production in the new plant at Zwickau near Chemnitz, in eastern Germany.

The first car made between 1900 and 1902, the 4-5, had its twin cylinder engine lying flat, with a chain drive to the rear wheels. Horch produced and sold around 10 of this model at a price of 2,300 marks. The second prototype, built at Reichenbach between 1902 and 1904, kept the twin cylinder layout, but with the engine running vertically. This model, with a tonneau-style body, cost 7,300 marks.

Horch suffered the fate of many car pioneers. An ardent technician, he fell out with his partners and shareholders, and left the firm A. Horch & Cie Motorwagenwerke AG in 1909. He had worked for Karl Benz before setting up on his own in 1900. Forbidden by contract to put his own name on a car ever again, he called his new production 'Audi', a Latinised version of his name 'Listen!' in German.

BODY
Open four-seater.
ENGINE
2 cylinders in line; front.
ENGINE STRUCTURE
Overhead inlet, side exhaust; 2 valves per cylinder; 1 gear driven side camshaft; cast iron cylinder head and block; 2 bearing crankshaft; single carburettor; water cooled.
TRANSMISSION
Rear wheel drive.
CHASSIS DETAILS
Separate steel chassis; steel and fabric body; front suspension, dead axle, semi-elliptic springs; rear suspension, live axle, semi-elliptic springs.
PERFORMANCE
Maximum speed 19mph (30km/h).

Right: Echoes of a small carriage and bicycle technology combined to create the first Horch prototypes. Pioneer motorists perched up in the dust and draught with the engine at the front, and gear drive underneath. A 4/5hp two-cylinder of 1901, one of ten built at Ehrenfeld. Body is by Utermöhle.

HORCH 14/17 1904

After producing the two prototypes, August Horch et Cie moved east from Cologne to Zwickau, close to the Czech border. It was here that the first true production models were built. The 14/17 used the paired cylinder type of construction, but still with the overhead inlet, side exhaust valve layout. Unusually for the period, this model also had a four-speed gearbox, with a shaft rather than chain drive to the rear axle.

A 16/20 version used the same sized engine, although with a slightly higher output.

BODY
Two-door; 4 seat; tonneau.
ENGINE
4 cylinders, in line; front; 85x100mm; 10.3kW(17bhp); 2680cc.
ENGINE STRUCTURE
Overhead inlet, side exhaust; 2 valves per cylinder; 1 gear driven side camshaft; cast iron cylinder head and block; 3 bearing crankshaft; single carburettor; water cooled.
TRANSMISSION
Rear wheel drive; separate 4 speed gearbox; spiral bevel final drive.
CHASSIS DETAILS
Separate steel chassis; steel and fabric body; front suspension, dead axle, semi-elliptic springs; rear suspension, live axle, semi-elliptic springs; 820x120 tyres.
DIMENSIONS
Wheelbase 218.0cm (85.8in).

Left and right: Horch's first production model followed the established chassis layout of the period. It was available with just one body style, a four-seater tonneau.

WANDERER 2-cylinder 1904

Wanderer was not registered as a company 'to produce motor cars and motor car parts' until 1906, but its founders Johann Winklhofer and Richard Jaenicke had been in the bicycle business since 1885. They brought in Eugen Buschmann to design their first prototype car. The original twin-cylinder model taught them many lessons, among which was the fact that with 1.9 litres, the running was hardly smooth. The chassis also needed improvement, with better braking and suspension. The No 1 prototype survived in the Dresden Motor Museum.

The change from repairing and selling English penny-farthing cycles, to manufacture of its own bicycles and then cars, brought about the transformation of the company from Chemnitzer-Veloziped-Fabrik Winklhofer und Jaenicke to Wanderer Fahrrad-Werke Winklhofer and Jaenicke in 1896. A fire in the workshop at Chemnitz in 1897 obliged the firm to move to larger premises in the Hartmannstrasse for production of its first three-wheeler.

BODY
4 door double phaeton, 4 seats; 600kg (1320lb).

ENGINE
2 cylinders in line; front; 100.0x120.0 mm, 1884cc; 8.8kW (12bhp) @ 1200rpm; 4.7kW/l (6.7bhp/l).

ENGINE STRUCTURE
Side valve; 2 valves per cylinder; one side camshaft; cast iron cylinder head and block; 2 bearing crankshaft; single carburettor; water cooled.

TRANSMISSION
Rear wheel drive; separate 3 speed gearbox.

CHASSIS DETAILS
Separate steel chassis, steel bodywork; front suspension, dead axle, semi-elliptic springs; rear suspension, live axle, semi-elliptic springs; single drum brake on transmission.

DIMENSIONS
Wheelbase 213.0cm (83.9in), front track 125.0cm (49.2in), rear track 125.0cm (49.1in), overall length 315.0cm (124.0 in), overall width 155.0cm (59.1 in), overall height 200.0cm (78.7in).

PERFORMANCE
Maximum speed 25 mph (40kph), 68.2kg/kW (50.0kg/bhp).

Right: Winklhofer and Jaenicke manufactory was an imposing building in Chemnitz between Leipzig and Dresden in the eastern part of Germany north of the Erzgebirge. *Far right:* Johann Baptist Winklhofer (left) and Richard Adolf Jaenicke set up a repair shop for the elegant but tricky solid-tyred penny-farthing.

Although NSU was becoming established as a maker of motor cycles, this was its first motor car. Rather than invest precious capital in designing an engine for its new model, the company chose to make the Belgian Pipe unit under licence. Its unusual feature was the rather complex arrangement needed to operate the inclined inlet and exhaust valves. Two gear driven camshafts were used, in line with the crankshaft. Long pushrods then actuated inverted rocker arms, which in turn operated the valves. The system worked well enough, except that the engine was physically very wide and extremely heavy.

NSU's survival in the years following the bicycle boom was due to its decision in 1901 to make motorcycles. It became a large company with a workforce of 400 in 1904, which rose to 1200 by 1911 by joining in the prosperity that came with the growing economic strength of the German Empire.

BODY
Four-door, four seat saloon; 1810kg (3982lb).

ENGINE
4 cylinders in line; front; 20.5kW(28bhp).

ENGINE STRUCTURE
Ohv; 2 valves per cylinder; 2 gear driven side camshafts; cast iron cylinder head and block; 3 bearing crankshaft; single carburettor; water cooled.

TRANSMISSION
Rear wheel drive; separate 4 speed gearbox; bevel final drive.

CHASSIS DETAILS
Separate steel chassis; steel and fabric body; front suspension, dead axle, semi-elliptic springs; rear suspension, live axle, semi-elliptic springs; rear wheel drum brakes; 810x90 tyres.

DIMENSIONS
Wheelbase 325.0cm (127.9in), front track 125.0cm (49.2in), rear track 125.0cm (49.2in).

PERFORMANCE
Maximum speed 41mph (65km/h); 88.3kg/kW (64.6kg/bhp).

Right: Following the example of its Belgian Pipe forebear, the early NSUs were tall, rather luxurious, and relatively expensive. The make's sporting achievements were confined to the 1904 Gordon Bennett Cup race when Hautvast finished 6th, an hour behind the winner.

After a few licence-built Pipe models were made, the company decided to design its own model, although retaining the curiously complex Pipe valve operation. The new model went under the title Original Neckarsulmer Motorwagen.

The Pipe layout used two low-mounted gear-driven camshafts, located either side of the engine, in line with the crankshaft. Exposed pushrods, operating top and bottom through rocker arms, actuated the valve gear. This meant that not only was the engine very wide, but also rather noisy. It was a typical long-stroke unit of the period, and the 'Original Neckarsulmer' had a three-speed gearbox, and semi-elliptic suspension front and rear. The small four-seater open body had a tall windscreen and basic hood.

BODY
2 door cabriolet; 4 seats; weight 600kg (1320lb).

ENGINE
4 cylinders in 2 pairs; in line, front; 68.0x90.0mm, 1420cc; 8.9kW (12bhp) @ 1650rpm.

ENGINE STRUCTURE
Ohv; 2 valves per cylinder; 2 side mounted camshafts, gear driven. Cast iron monoblocks; 3 bearing crankshaft; NSU carburettor; water cooled.

TRANSMISSION
Rear wheel drive; 3 speed gearbox; spiral bevel final drive.

CHASSIS DETAILS
Separate chassis; steel bodywork; front suspension, dead axle, semi-elliptic springs; rear suspension, live axle, semi-elliptic springs; worm steering; rear wheel drum brakes; 700x85 tyres.

DIMENSIONS
Wheelbase 200.0cm (78.7in), front track 115.0cm (45.3in), rear track 115.0cm (45.3in).

PERFORMANCE
Maximum speed 40mph (65kph) 67.4kg/kW (50.0kg/bhp).

Right: Later NSU. The 10/20 of 1909 with double phaeton bodywork, and 2608cc engine.

HORCH 35/40 1906

The infant motor industry quickly learned the advantages to be gained by successful performances in competition. The 35/40 also signalled Horch's preference towards larger engined models.

As was customary at this period, the cylinders were cast in pairs and then attached to the crankcase, with the valves – overhead inlet, side exhaust – operated by a gear driven low-mounted camshaft. The three-speed gearbox was also separate, driven from the engine by a short shaft.

A simple semi-elliptic suspension arrangement was used, with the driver having to rely on rear wheel brakes alone. The Herkomer trials in which the model was entered were held in Munich, not far from the home of Daimler-Benz.

As with most car manufacturers of the period, Horch sent complete chassis and engine out to specialist coach-builders for a variety of bodywork styles from enclosed limousine to the sketchy open bodies and flared wings of the sports version.

BODY
4 doors; phaeton; 4 seats; weight 1100kg (2420lb).

ENGINE
4 cylinders in 2 pairs, in line, front; 115.0x140.0mm, 5810cc; 29.8kW (40bhp) @ 1400rpm. 5.1kW/l (6.9bhp/l).

ENGINE STRUCTURE
Overhead inlet, side exhaust; 2 valves per cylinder; 1 gear driven side camshaft; cast iron monoblock; 3 bearing crankshaft; water cooled.

TRANSMISSION
Rear wheel drive; separate 3-speed gearbox.

CHASSIS DETAILS
Separate chassis; steel and fabric body; front suspension, dead axle, semi-elliptic springs; rear suspension, live axle, semi-elliptic springs; rear wheel brakes; worm steering; 880x1215 tyres.

DIMENSIONS
Wheelbase 325.0cm (127.9in), front track 140.0cm (55.1in), rear track 140.0cm (55.1in).

PERFORMANCE
Maximum speed 53-56mph (85-90kph); 36.9kg/kW (27.5kg/bhp).

Right: The 18/22 Horch a 2725cc modest forerunner of the 35/40 won the 1906 Herkomer Trial. Dr Stöss the victorious driver is at the wheel. August Horch leans proprietorially on left of the car.

HORCH 31/60 1907

This was the largest, most powerful and, more importantly, the fastest Horch model yet. It stayed with the overhead inlet, side exhaust layout and the cylinders cast in pairs, with no detachable cylinder head. The earlier models had a three-speed gearbox, but later Horch decided that a four-speed box would make the new model even more attractive.

Unusually for this period, the 31/60 also featured brakes on all four wheels. In 1907 August Horch, a believer in doing things for himself, entered a specially-bodied version of the car in the Kaiserpreis race in the Taunus mountain area near Wiesbaden. The standard body used a double phaeton design. Chassis price was 184,000 marks.

BODY
4 door double phaeton; 4 seats; 1250kg (2750lb).

ENGINE
6 cylinders in 3 pairs; in line; front;,115.0x140.0mm, 8720cc; 48.5kW (65bhp) @ 1400rpm; 6.2kW/l (8.3bhp/l).

ENGINE STRUCTURE
Overhead inlet, side exhaust; 2 valves per cylinder; 1 spur gear driven side camshaft; cast iron monoblock; 5 bearing crankshaft; water cooled.

TRANSMISSION
Rear wheel drive; 3 speed gearbox. spiral bevel final drive.

CHASSIS DETAILS
Separate chassis; steel and fabric body; front suspension, dead axle, semi-elliptic brakes; rear suspension, live axle, semi-elliptic springs; drum brakes front and rear; worm steering; 875x105 tyres.

DIMENSIONS
Wheelbase 340.0cm (136.0in), front track 140.0cm (55.1in), rear track 140.0cm (55.1in).

PERFORMANCE
Maximum speed 61mph (100kph); 25.8kg/kW (19.2kg/bhp).

Right: Imperial magnificence in the Colonies. Liveried chauffeur with a Horch 31/60 in the tropics.
Left: A Horch prototype 22/25 of 1905.

HORCH 4 cylinder 1907

In 1907 Horch produced a whole range of 4 cylinder cars based on essentially the same design. The practice of using a separate chassis allowed the cars to be tailored in size to their engine capacity. This ranged from the 1588cc 6/18 to the massive 6.4 litre 25/60. All the engines used the double cast iron cylinder design with just the smallest having a chain driven camshaft and a Cundell GA carburettor.

The 6/18 was also different, and for a short period it used three-quarter elliptic springs, later reverting to the semi-elliptic layout used by the remainder of the range. Transmission was by four-speed gearbox across the whole of the new range.

August Horch believed strongly in solving his own technical problems rather than merely copying solutions arrived at elsewhere. He made its own automatic carburettor and duplex ignition. There was a camshaft-driven coolant pump, and exhaust gas pressure was used for engine lubrication and fuel feed.

BODY
4 door double phaeton; 4 seats; weight 1200kg (2640lb).
ENGINE
4 cylinders in 2 pairs; front; in line; 85.0x115.0mm, 2608cc; 22.4kW (30bhp) @ 1600rpm; 8.6kW/l (11.5bhp/l).
ENGINE STRUCTURE
Overhead inlet, side exhaust; 2 valves per cylinder; 1 gear driven side camshaft; cast iron monoblock in 2 pairs; 3 bearing crankshaft; Horch carburettor, water cooled.
TRANSMISSION
rear wheel drive; separate 4 speed gearbox; spiral bevel final drive.
CHASSIS DETAILS
Separate chassis; steel and fabric body; front suspension, beam axle, semi-elliptic springs; rear suspension, live axle, semi-elliptic springs; rear wheel drum brakes; worm steering; 810x90 tyres.

DIMENSIONS
Wheelbase 310.0cm (122.0in), front track 130.0cm (51.2 in), rear track 130.0cm (51.2 in).
PERFORMANCE
Maximum speed 47mph (75kph): 53.5kg/kW (40.0kg/bhp).

Right: The 1907 limousine featured a speaking-tube as a means of communication from the occupants, cosily ensconced in the rear compartment, to the driver who was exposed to the elements and heard instructions through a trumpet by his right ear.
Far right: 1906 Herkomer Trial team line up outside factory.

HORCH 25/60 1907

It did not take manufacturers long to realise the importance of competition success, especially in the long distance events of this period. August Horch designed the 25/55 and 25/60 with the prestigious Kaiserpreis in mind, building just six examples, three of which were entered, with Horch himself driving.

The standard model was a 25/60, with the six-cylinder engine made up of three two-cylinder castings, with overhead inlet and side exhaust valves. The Kaiserpreis models were rated as 31/60, with a top speed of 62mph, against the lower-powered model's 56mph.

It was Horch's last design with the overhead inlet, side exhaust layout.

The 1907 Herkomer Trials, won by Horch in 1906, were followed by failure in the Kaiserpreis. The directors blamed the manager, as they often do when sporting endeavours go wrong, and demanded a more cautious policy. They wanted to lower prices instead of taking part in racing. Horch had to go.

BODY
2 door open coupe, 1250kg (2750lb).

ENGINE
6 cylinders in three pairs, in line; front; 115.0x155.0mm, 6440cc; 44.1kW/60bhp @ 1600rpm; 6.8kW/l (9.4bhp/l).

ENGINE STRUCTURE
Overhead inlet, side exhaust; 2 valves per cylinder; 1 gear driven side camshaft; cast iron cylinder head and block; 5 bearing crankshaft; water cooled.

TRANSMISSION
Rear wheel drive; separate 3 or 4 speed gearbox; hypoid bevel final drive.

CHASSIS DETAILS
Separate steel chassis; front suspension, dead axle, semi-elliptic springs; rear suspension, live axle, semi-elliptic springs; rear wheel drum brakes; worm steering; 8875x105 tyres.

DIMENSIONS
Wheelbase 340.0cm (133.9in), front track 140.0cm (55.1in), rear track 140.0cm (55.1in).

PERFORMANCE
Maximum speed 56mph (90km/h); 28.3kg/kW (20.8kg/bhp).

Left: August Horch.
Right: Three 31/60 models, more powerful versions of the production 25/60, were entered in the 1907 Kaiserpreis, with August Horch heading the team.

WANDERER 4-cylinder Prototype 1907

This second prototype was to prove much closer to the ideas Winklhofer and Jaenicke were pursuing. The smaller engine, now with four cylinders and a capacity of 1.2 litres, produced as much power as the twin cylinder in their original model.

    The new car was also much more compact, although it stayed with the three-speed gearbox. The rear suspension too was much modified, now running with an unusual arrangement of three-quarter elliptic springs. In 1912, after the company was restarted, this second prototype was to form the basis of the first production car, the 5/12 'Püppchen'.

    When many of the new cars of this era were in the 'heavyweight' sector, the new Wanderer was a true lightweight, so that even with the small engine, performance was remarkably good. The one weak feature was the single foot-operated brake working on the transmission.

BODY
Open two-seater; 500kg (1100lb).

ENGINE
4 cylinders in line; front; 62.0x95.0 mm, 1147cc; 8.8kW (12bhp) @ 1800rpm; 7.7kW/l (10.5bhp/l).

ENGINE STRUCTURE
Overhead inlet and side exhaust valves; 2 valves per cylinder; cast iron cylinder head and block; 3 bearing crankshaft; single carburettor; water cooled

TRANSMISSION
Rear wheel drive; separate 3 speed gearbox.

CHASSIS DETAILS
Separate U-section steel chassis, steel bodywork; front suspension, dead front axle, semi-elliptic springs; rear suspension, live axle, three-quarter elliptic springs; single drum brake on transmission.

DIMENSIONS
Front track 107.0cm (42.1in), rear track 107.0cm (42.1in), overall length 360.0cm (141.7 in), overall height 190.0cm (74.8in), overall width 130.0cm (51.2 in).

PERFORMANCE
Maximum speed 44mph (70km/h), 56.8kg/kW (41.7kg/bhp).

Right: There was a hint of Model T Ford about this Wanderer, although the engineering was relatively sophisticated. The overhead inlet and side exhaust valve layout became a firm favourite of luxury car makers in the 1930s to 1950s.

HORCH 23/40 1908

Competition successes were important in establishing a marque's name in these early days of motoring. The Prince Henry Trial was a severe test of reliability as well as speed and 1908 was to see the first of a series of three wins for Horch. A special torpedo body was developed for the Trial car, but the normal production version had an open tonneau-style coachwork. The 23/40 had the largest engine so far built by the company, with the 5.8 litre developing 29.4kW at 1400rpm. Yet while success may have put Horch on the map, it hardly helped sales, with the 23/40 managing just 156 units during its five years in production.

BODY
2 door, 4 seat tonneau.

ENGINE
4 cylinders in line; front; 115.0x140.0, 5817cc; 29.4kW (40bhp) @ 1400rpm; 5.1kW/l (6.9bhp/l).

ENGINE STRUCTURE
Overhead inlet, side exhaust; 2 valves per cylinder; 1 gear driven side camshaft; cast iron cylinder head and block; 3 bearing crankshaft; single carburettor; water cooled.

TRANSMISSION
Rear wheel drive; separate 4 speed gearbox; spiral bevel final drive.

CHASSIS DETAILS
Separate steel chassis; steel and fabric body; front suspension, dead axle, semi-elliptic springs; rear suspension, live axle, semi-elliptic springs; 880x125 tyres.

DIMENSIONS
Wheelbase 325.0cm (128.0in), front track 140.0cm (55.1in), rear track 140.0cm (55.1in).

PERFORMANCE
Maximum speed 53-56mph (85-90km/h).

Right: Horch was not only among the first engineers to use shaft drive instead of chains, he also saw the virtue of low aerodynamic drag. A special 'Torpedo' model was built for the 1908 Prince Henry Trial. *Left:* Production cars were rather more mundane. The origins of the sports car were being created.

NSU 6/12, 6/18 1908

At the 1907 Berlin motor show NSU displayed three versions of what was essentially the same car with engines of different capacities.

The 6/12 was the smallest, with a capacity of just 1540cc. It had a side valve layout and gear-driven camshaft. While the larger-engined models used four-speed gearboxes, the 6/12 had just a three-speed unit. This same basic engine design remained in use by NSU until 1911.

NSU had decided quite early on that the Pipe engine, with its complex side valve operation and twin camshafts, was too big. The 6/12 engine designed instead followed a more conventional pattern, with a single gear-driven camshaft for its side valve layout. The 1.6 litre engine drove through a three-speed gearbox, giving a top speed in the region of 34-38mph, depending on the type of bodywork. As was usual at the time, the car was sold as a chassis, with the option of a range of body styles from coupe to imposing limousine.

The 6/18 smaller chassis had a wider range of body styles, including the four-seater double phaeton.

BODY
4 door double phaeton, 4 seats; 1560kg (3432lb).

ENGINE
4 cylinders in line; front; 70.0x100.0 mm, 1539cc; 9.6kW (13bhp); 6.2kW/l (8.4bhp/l).

ENGINE STRUCTURE
Side valve; 2 valves per cylinder; one gear driven side camshaft; cast iron cylinder head and block; 3 bearing crankshaft; single carburettor; water cooled

TRANSMISSION
Rear wheel drive; separate 3 speed gearbox; hypoid bevel final drive, 5.1.

CHASSIS DETAILS
Separate steel chassis, steel and fabric bodywork; front suspension, dead front axle, semi-elliptic springs; rear suspension, live axle, semi-elliptic springs; drum brakes on rear wheels, mechanically operated; worm steering.

DIMENSIONS
Wheelbase 263.5cm (103.7in), front track 115.0cm (45.3in), rear track 115.0cm (45.3).

PERFORMANCE
Maximum speed 34-38 mph (55-60km/h), 162.5 kg/kW (120.0kg/bhp).

Right: Neckarsulmer Strickmaschinen Union, a weaving machine conglomerate on the River Neckar, created the NSU marque to put industrial Germany on wheels. Its first cars were staid affairs for factory owners and the wealthy middle class.

The principal difference between this and the 6/12, with which it shared the same chassis, was a larger engine. The 2.3 litre unit, with an output of 11.8kW, meant that the 8/15 had a higher top speed, and was capable of reaching 40mph with one of the lighter bodies. Yet it remained with drum brakes on the rear axle alone for slowing. The same range of body styles as the smaller engined model were available.

This was a larger version of the new engine originally developed for the 6/18. The bore was opened out by 15mm, with the stroke remaining at 100mm. As was common at this period, the four-cylinder block was cast as a single unit, with a single camshaft operating the side valves.

BODY
4 door landaulette, 4 seats; 1600kg (3520lb).

ENGINE
4 cylinders in line; front;85.0x100.0mm, 2269cc; 11.8kW (16bhp); 5.2kW/l (7.1bhp/l).

ENGINE STRUCTURE
Side valve; 2 valves per cylinder; 1 gear driven side camshaft; cast iron cylinder head and block; 3 bearing crankshaft; single carburettor; water cooled.

TRANSMISSION
Rear wheel drive; separate 3 speed gearbox; hypoid bevel final drive, 5.0.

CHASSIS DETAILS
Separate steel chassis, steel bodywork; front suspension, dead front axle, semi-elliptic springs; rear suspension, live axle, semi-elliptic springs; rear wheel drum brakes.

DIMENSIONS
Wheelbase 263.5cm (103.7in), front track 115.0cm (45.3in), rear track 115.0cm (45.3in).

PERFORMANCE
Maximum speed 38-40mph (60-65kph), 135.6kg/kW (100.0kg/bhp).

Right: **The Landaulette body had all the elegance and appointments of the horse-drawn coach including carriage lamps to illuminate the step. And the postillion at least had a roof.**

Until now Horch had been using the early-style overhead inlet, side exhaust layout. This new engine, for the Type H model, switched to a side-valve system, which made maintenance easier with the one-piece block and cylinder head. It was this model which gave the company its second victory in the Prince Henry Trials. But for the more conservative clients, Horch retained the original valve system for the lower-powered 17/32. As well as the usual range of passenger-car bodies, the 17/42 was also sold as a light van which outsold the cars ten to one.

August Horch's contract was terminated on June 19 1909. In compensation he received 20,000 Reichsmarks on condition that he never used his own name on a car again. He had adopted aluminium for engine castings, and light weight construction for engines and gearboxes. He was determined to return to car manufacture.

BODY
Open four-seater.
ENGINE
4 cylinders in line; front; 100.0x135.0cc, 4240cc; 33.1kW(45bhp); 7.8kW/l (10.6bhp/l).
ENGINE STRUCTURE
Side-valve; 2 valves per cylinder; one gear driven side camshaft; cast iron cylinder head and block; 3 bearing crankshaft; single carburettor; water cooled.
TRANSMISSION
Rear wheel drive; 4 speed gearbox, spiral bevel final drive.
CHASSIS DETAILS
Separate steel chassis; steel and fabric body; front suspension, dead axle, semi-elliptic springs; rear suspension, live axle, semi-elliptic springs.

Right: **Prince Henry car. The 1910 team was composed of i.o.e. 17/32s.**

HORCH 18/50 1909

With the cylinder stroke increased from 135.0 to 150.0mm, the capacity of the 17/45 4.2 litre engine which had won Horch's second victory in the Prince Henry Trials was increased to 4.7 litres, and the power output to 40.4kW. The chassis remained much as before, with the Type P using a separate four-speed gearbox and rear wheel brakes. This model was also available, like the 14/45, as a passenger car or a light commercial vehicle.

BODY
Open four-seater.

ENGINE
4 cylinders, in line; front; 100.0x150.0mm, 4712cc; 40.4kW (55bhp) @ 1800rpm; 8.6kW/l (11.7bhp/l).

ENGINE STRUCTURE
Side valve; 2 valves per cylinder; 1 gear driven side camshaft; cast iron cylinder head and block; 2 bearing crankshaft; single carburettor; water cooled.

TRANSMISSION
Rear wheel drive; 4 speed gearbox.

CHASSIS DETAILS
Separate steel chassis; steel and fabric body; front suspension, dead axle, semi-elliptic springs; rear suspension, live axle, semi-elliptic springs; 987x105 tyres.

PERFORMANCE
Maximum speed 56mph (90km/h).

Right: Severe lines of an 18/50 Phaeton of 1921. The series lasted until 1922 when post-war parsimony dictated smaller, more economical, and cheaper cars. Left: August Horch poses with the workers in the middle of the front row.

NSU Neckarsulmer 10/20 1909

The new engine was a far simpler design, with a side-valve layout, single-piece cast iron block and cylinder head and three bearing crankshaft. It was unique among the NSU models produced in 1909, in having a four rather than three speed gearbox, resulting in a leisurely top speed of 43mph. As was becoming common, a variety of body styles was available.

The Neckarsulmer used the largest version of the simple four-cylinder side valve engine, which had been designed to replace the bulky and mechanically rather complex T-head Pipe engine, used in earlier NSU models.

BODY
Two-door, four seat phaeton; 1700kg (3740lb).

ENGINE
4 cylinders in line; front; 85.0x115.0mm, 2608cc; 14.7kW(20bhp) @ 1400rpm; 5.6kW/l (7.7bhp/l).

ENGINE STRUCTURE
Side valve; 2 valves per cylinder; 1 gear driven side camshaft; cast iron cylinder head and block; 3 bearing crankshaft; single carburettor; water cooled.

TRANSMISSION
Rear wheel drive; separate 4 speed gearbox; bevel final drive.

CHASSIS DETAILS
Separate steel chassis; steel and fabric body; front suspension, dead axle, semi-elliptic springs; rear suspension, live axle, semi-elliptic springs; rear wheel drum brakes; 810x90 tyres.

DIMENSIONS
Wheelbase 310.0cm (122.0in), front track 130.0cm (51.2in), rear track 130.0cm (51.2in).

PERFORMANCE
Maximum speed 43mph (70km/h); 115.6kg/kW (85.0kg/bhp).

Right: The 1909 production NSU belies the sporting pedigree the firm was fostering.

After a disagreement with his fellow directors, August Horch left the firm he had founded. Two years later he revealed the first model to bear the Audi name. Perhaps not surprisingly, there was a lot of Horch engineering design in the new model. The four cylinder engine had its cylinders cast in pairs, with the valves operated by pushrods from a side mounted, gear-driven camshaft. The overhead inlet valve used a small rocker arm to transfer the action through 90deg. Ignition could be by either magneto or battery and trembler coil, each system having its own individual sparking plug. Audi's first model was priced at 8500 marks, with an imposing double phaeton body.

One of the first cars went to Sweden in 1910 for the 8-days Trial and finished first. The 10/22 also known as the Type A was the first product of August Horch Automobilwerke GmbH, Zwickau, later Audi Automobilwerke GmbH.

BODY
Two-door double phaeton; 4 seats; weight 830kg (1826lb).

ENGINE
4 cylinders in 2 pairs; in line, front; 80.0x130.0mm, 2612cc; 16.6kW (22bhp) @ 1800rpm. 6.4kW/l (8.4bhp/l).

ENGINE STRUCTURE
Overhead inlet, side exhaust; two valves per cylinder; 1 gear-driven side camshaft; cast iron monoblock; 3 bearing crankshaft; Zenith carburettor; water cooled.

TRANSMISSION
Rear wheel drive; separate 4 speed gearbox; spiral bevel final drive; 3.71.

CHASSIS DETAILS
Separate steel chassis; steel and wood body. front suspension, semi-elliptic springs; rear suspension, semi-elliptic springs; rear wheel brakes; worm steering; 815x105 tyres.

DIMENSIONS
Wheelbase 305.0cm (120.1in), front track 130.0cm (51.2in), rear track 130.0cm (51.2in).

PERFORMANCE
Maximum speed 47mph (75kph); 50.0kg/kW (37.7kg/bhp).

Right and left: Flat radiator. The Audi's distinctive pointed radiator was not adopted until 1914.

Horch did not immediately capitalise on its competition success with the original six-cylinder 25/60. Three years were to pass before the next six cylinder model was to appear. The Type M 25/60 used the same cylinder dimensions as the original. Two versions were available, the less powerful model being the 25/55 with four cylinders.

The wheelbase was the same as that of the 'short chassis' Kaiserpreis cars, but now the four-speed gearbox was standard. Unlike the original 25/60, of which just six were built (including the three Kaiserpreis cars), the new model was rather more successful with 122 being sold in chassis form each costing 5,000 Marks.

BODY
Two-door, four-seat cabriolet; weight 1600kg (3520 lb).

ENGINE
4 cylinders, in line; front; 115.0x155.0mm, 6440cc; 44.1kW (60bhp) @ 1400rpm; 6.4kW/l (8.6bhp/l).

ENGINE STRUCTURE
Overhead inlet, side exhaust; 2 valves per cylinder; 1 gear driven side camshaft; cast iron cylinder head and block; 5 bearing crankshaft; single carburettor; water cooled.

TRANSMISSION
Rear wheel drive; 4 speed gearbox; spiral bevel final drive.

CHASSIS DETAILS
Separate steel chassis; steel and fabric body; front suspension, dead axle, semi-elliptic springs; rear suspension, live axle, semi-elliptic springs; rear wheel drum brakes; 875x105 tyres.

DIMENSIONS
Wheelbase 338.0cm (133.1in), front track 140.0cm (55.1in), rear track 140.0cm (55.1in).

PERFORMANCE
Maximum speed 62mph (100km/h).

Right: The four cylinder range had a long shelf life. This is a 10/30 of 1913 pressed into the service of the Imperial army. This model had a ten year span, and similar cars continued in production well into the 1920s.

AUDI Type B 10/28 1911

Just a year after setting up on his own, August Horch won the 1911 Austrian Alpine Rally with a new version of his first Audi. The Type B had an increased power output, from 22 to 28bhp, still with the cylinders cast in pairs. The double phaeton body, with a curved, fixed panel across the car between front and rear seats, had a hood but no windows to protect the passengers, and there was a steel chassis and simple suspension, with semi-elliptic springs front and rear. Audi also produced a shorter, 290cm, wheelbase version of this model.

BODY
4 door double phaeton; 4 seats; 830kg (1826lb).

ENGINE
4 cylinders in 2 pairs; in line, front; 80.0x130.0mm, 2612cc; 21kW (28bhp) @ 1800rpm; 8.0kW/l (10.7bhp/l).

ENGINE STRUCTURE
Overhead inlet, side exhaust; 2 valves per cylinders; 1 gear driven side camshaft; cast iron monoblock; 3 bearing crankshaft; water cooled.

TRANSMISSION
Rear wheel drive; separate 3-speed gearbox; spiral bevel final drive; 3.71.

CHASSIS DETAILS
Separate steel chassis; steel and fabric body; front suspension, dead axle, semi-elliptic springs; rear suspension, live axle, semi-elliptic springs; rear wheel brakes; worm steering; front mounted fuel tank; 815x105 tyres.

DIMENSIONS
Wheelbase 305.0cm (120.1in), front track 130.0cm (51.8in), rear track 130.0cm (51.8in).

PERFORMANCE
Maximum speed 56mph (90kph); 39.5kg/kW (29.6kg/bhp).

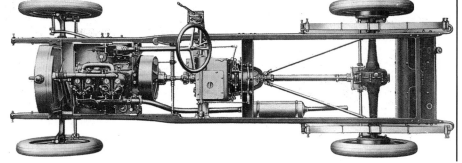

Left: Original Audi chassis from above

AUDI Type C 14/35 1911

Hard on the heels of the 1911 Type B came the Type C, in most essentials little more than a larger version. The same overhead inlet, side exhaust layout was used, operated by long pushrods from a gear-driven camshaft set low in the block. The Type C was offered with short and long wheelbase chassis, and won three Alpine Rallies in succession, 1912, 1913, 1914, establishing Audi's sporting credentials. A double phaeton style body was offered with a stiffening panel running across the car between the front and rear seats, plus a 40bhp version of the engine.

BODY
4 door phaeton; 4 seats; 920kg (2024lb).

ENGINE
4 cylinders in pairs; in line; front; 90.0x140.0mm, 3564cc; 26.1kW (35bhp) @ 1700rpm; 7.3 kW/l (13.7bhp/l).

ENGINE STRUCTURE
Overhead inlet, side exhaust; 2 valves per cylinders, gear driven side camshaft; cast iron monoblock; 3 bearing crankshaft; Zenith carburettor; water cooled.

TRANSMISSION
Rear wheel drive; separate 4 speed gearbox; spiral bevel final drive; 3.25.

CHASSIS DETAILS
Separate steel chassis; steel and fabric body; front suspension, dead axle, semi-elliptic springs; rear suspension, live axle, semi-elliptic springs; rear wheel drum brakes;worm steering; 820x120 tyres.

DIMENSIONS
Wheelbase 305.0cm (120.1in), front track 130.0cm (51.2in), rear track 130.0cm (51.2in).

PERFORMANCE
Maximum speed 56mph (90kph); 35.2kg/kW (26.3kg/bhp).

Left: Competition versions of the Type C had engines of 30kW (40bhp), and were able to reach speeds of 62mph (100kph). An example, one of the Alpine winners and August Horch's personal car throughout the war, survives in the Deutsches Museum in Munich.
Right: Chassis picture shows cylinders cast in pairs.

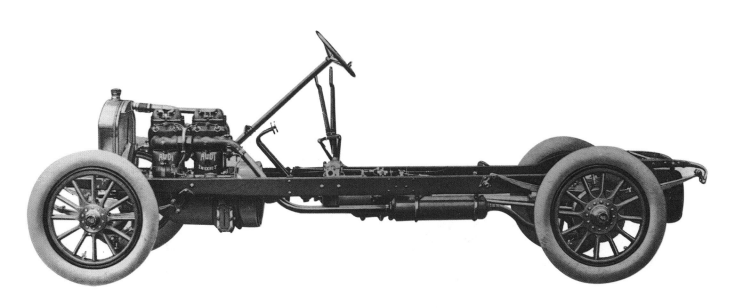

HORCH 8/24 1911

This was one of several Horch models spanning the period of the 1914-1918 war, with production running from 1911 through to 1921; it was also the first Horch to approach selling 1,000 units in its lifetime. The L-head side valve arrangement was a classic design, with a low-mounted gear-driven camshaft.

There was a less-powerful version of the C type Horch, the 6/18, with the very short, for the time, stroke of just 90mm, with the identical 74.5mm bore. This 1588cc engine had an output of just 13.2kW. The wheelbase too was shorter than that of the larger model.

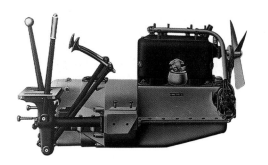

BODY
4 door, 4 seat limousine; weight 1250kg (2750lb).

ENGINE
4 cylinders, in line; front; 74.5x120.0mm, 2080cc; 17.6kW (24bhp) @ 1800rpm; 8.46kW/l (11.5bhp/l).

ENGINE STRUCTURE
Side valve; 2 valves per cylinder; 1 gear driven side camshaft; cast iron cylinder head and block; 3 bearing crankshaft; single Cundell GA carburettor; water cooled.

TRANMISSION
Rear wheel drive; 4 speed gearbox, spiral bevel final drive, 3.6.

CHASSIS DETAILS
Separate steel chassis; steel body; front suspension, dead axle, semi-elliptic springs; rear suspension, live axle, semi-elliptic springs; 765x105 tyres.

DIMENSIONS
Wheelbase 310.0cm (122.0 in), front track 130.0cm (51.2in), rear track 130.0cm (51.2in).

PERFORMANCE
Maximum speed 47mph (75km/h).

Right: Sturdy open bodywork for an 8/24 with flexible separate exhaust pipes and wide running board. Side lights were carefully faired into the scuttle and there was no fixed windscreen.
Left: Engine in unit with clutch and gearbox.

WANDERER 5/12 "Puppchen" 1911

After the two protypes produced during 1905 and 1907, Wanderer finally decided on the four-cylinder engine for its first production model. The long-stroke 1147cc side-valve unit produced just 9kW (12bhp), satisfactory for such a small car which was advanced enough to use a pump, rather than rely on thermosyphon to drive water round the cooling system.

The body was unusual, using a tandem seating layout, with no hood, so that the driver had to rely on just the tall, vertical windscreen, with no wiper, for protection. Drive to the rear wheels was through a non-synchromesh three-speed gearbox, while the footbrake operated a single, external contracting drum on the propeller shaft. There was, however, a mechanical parking (or emergency) brake working on the rear wheels.

This was the famous "Puppchen" (little doll), a nickname taken from a popular song of the time. Ettore Bugatti was reputed to have influenced it, but the only evidence that he did lay in a visit to Saxony he made, trying to sell engine designs.

BODY
2 seat open body; weight 500kg (1100lb).

ENGINE
4 cylinders, in line; front 62.0x95.0mm, 1147cc; 9kW (12bhp) @ 1800rpm; 7.8kW/l (10.5bhp/l).

ENGINE STRUCTURE
Overhead inlet, side exhaust valves; 2 valves per cylinder; 1 gear driven side camshaft; cast iron cylinder head and block; 3 bearing crankshaft; Zenith carburettor; water cooled.

TRANSMISSION
Rear wheel drive; 3 speed gearbox; spiral bevel final drive, 4.60.

CHASSIS DETAILS
Separate box-section chassis; steel bodywork; Front and rear suspension, semi-elliptic springs. Foot brake acting on external contracting drum on propeller shaft; handbrake on rear wheel drums; 20l (4.4 Imp gal) (5.3 US gal) fuel tank; 760x90 tyres.

DIMENSIONS
Wheelbase 225.0cm (88.6in), front track 107.0cm (41.2in), rear track 107.0cm (41.2in), overall length 310.0cm (122.1in), overall width 133.0cm (53.4in), overall height 150.0cm (59.0in).

PERFORMANCE
Maximum speed 43mph (70 kph); 55.6kg/kW (41.7kg/bhp); average fuel consumption 35.3mpg (8l/100km) manufacturer's fig.

Right: There is more than a passing resemblance to Bébé Peugeot in the 1911 "Doll" from Wanderer.

AUDI Type D 14/45 1912

With confidence increasing after the wins in the Alpine Trials, August Horch again increased the capacity and power of the four cylinder engine. The extra vigour enabled the company to use an even bigger upright saloon body, with the car running on a very long 332cm (130.7in) wheelbase. A shorter 317cm (124.8in) wheelbase version was available for the phaeton. The high final drive ratio, allied with the very long stroke engine, gave excellent torque right through the limited rev range, providing the Type D with a relatively relaxed air although capable of being driven in a spirited sporting manner.

BODY
4 door phaeton; 4 seats (1200kg/2640lb).

ENGINE
4 cylinders in pairs; 100.0x150.0mm, 4680cc; 33.6kW (45bhp) @ 1650rpm; 7.2kW/l (9.6 bhp/l).

ENGINE STRUCTURE
Overhead inlet, side exhaust; 2 valves per cylinder; 1 gear driven side camshaft; cast iron monoblock; 3 bearing crankshaft, Zenith carburettor; water cooled.

TRANSMISSION
Rear wheel drive; 4 speed gearbox, spiral bevel final drive; 2.89.

CHASSIS DETAILS
Separate steel chassis; steel bodywork; front suspension, dead axle, semi-elliptic springs; rear suspension, live axle, semi-elliptic springs; rear wheel drum brakes; worm steering, 880x120 tyres.

DIMENSIONS
Wheelbase 332.0cm (130.7in), front track 140.0cm (55.2in), rear track 140.0cm (55.2in).

PERFORMANCE
Maximum speed 59mph (95kph); 35/7kg/kW (26.7kg/bhp).

Right: Substantial coachwork for an Alpine winner. Cross-bracing between front and rear seats steadied the body for the Triennial Cup victors. *Left:* Chassis classic layout with gearbox still separate from engine and clutch. Four cylinders cast in two pairs.

NSU 8/24 1912

The 8/24 came in the middle of the five-strong range of NSUs at this period. As well as the larger 2.1 litre engine, the model also had a four-speed gearbox. The wheelbase too was longer, with a slightly wider track. But the chassis and running gear remained essentially unchanged. The foot brake remained working on the rear wheels alone, but the tyres were wider and the wheels larger. The body styles varied from the basic two-seater, through the double phaeton to the saloon and limousine. Prices ranged from 6,200 Marks for the chassis alone to 9,500 Marks for the phaeton-landaulette with a second windscreen for the rear passengers.

NSU's car production took time to get under way. Only 20 cars were made in 1906 when bicycle output reached 13,858. By 1910 NSU was making 2,500 motorcycles, in 1914 3,600 and 27,000 bicycles, as well as 432 cars. By 1914 the company had made over 30,000 motorcycles, many for the German army.

BODY
4 door double phaeton, 4 seats; 950kg (2090lb).

ENGINE
4 cylinders in line; front; 80.0x104.0 mm, 2100cc; 17.6kW (24bhp)@ 1800rpm; 11.4kW/l (11.4bhp/l).

ENGINE STRUCTURE
Side valves; 2 valves per cylinder; 1 gear driven side camshaft; cast iron cylinder head and block; 3 bearing crankshaft; single carburettor; water cooled.

TRANSMISSION
Rear wheel drive; 4 speed gearbox; hypoid bevel final drive.

CHASSIS DETAILS
Separate steel chassis, steel bodywork; front suspension, dead axle, semi-elliptic springs; rear suspension, live axle, C-springs; rear wheel drum brakes; 60.0l (37.3 Imp gal) (44.8US gal) fuel tank; 810x100 tyres.

DIMENSIONS
Wheelbase 290.0cm (114.2in), front track 125.0cm (49.2in), rear track 125.0cm (49.2in), overall length 410.0cm (161.4in); overall width 150.0cm (59.1in), overall height 220.0cm (86.6in); overall width 150.0cm (59.1in)

PERFORMANCE
54.0kg/kW (39.5kg/bhp).

Right: **Fashionable flared bodywork for pre-war tourer with hood.**

AUDI Type E 22/50 1913

The largest engine ever built by Audi for a production car was still based on Horch's original 1910 design. The extra capacity was obtained by the simple expedient of widening the bores of the Type D engine from 100 to 110mm, which resulted in a power output of 41.0kW or 55bhp, making it the the most powerful model so far. The new model retained the same chassis dimensions as the Type D and despite the additional performance continued with only rear wheel brakes. The saloon body was heavier, but the new model was, in the right circumstances, able to reach speeds in excess of 100kph (62mph).

A feature of the phaeton was the way the hood folded virtually flush with the body, giving a neat appearance. As was usual for larger cars of the period, the spare tyre was carried on the front wing, with a tool box set into the running board.

BODY
4 door; saloon and phaeton; 4 seats; 1225kg (2695lb).

ENGINE
4 cylinders in pairs; 110.0x150.0cc, 5720cc; 41.0kW (55bhp) @ 1650cc; 24.7kW/l (9.6bhp/l).

ENGINE STRUCTURE
Overhead inlet, side exhaust; 2 valves per cylinder; 1 gear-driven side camshaft; cast iron monoblock; 3 bearing crankshaft; Zenith caburettor, water cooled.

TRANSMISSION
Rear wheel drive; separate 4 speed gearbox; spiral bevel final drive; 2.74.

CHASSIS DETAILS
Separate steel chassis; steel bodywork; front suspension, dead axle, semi-elliptic springs; rear suspension, live axle, semi-elliptic springs; rear wheel drum brakes; worm steering, 880x125 tyres.

DIMENSIONS
Wheelbase 332cm (130.1in), front track 140cm (55.1in), rear track 140cm (55.1in).

PERFORMANCE
Maximum speed 62-65 mph (100-105kph); 29.9kg/kW (22.3kg/bhp).

Left: Cylinders in pairs, side exhaust manifold.

Unusually, Horch returned to the 'pioneer' system, with the engine block cast with two pairs of two cylinders. Yet when most engines still relied on thermosyphon cooling and a large radiator, the 10/30 used a water pump to give a constant coolant flow round the engine.

The 10/30 Type B model was available with the usual range of contemporary body styles, from phaeton to limousine. Introduced in 1911, this was the only model of that year not to be continued after the First World War, with production ending in 1914 after just 168 were built.

At the same time, Horch also launched the Type N 10/30, which used a conventional single-unit four-cylinder block and an inlet over exhaust valve layout. Capacity was very slightly larger than the Type B's, but power output remained at 22.1kW. This version, with a longer wheelbase and wider track, was more successful than the original, with 767 being built during the production run which finally ended in 1921.

BODY
4 door 4 seats limousine; 1200kg (2400lb).

ENGINE
4 cylinders in pairs, in line; front; 85.0x115.0mm, 2608cc; 22.1kW (30bhp) @ 1600rpm; 8.5kW/l (11.5bhp/l).

ENGINE STRUCTURE
Side valve; 2 valves per cylinder; 1 gear driven side camshaft; cast iron cylinder head and block; 3 bearing crankshaft; single carburettor; water cooled.

TRANSMISSION
Rear wheel drive; separate 4 speed gearbox; spiral bevel final drive, 3.7.

CHASSIS DETAILS
Separate steel chassis; steel body; front suspension, dead axle, semi-elliptic springs; rear suspension, live axle, semi-elliptic springs; rear wheel drum brakes; 810x90 tyres.

DIMENSIONS
Wheelbase 280.0cm (110.2in), front track 125.0cm (49.2in), rear track 125.0cm (49.2in).

PERFORMANCE
Maximum speed 47mph (75km/h); 54.3kW/kg (40.0bhp/kg).

Right: A viersitzer (four seater) 10/30 with hooded headlamps and no windscreen. Most models had a folding screen and sidemounted spare wheels on driver's side, still the right in 1913.
Far right: Tandem seating for mechanic in 10/30 racer.

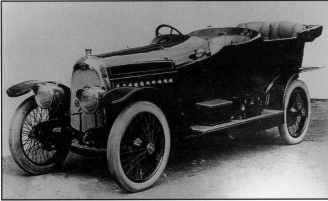

AUDI 14/35 Type C 1914

August Horch put his new Audi cars much to the fore with some remarkable competition successes, one of the toughest being the Austrian Alpenfahrt. He won the 1911 event with the Type B and in 1914 repeated his success with the Type C, which he promptly named the Alpensieger – Alpine Winner. As well as the standard 305cm wheelbase version, Audi also produced short and long wheelbase versions with 290 and 320cm. The competition version, similar to the car which had won the Austrian Alpine event, developed 29.8kW, which gave a top speed of 62mph.

The 1914 event was a triumph for Audi, winning outright for the fourth year running, winning the team prize for the second time in a row and winning the Triennial Challenge Trophy.

BODY
4 door tourer; 4 seats; weight 920kg (2024lb).

ENGINE
4 cylinders; in line; front; 90.0x140.0mm, 3564cc; 26.1kW (35bhp) @ 1700rpm; 7.3kW/l (9.8bhp/l).

ENGINE STRUCTURE
Overhead inlet, side exhaust; 2 valves per cylinder; gear driven side camshaft; cast iron monoblock; 3 bearing crankshaft; Zenith carburettor; water cooled.

TRANSMISSION
Rear wheel drive; separate 4 speed gearbox; spiral bevel final drive, 3.25.

CHASSIS DETAILS
Box section chassis; steel and fabric body; front suspension, beam axle, semi-elliptic springs; rear suspension, live axle, semi-elliptic springs; worm steering, rear wheel drum brakes; 8.20x120 tyres.

DIMENSIONS
Wheelbase 305.0cm (120.1in), front track 130.0cm (51.2in), rear track 130.0cm (51.2in).

PERFORMANCE
Maximum speed 56mph (90kph); 35.2kg/kW (26.3kg/bhp).

Right: **Boat-tailed Alpensieger ensured Audi's sporting pedigree. Body made by Kathe of Halle.**

AUDI 8/22 Type G 1914

In the three years since he established Audi, August Horch used the Alpine trial events as a showplace for his new cars. But now the time had come for him to show that he could also produce a very much more everyday type of car – and at a rather more everyday price than he had been charging for previous models.

The Type G 8/22 had a simple side valve engine, with magneto ignition and four-speed gearbox. The chassis was straightforward, with semi-elliptic springs and only rear wheel brakes. The large and heavy saloon body was perhaps rather more impressive than the Type G, but its great weight affected its performance and it could barely reach 40mph. For the first Type G, life was to be short, with production stopping on the outbreak of the Great War in August 1914.

Production was revived in 1920 together with the 14/35, 18/45, and 22/50. August Horch resigned from the company in 1920 becoming a member of the supervisory board when he joined the ministry of transport in Berlin.

BODY
4 door saloon; 4 seats; 1250kg (2750lb).

ENGINE
4 cylinders, in line; front; 75.0x118.0mm, 2071cc; 16.4kW (22bhp) @ 1900rpm; 8.0kW/l (10.6bhp/l).

ENGINE STRUCTURE
Side valve; 2 valves per cylinder; 1 gear driven side camshaft; cast iron monoblock; 3 bearing crankshaft; Zenith carburettor, water cooled.

TRANSMISSION
Rear wheel drive; 4 speed gearbox; spiral bevel final drive, 4.45.

CHASSIS DETAILS
Box section chassis; steel and fabric body; front suspension; beam axle, semi-elliptic springs; rear suspension, live axle, semi-elliptic springs; rear wheel drum brakes; worm steering; 8.20x120 tyres.

DIMENSIONS
Wheelbase 229.5cm (117.9in), front track 125.0cm (49.2in), rear track 125.0cm (49.2in).

PERFORMANCE
Maximum speed 40mph (65kph); 76.2kg/kW (56.8kg/bhp).

Right: Audi's role as touring car emphasised by luggage trunks on rear and mounted at side of the body. Passengers gained access from right side only.

With demand growing, Wanderer replaced its original 5/12 tandem-bodied model with the larger engined 5/15. Power was raised to 11kW, with larger bore and stroke and a capacity of 1286cc.

The same three-speed gearbox and propeller shaft braking system were retained, and although the 5/15 was heavier the extra power gave it about the same performance as the previous model. The 5/15 had a 10.0cm longer wheelbase, but retained the same track dimensions.

Wanderer decided to retain the curious tandem seating layout, but also offered the 5/15 with the option of either side-by-side two-seater or three-seater open body styles, the latter weighing around 150kg more.

Production of the 5/15 was interrupted shortly after its launch by the start of the First World War in August 1914.

BODY
2 seater open; 2 doors; 600kg (1320lb)

ENGINE
4 cylinders in line; front; 64.0x100.0mm, 1286cc; 11kW (15bhp) @ 1800rpm; 8.5kW/l (11.7bhp/l).

ENGINE STRUCTURE
Overhead valves; 2 valves per cylinder; 1 gear driven side camshaft; 3 bearing crankshaft; Zenith carburettor, water cooled.

TRANSMISSION
Rear wheel drive; 3 speed gearbox; spiral bevel final drive, 4.60.

CHASSIS DETAILS
U beam separate chassis; steel bodywork; front and rear suspension, semi-elliptic springs; Foot brake acting on external contracting drum on propeller shaft; handbrake on rear wheel drums; 20.0l (4.4 Imp gal) (5.3 US gal) fuel tank; 710x90 tyres.

DIMENSIONS
Wheelbase 235.0cm (92.5in), front track 107.0cm (42.1in), rear track 107.0cm (42.1in), overall length 310.0cm (122.0in), overall width 133.0cm (52.5in), overall height 155.0cm (61.0in).

PERFORMANCE
Maximum speed 43mph (70kph); 54.5kg/kW (40.0kg/bhp); average fuel consumption 35.3mpg (8.0 l/100km).

Right: Curved body sides gave extra elbow room, following fashion set by Austro-Daimler.

A very straightforward model, with the three-speed gearbox still separated from the engine, driving the live rear axle through a single-piece propeller shaft. The side-valve engine had the single camshaft on the left-hand side gear driven from the front of the three-bearing crankshaft; a skew gear took drive down to the oil pump. The 5/15 was made in right-hand drive form only, as was common with many German cars at the time. For emergency braking – the foot brake worked on the rear wheels alone – the hand brake operated through an outboard lever with rods acting on a cross-shaft ahead of the rear axle.

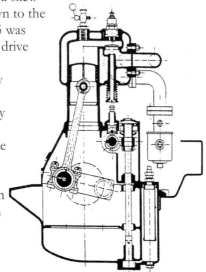

BODY

4 door double phaeton, 4 seats.

ENGINE

4 cylinders in line; front; 66.0x90.0 mm, 1232cc; 11.0kW (15bhp); 7.3kW/l (10.0 bhp/l).

ENGINE STRUCTURE

Side valve; 2 valves per cylinder; 1 gear driven camshaft; cast iron cylinder head and block; 3 bearing crankshaft; water cooled.

TRANSMISSION

Rear wheel drive; 3 speed gearbox; hypoid bevel final drive.

CHASSIS DETAILS

Separate steel chassis, steel bodywork; front suspension, dead axle, semi-elliptic springs; rear suspension, live axle, semi-elliptic springs; rear wheel drum brakes; worm and sector steering; 700x85 tyres.

DIMENSIONS

Wheelbase 245.0cm (96.5in); front track 115.0cm (45.3in); rear track 115.0cm (45.3in); overall length 330.0cm (129.9in); overall width 142.5cm (56.1in).

Left: Exposed valve gear made tappet adjustment easy. Spark plug over inlet valve.
Right: Sturdy side-valve engine of NSU 5/15 had block and cylinder head cast integrally and three bearing crank.

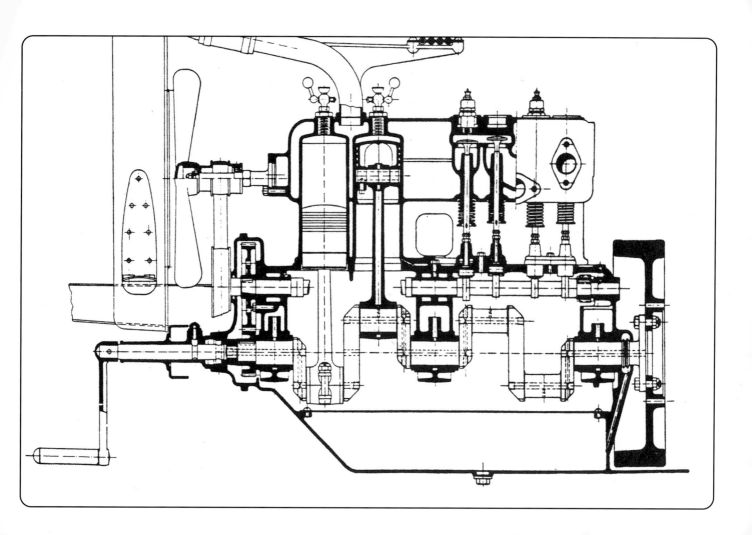

The 6/18 was the smallest capacity and lowest powered model of NSU's 1914 range, but nevertheless it shared the same range of bodies as the larger ones. These ranged from a two-seater sports car, through the double phaeton to the choice of owner-driver or chauffeur driven limousines, the latter with a glass division. The monoblock engine used thermosyphon cooling, without a water pump.

BODY
2 door double phaeton, 4 seats; 680kg (1496lb).

ENGINE
4 cylinders, in line; front; 75.0x 88.0mm, 1555cc; 13.2kW (18bhp) @ 1800rpm; 8.5kW/l (11.5bhp/l).

ENGINE STRUCTURE
Side valve; 2 valves per cylinder; 1 gear driven side camshaft; cast iron cylinder head and block; 3 bearing crankshaft; water cooled.

TRANSMISSION
Rear wheel drive; 3 speed gearbox; hypoid bevel final drive.

CHASSIS DETAILS
Separate steel chassis, steel bodywork front suspension, semi-elliptic springs; rear suspension, live axle, C-springs; rear wheel drum brakes; 37.0l (8.1Imp gal) (9.8US gal) fuel tank; 750x85 front, 760x90 rear tyres.

DIMENSIONS
Wheelbase 265.0cm (104.3in), front track 115.0cm 42.3(in), rear track 115.0cm (42.3in) overall length 380.0cm (149.6in); overall width 145.0cm (57.1in), overall height 215.0cm (84.6in).

PERFORMANCE
51.5kg/kW (37.8kg/bhp).

Right: It is not clear if the two military gentlemen behind the driver are crouching in a rear seat or, a more likely explanation standing on the far side of the car.

NSU 10/20 1914

This was one of the larger NSU models to be produced before WW1, again with a very wide range of body styles, seating up to six people, available on the standard chassis. Struggling with heavy limousine bodywork severely limited the 10/20's performance.

'Neckarsulmer Strickmaschinen Union' became NSU in 1892 but its car production was tentative and its low-priced cars failed to catch the public's imagination, and its larger models were regarded as over-priced. Technical director Ernst Lehmann was engaged in 1910 to design the 3.3 litre 13/35 but it was not until the 1920s that NSU made its mark with cars.

BODY
2 door, 4 seater landaulette; 1650kg (3300lb).

ENGINE
4 cylinders, in line; front; 85.0x115.0, 2610cc; 16.2kW (22bhp); 6.2kW/l (8.4bhp/l).

ENGINE STRUCTURE
Overhead inlet, side exhaust; 2 valves per cylinder; 1 gear driven side camshaft; cast iron cylinder head and block; 3 bearing crankshaft; single carburettor; water cooled

TRANSMISSION
Rear wheel drive, separate 4 speed gearbox; spiral bevel final drive, 5.0.

CHASSIS DETAILS
Separate steel chassis; steel and fabric body; front suspension, dead axle, semi-elliptic springs; rear suspension, live axle, semi-elliptic springs; rear wheel drum brakes.

DIMENSIONS
Wheelbase 302.0cm (118.9in), front track 130.0cm (51.2in), rear track 130.0cm (51.2in)

PERFORMANCE
Maximum speed 41-44mph (65-70km/h); 101.9kg/kW (75.0bhp/kg).

Right: Never strikingly pretty, NSUs of before the First World War tended to be severely practical. Tall narrow bodywork, with scant regard for fashion, weakened their market appeal.

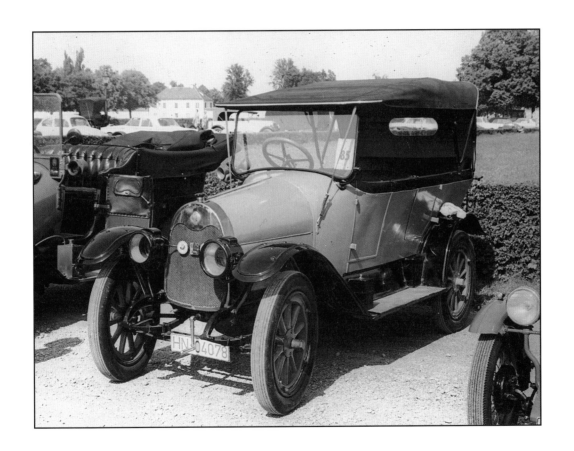

There was a trend towards larger-engined cars during this period, although NSU stayed with a four-cylinder design for its new 13/35, with which it intended to complement the slightly smaller 10/30. Overhead inlet valves with side exhaust valves were used, both operated by a single gear-driven low-mounted camshaft. The original model used an NSU carburettor, but later the move was made to Zenith. With more power, the 13/35 was able to carry a larger body, including an imposing four-door limousine of impressive dimensions.

NSU's fortunes improved with the development of the 5/12. It was put into production with a four cylinder engine of 1163cc and was a true miniature car like the Bébé Peugeot designed by Bugatti. The 5/12 evolved into the 5/15 and then the 5/20, and its popularity continued for ten years.

BODY
4 door limousine, 4 seats; weight 1350kg (2970lb).

ENGINE
4 cylinders in two pairs, in line; front; 97.0x115.0mm, 3300cc; 25.7kW/35bhp @ 1700rpm; 7.8kW/l (10.6bhp/l).

ENGINE STRUCTURE
Overhead inlet, side exhaust; 2 valves per cylinder; 1 gear driven side camshaft; cast iron cylinder head and block; 3 bearing crankshaft; water cooled.

TRANSMISSION
Rear wheel drive; separate 4 gearbox; hypoid bevel final drive, 3.3.

CHASSIS DETAILS
Separate steel chassis; steel body; front suspension, dead axle, semi-elliptic springs; rear suspension, live axle, three-quarter elliptic springs; rear wheel drum brakes; worm steering; 820x120 tyres.

DIMENSIONS
Wheelbase 320.0cm (126.0in), front track 137.5cm (54.1in), rear track 137.5cm (54.1in).

PERFORMANCE
Maximum speed 53mph (85km/h); 52.5kg/kW (38.6kg/bhp).

Right: Claims for the NSU on sales material "overreaches the highest promises.. has the honourable distinctions of beauty, speed, and reliability. The NSU motor car received great acclaim at the Berlin Motor Show."

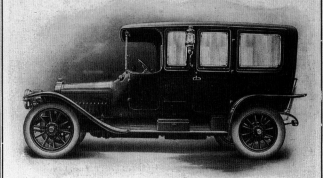

AUDI Type G 4-cylinder 1919

For Audi, as with the rest of Germany's motor industry, the sole object at the end of the Great War was to pick up the pieces and start again. Rather than spend time and resources on developing a new model, Audi simply started to build a slightly revised version of the Type G it had been producing before the start of hostilities. Power was raised from 16.4 to 20.1kW, with the four cylinder engine now revving to 2200rpm.

The rest of the mechanical side of the G4 remained unchanged, with Bosch magneto ignition and fuel supply to the Zenith carburettor through a Pallas Autovac. But rather than the heavy saloon coachwork used on pre-war models, the G4 was now built with a lighter open four-seater touring body.

Despite a new model programme, by the 1920s Audi was in financial difficulties. A takeover, ironically by Horch, was proposed but came to naught. In October 1926 Audi was restructured but the losses persisted.

BODY
2 door tourer; 4 seats; 900kg (1980lb).

ENGINE
4 cylinders, in line; front; 75.0x118.0mm, 2071cc; 20.1kW (28bhp) @ 1900rpm; 10.1kW/l (13.5bhp/l).

ENGINE STRUCTURE
Side valve; 2 valves per cylinder; 1 gear drive side camshaft; cast iron monoblock; 3 bearing crankshaft; Zenith 30 Type carburettor; water cooled.

TRANSMISSION
Rear wheel drive; 4 speed gearbox; spiral bevel final drive, 4.45.

CHASSIS DETAILS
Box-section chassis; steel and fabric bodywork; front suspension, beam axle, semi-elliptic springs; rear suspension, live axle, semi-elliptic springs; rear wheel drum brakes; worm steering; 8.20x120 tyres.

DIMENSIONS
Wheelbase 299.5cm (117.9in), front track 125.0cm (49.2in), rear track 125.0cm (49.2in).

PERFORMANCE
Maximum speed 40mph (65kph); 44.7 kg/kW (32.1kg/bhp).

Right: **Proud prow. The Audi radiator had a flagstaff style of mascot on top, which was a stylised figure '1'.**

DKW SB 1919

After the fiasco of the Dampfkraftwagen, an attempt to make a steam car, Rasmussen's first production car was a very different vehicle. At the 1923 Berlin Motor Show, DKW exhibited two similar models, one electric-powered, the other with a motor cycle engine. The car's origins went back rather earlier, when Slaby Beringer developed a tiny electric vehicle, with tiller steering. The SB had a lightweight steel chassis and very basic plywood bodywork; four and six-wheel versions were made. Rasmussen acquired Slaby Beringer GmBH when the company went bankrupt in 1922, offering Beringer a position on the board of DKW and making Rudolf Slaby chief engineer of Zschopau Engine Works.

The 'new' SB now had a steering wheel, and was powered by a 175cc single cylinder two-stroke DKW motor cycle engine developing 2.5bhp at 3500rpm. The chain drive to the rear wheel was through a two-speed gearbox. The SB's bodywork remained as basic as before, retaining the plywood side panels and steel cover over the driver's legs. Before production of the electric SB was ended in 1923, 2005 had been exported to the Far East, through a company called the Japan and

German Electric Car Co.

Stanley and Doble technology from the United States went into the Dampfkraftwagen, the original DKW. Its two cylinder engine wanted a 100 Bar atmospheric pressure, or 1450 p.s.i. of steam from the oil fuelled vertical tube boiler. Its 500 litre water tank gave it a range of 56 miles (90km). Rasmussen persevered with the Dampf Kraft Wagen, or steam powered car, until the 1920s.

HORCH 10/35 1921

Although aluminium was used in aero engines, it was still a comparatively rare material for car engine designers. Horch made the most of supercharger expert Arnold Zoller's experience to produce a new engine using this material, but Zoller resigned before the job was finished. It was left to Paul Daimler to develop the 10/35 into the 10/50.

It was a conventional enough long stroke design, with a side valve layout and three bearing crankshaft. The benefit of using aluminium was reflected in the relatively low overall weight of the 10/35, at just 1300kg, but difficulties encountered in working with it meant that Horch went back to cast iron for subsequent models. The first 10/35 ran with three-quarter elliptic rear springs, which changed to a semi-elliptic layout from 1923 onwards.

The company's name changed from A Horch & Cie Motorenwagen-Werke AG Zwickau:Sa to Horch-Werke AG under its new managing director Jacob Holler. Profits reached a million Marks and the capital value of the company went up to more than 2.25 million Marks.

BODY
Four-door, four seat saloon; weight 1300kg (2600lb).

ENGINE
4 cylinders, in line; front; 80.0x130.0mm; 2630cc; 25.7kW (35bhp) @ 2000rpm; 9.8kW/l (13.3bhp/l).

ENGINE STRUCTURE
Side valve; 2 valves per cylinder; 1 gear driven side camshaft; aluminium alloy cylinder head and block; 3 bearing crankshaft; single Pallas carburettor; water cooled.

TRANSMISSION
Rear wheel drive; 4 speed gearbox; bevel final drive, 4.67.

CHASSIS DETAILS
Separate U-section steel chassis; steel body; front suspension, dead axle, semi-elliptic springs; rear suspension, live axle, three-quarter elliptic springs; rear wheel drum brakes; 820x120 tyres.

DIMENSIONS
Wheelbase 322.0cm (126.8in), front track 138.0cm (54.3in), rear track 138.0cm (54.3in), overall length 455.0cm (179in), overall width 160.0cm (63.0in), overall height 225.0cm (88.6in)

PERFORMANCE
Maximum speed 50mph (80kph); 50.6kg/kW (37.1kg/bhp), fuel consumption 19mpg (14.9l/100km) manufacturer's fig.

Right: Horch exports amounted to half its output before the war. In 1919 they rose further and by 1925 they were three times the 1913 figure.

It was three years after the Armistice at the end of the First World War before Wanderer was able to restart production. The W6 6/18 was a large car, with a very tall and upright two-door saloon body on a longer wheelbase version of the 5/15 chassis. The 1551cc engine was also based on the one used in the previous model, but now using a Pallas carburettor.

Despite the increases in size and weight, the W6 had to rely on the single transmission foot brake for stopping. But after the rather basic earlier models, with ponderous saloon styling, the W6 pointed to the way in which Wanderer would develop in the years to come.

Wanderer was a leading supplier of motorcycles and bicycles to the German army, and its tandem-seat Püppchen reconnaissance vehicle was approved of by staff officers. Adapting to peacetime demand proved problematical however, and after good results in 1920 and 1921, layoffs and financial crises continued for several years.

BODY
2 door saloon; 4 seats; weight 700kg (1540lb).

ENGINE
4 cylinders, in line; front; 67.0x110.0mm, 1551cc; 13kW (18bhp) @ 1800rpm; 8.4kW/l (11.6bhp/l).

ENGINE STRUCTURE
Side valve, 2 valves per cylinder; 1 gear driven side camshaft; cast iron cylinder head and block; 3 bearing crankshaft; Pallas carburettor; water cooled.

TRANSMISSION
Rear wheel drive; 4 speed gearbox; spiral bevel final drive, 4.50.

CHASSIS DETAILS
U beam separate chassis; steel bodywork; front and rear suspension, semi-elliptic springs; Foot brake acting on external contracting drum on propeller shaft; handbrake on rear wheel drums; 30.0l (6.7 Imp gal) (7.9 US gal) fuel tank; 760x100 tyres.

DIMENSIONS
Wheelbase 275.0cm (108.3in), front track 118.0cm (46.5in), rear track 118.0cm (46.5in), overall length 385.0cm (151.6in), overall width 139.0cm (54.7in), overall height 142.0cm (55.9in).

PERORMANCE
Maximum speed 50mph (80kph); 53.8kg/kW (38.9kg/bhp); average fuel consumption 31.3mpg (9.0l/100km) manufacturer's fig.

WANDERER W8 1921

If Audi and Horch were now moving up market, Wanderer seemed determined to follow its own path. Many manufacturers were using detachable cylinder heads, but Wanderer stubbornly continued with a single-piece engine block casting, with overhead valves and chain driven camshaft. Wanderer also continued with some off-beat body styles, with the two seater now having the driver on the right, while the passenger seat was behind and to the left; the spare wheel was strapped alongside the driver's right elbow. There was just one door, on the left.

A Sportwagen version, called the Targa Florio, used a longer stroke, 1498cc version of the engine, with 29.8kW output. But this even this model stayed with the W8's rear wheel drum brakes.

BODY
2 door tourer; 4 seats; 850kg (1870lb).

ENGINE
4 cylinders, in line; front; 64.5x100.0mm, 1306cc; 14.9kW (20bhp) @ 2000rpm; 11.4 kW/l (15.3bhp/l).

ENGINE STRUCTURE
Ohv; 2 valves per cylinder; 1 chain driven side camshaft; cast iron monoblock; 3 bearing crankshaft; Pallas carburettor; water cooled.

TRANSMISSION
Rear wheel drive; 3 speed gearbox; spiral bevel final drive, 4.60.

CHASSIS DETAILS
Section chassis, steel and fabric body; front suspension, beam axle, semi-elliptic springs; rear suspension; live axle, semi-elliptic springs; worm steering; rear wheel drum brakes; 7.10x1300 tyres.

DIMENSIONS
Wheelbase 239.5cm (94.3in), front track 108.0cm (42.5in), rear track 108.0cm (42.5in), overall length 325.0cm (128.9in), overall width 133.0cm (52.4in), overall height 142.0cm (55.9in).

PERFORMANCE
Maximum speed 48mph (78kph); 57.1kg/kW (42.5kg/bhp); average fuel consumption 33mpg (8.5 l/100km) manufacturer's fig.

Advancing technology meant that NSU was now using a separate cylinder head and block, both in cast iron. However, the conventional side valve layout was retained, as was thermosyphon cooling, without the benefit of a water pump. Mechanically-operated wheel brakes on the rear axle alone had to provide all the stopping power.

A variety of bodies were listed, from the sports two-seater through double phaeton to the phaeton-landaulette. The chasis price was 6300 marks, with bodies costing from between 500 to 3300 marks.

NSU's car production was growing. By 1923 it was making a car every two hours, a motorcycle every 20 minutes, and bicycle every 5 minutes. Car sales received a boost when the 5/15 scored competition successes.

BODY
4 door double phaeton, 4 seats; weight 1700kg (3740lb).

ENGINE
4 cylinders, in line; front; 80.0x 104.4mm, 2091cc; 17.6kW (24bhp); 8.4kW/l (11.5bhp/l).

ENGINE STRUCTURE
Side valve; 2 valves per cylinder; 1 gear driven side camshaft; cast iron cylinder head and block; 3 bearing crankshaft; single carburettor; water cooled

TRANSMISSION
Rear wheel drive; separate 4 speed gearbox; hypoid bevel final drive, .

CHASSIS DETAILS
Separate steel chassis, steel bodywork; front suspension, dead front axle, semi-elliptic springs; rear suspension, live axle, semi-elliptic springs; rear wheel drum brakes; 810x100 rear tyres.

DIMENSIONS
Wheelbase 290.0cm (144.2in), front track 125.0cm (49.2in), rear track 125.0cm (49.2in), overall length 410.0cm (161.4in), overall width 150.0cm (59.1in).

PERFORMANCE
95.6kg/kW (70.8kg/bhp).

Right: Folding windscreen, faired sidelights, and serpentine bulb horn are features of this elegant 8/24 Double Phaeton along with upholstered "club" seats in the back.

AUDI 14/50 Type K 1922

The preceding Type G was something of a stopgap model hurriedly conceived in the year after WW1 ended. This gave time for Audi to design its most ambitious model so far. The cylinder block was cast in aluminium alloy, with steel cylinder bore liners, while a gear-driven camshaft operated the overhead valves by means of pushrods. Ignition was by Bosch magneto, and fuel was fed to the carburettor by a Pallas Autovac system.

Audi kept chassis weight down by using aluminium for the rear axle casing, so that the Type K saloon weighed only 1400kg.

The engine, gearbox, radiator and steering box were mounted in a unit. If the engine was technically advanced, the chassis was rather less so. The driver had to rely on rear wheel brakes alone, while the suspension was by simple semi-elliptic springs front and rear. The Type K caught the public imagination and 750 were sold in its short, two year life-span.

The company's financial situation continued to be worrying, and in the difficult economic times, demand for large cars was bound to diminish.

BODY
4 door saloon; 4 seats; weight 1400kg (3080lb).

ENGINE
4 cylinders, in line; front; 90.0x140.0mm, 3562cc; 37.3kW/l (50bhp/l) @ 3000rpm; 10.7kW/l (14.3bhp/l).

ENGINE STRUCTURE
Ohv; 2 valves per cylinder; 1 gear driven side camshaft; cast iron head; aluminium alloy block with steel cylinder liners; 3 bearing crankshaft; Zenith TD36 carburettor; water cooled.

TRANSMISSION
Rear wheel drive; separate 4 speed gearbox; spiral bevel final drive, 4.30.

CHASSIS DETAILS
Separate box section chassis; steel body; front suspension, beam axle, semi-elliptic springs; rear suspension, live axle, semi-elliptic springs; rear wheel drum brakes; worm steering; 8.95x135 tyres

DIMENSIONS
Wheelbase 353.0cm (140.0in), front track 140.0cm (55.1in), rear track 140.0cm (55.1in).

PERFORMANCE
Maximum speed 59mph (95kph); 37.5kg/kW (28.0kg/bhp).

Right: Audi Phaeton with rather severe lines. *Above:* Advertisement for 14/35, 1919.

This was another Arnold Zoller-designed engine, but instead of using aluminium as he had done for the 1921 car, this was a new but conventional cast iron design, with side valves; later this same design would be developed into a six cylinder unit.

The 10/35 was a big car in the Horch tradition, with a choice of bodies, the most imposing of which was a tall, upright limousine. The original model used three-quarter elliptic springs for the rear suspension, but in 1923 this was changed to an underslung semi-elliptic layout.

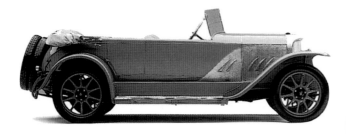

BODY
4 door saloon, 1050kg (2310lb)
4 cylinders in line; front;
80.0x130.0mm, 2630cc; 25.7kW/35bhp @ 2000rpm; 9.8kW/l (13.3bhp/l).

ENGINE STRUCTURE
Side valves; 2 valves per cylinder; 1 gear driven side camshaft; cast iron cylinder head and block; 3 bearing crankshaft; Pallas carburettor; water cooled.

TRANSMISSION
Rear wheel drive; 4 speed gearbox; hypoid bevel final drive, 4.67.

CHASSIS DETAILS
Separate steel chassis; front suspension, dead axle, semi-elliptic springs; rear suspension, live axle, three-quarter elliptic springs; drum brakes; worm steering; 820x120 tyres.

DIMENSIONS
Wheelbase 322.0cm (126.8in), front track 138.0cm (54.3in), rear track 138.0cm (54.3in); overall length 455.0cm (179.1in), overall width 160.0cm (62.9in), overall height 225.0cm (88.6in).

PERFORMANCE
Maximum speed 50mph (80km/h); 40.9kg/kW (30kg/bhp); average fuel consumption 118.8mpg manufacturer's fig.

Left and right: **Horch meant its cars to last. Magnificent 10/35 with open bodywork.**

NSU 14/40 Tourer 1922

This was the largest engine NSU was to use in its current series and, thanks to the flexibility a separate chassis allowed, the largest car. The 2.3 litre side-valve engine developed 29.4kW, and the three-speed gearbox remained as a separate unit from the engine, with a single-piece propeller shaft to the live rear axle.

  With its longer chassis and wider track, the 14/40 was offered with a range of bodies from a sports two seater to an imposing and very upright limousine. Exactly how many of each were sold is not recorded, but during the four years the model was in production in the years following WW1, a total of 275 chassis were built, gaining a fine reputation as a long-distance touring car. NSU made 3,500 cars in 1921, 4,650 in 1924, falling back to 4,000 in 1926 at the end of the motoring boom.

BODY
4door convertible; 4 seats; weight 1300kg (2860lb).

ENGINE
4 cylinders in line; front;85.0x100.0mm, 2269cc; 29.4kW (40bhp) @ 3200rpm; 12.9kW/l (17.6bhp/l).

ENGINE STRUCTURE
Side valve; 2 valves per cylinder; 1 gear driven side camshaft; cast iron cylinder head and block; 3 bearing crankshaft; single carburettor; water cooled.

TRANSMISSION
Rear wheel drive; separate 3 speed gearbox; hypoid bevel final drive, 5.0.

CHASSIS DETAILS
Separate steel chassis, steel bodywork; front suspension, dead front axle, semi-elliptic springs; rear suspension, live axle, semi-elliptic springs; rear wheel drum brakes.

DIMENSIONS
Wheelbase 263.5cm (103.7in), front track 115.0cm (45.3in), rear track 115.0cm (45.3in).

PERFORMANCE
Maximum speed 38-40mph (60-65kph), 135.6kg/kW (100.0kg/bhp).

Right: Once again the tulip shape for the body sides was a useful means of gaining width without sacrificing the practicality of running boards and mudguards. Oval window and frilled curtains hinted at railway carriage solidarity.

The vogue for long stroke engines during this period was brought about by a demand for good torque or pulling power throughout the limited rev range. With no synchromesh, drivers would hold on to gears for as long as possible when going up slopes, rather than go through the complex process of changing down. No torque figures were quoted for Paul Daimler's engine design, but the 130mm stroke was long by any standard current at the time.

Light alloys for engine structures were still new and Horch did pioneering work in developing a material it called Silumin for the new car's cylinder block. An alloy of aluminium and silicon it was cast with steel cylinder liners.

The rest of the design was conservative enough, with the 10/50 available with either an uncompromisingly upright saloon or a much lighter soft-top touring model. The suspension, with semi-elliptic springs front and rear, was conventional, but both models featured drum brakes on all four wheels which were starting to become common throughout the industry.

BODY
4 door saloon, 2 door touring; 4 seats; 2100kg (4621lb).

ENGINE
4 cylinders, in line; front; 80.0x130.0mm, 2630cc; compr 5.4:1; 37kW (50bhp) @ 2800rpm; 14.1kW/l (19.0bhp/l).

ENGINE STRUCTURE
Ohc; 2 valves per cylinder; 1 gear driven overhead camshaft; aluminium cylinder head and silumim block; 3 bearing crankshaft; Zenith 36 carburettor; water cooled.

TRANSMISSION
Rear wheel drive; 4 speed gearbox; spiral bevel final drive; 4.78.

CHASSIS DETAILS
U-section chassis; steel bodywork; front and rear suspension, semi-elliptic springs; friction dampers; drum brakes, mechanically operated; 55.0l (12.1 Imp gall) (15.5 US gall) fuel tank;

820x133 tyres.

DIMENSIONS
Wheelbase 330.0cm (129.9in), front track 138.0cm (54.3in), rear track 138.0cm (54.3in), overall length 450.0cm (177.2in), overall width 173.0cm 68.1(in), overall height 200.0cm (78.7in).

PERFORMANCE
Maximum speed 59mph (95kph); 57.8kg/kW (42.0kg/bhp); average fuel consumption 18.8 mpg (15.0l/100km).

Above: **Access to the rear was helped by tipping middle row of seats.**

Audi was gambling on its larger version of the Type K being a success, but in three years of production just 300 were made. The engine was seen as very advanced, with its aluminium alloy block using steel cylinder liners and duralumin connecting rods. There was more aluminium alloy for the rear axle casing, all of which managed to keep the Type M weight down to just 1700kg, even when carrying an imposing four-door limousine body.

Technical innovations on the chassis included hydraulically-operated drum brakes with servo assistance; while hydraulic dampers smoothed out the ride given by the simple semi-elliptic non-independent suspension. When production stopped in 1927, the far less complex Type R was ready to take its place. Probably the best Audi yet.

BODY
4 door limousine; 4 seats; 1700kg (3740lb).

ENGINE
6 cylinders, in line; front; 90.0x122.0mm, 4655cc; 52.2kW (70bhp) @ 3000rpm; 11.2kW/l (15.0 bhp/l).

ENGINE STRUCTURE
Ohv; 2 valves per cylinder; 1 gear driven camshaft; cast iron cylinder head; aluminium alloy block, with steel liners; 7 bearing crankshaft; Zenith 36DK carburettor; water cooled.

TRANSMISSION
Rear wheel drive; 4 speed gearbox; spiral bevel final drive.

CHASSIS DETAILS
Box-section chassis; steel body; front suspension, beam axle, semi-elliptic springs; rear suspension, live axle, semi-elliptic springs; hydraulic dampers; drum brakes; single hydraulic circuit with servo assistance; worm steering; 8.95x135 tyres.

DIMENSIONS
Wheelbase 375.0cm (147.6in), front track 145.0cm (57in), rear track 145.0cm (57in).

PERFORMANCE
Maximum speed 75mph (120kph); 35.7kg/kW (24.3kg/bhp).

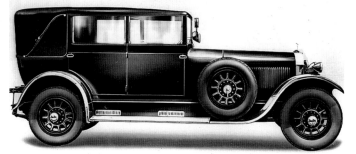

Right: Light weight engine. Audi's enthusiasm for radical light-metal design began in 1920s.

WANDERER S4 1924

The S4, also known as the W9, was the first Wanderer model to have a detachable cylinder head, but this apart the new 1.5 litre engine had a good deal in common with the smaller one from the W8, even staying with magneto ignition. But now there was a four-speed gearbox and, from late 1925, four wheel mechanically-operated drum brakes. The chassis, however, followed very conventional lines, since Wanderer seemed to have finally shed its 'cyclecar' image as far as body design was concerned. The W8 now had a straightforward two-door, four seater tourer style.

Company policy was continous througout the 1920s when survival rather than profit had to be uppermost in management's minds. Wanderer undertook a number of worthy but rather dull designs of which the W9 was first.

BODY
2 door tourer; 4 seats; 950kg (2090lb).

ENGINE
4 cylinders; in line; front; 67.0x110.0mm, 1551cc; 17.9kW (22bhp) @ 2800rpm; 11.5kW/l (15.5bhp/l).

ENGINE STRUCTURE
Ohv; 2 valves per cylinder; 1 chain driven side camshaft; cast iron cylinder head and block; 3 bearing crankshaft; Pallas carburettor; water cooled.

TRANSMISSION
Rear wheel drive; 4 speed gearbox; spiral bevel final drive; 4.50.

CHASSIS DETAILS
U-section chassis, steel body; front suspension, beam axle, semi-elliptic springs; rear suspension, live axle, semi-elliptic springs; worm steering; 765x105 tyres.

DIMENSIONS
Wheelbase 275.0cm (108.3in), front track 118.0 cm (46.5in), rear track 118.0cm (46.5in).

PERFORMANCE
Maximum speed 53mph (85kph); 53.1kg/kW (39.6kg/bhp); average fuel consumption 30mpg (29.7l/100km) manufacturer's fig.

Right: Bicycles, motorcycles, and cars. Wanderer's product lines from Schönau put post-war Germany on its wheels.

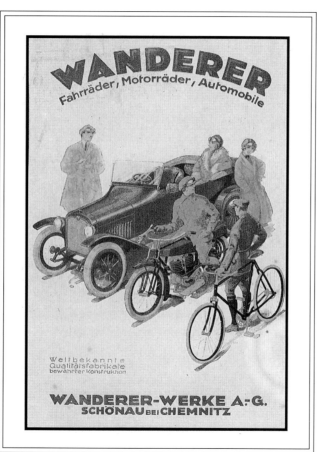

Technically the W10 was the most advanced Wanderer model to date. The side valve layout which had been used on some previous Wanderers was replaced by a new single overhead camshaft to operate the valves. Bevel drives from the nose of the crankshaft, via a vertical shaft to the camshaft, did away with the need for pushrods and reduced weight.

This new engine developed almost twice the power of the W6 engine, and was able to rev 1000rpm higher. This greater flexibility allowed Wanderer to go back to using a three-speed gearbox. Changing gear needed skill in the days before synchromesh, so the less changes needed, the easier it was to drive. The W10 was available as a four door open model or a more grand four door limousine, both running on broad spoked artillery wheels instead of the more usual wire-spoked variety.

The car sold successfully, and enabled its makers to pay shareholders a small dividend and start work on new factory buildings in Seigmar. Gläser of Dresden built the drophead models.

BODY
2 door open; 4 door saloon; 4 seats; weight 875kg (1929lb).

ENGINE
4 cylinders, in line; front; 6.70x110mm, 1551cc; compr 5.3:1; 22kW (30bhp) @ 2800rpm.

ENGINE STRUCTURE
Ohv; 2 valves per cylinder; 1 shaft-driven ohc; cast iron cylinder head and block; 3 bearing crankshaft; Pallas SA11 carburettor; water cooled.

TRANSMISSION
Rear wheel drive; 3 speed gearbox; spiral bevel final drive, 5.33.

CHASSIS DETAILS
Separate box section chassis; steel bodywork; front and rear suspension semi-elliptic springs; friction dampers; 4 wheel drum brakes; 45.0l (9.9 Imp gal) (11.9 US gal) fuel tank; 730x130 tyres.

DIMENSIONS
Wheelbase 280.0cm (110.2in), front track 125cm (49.2in), rear track 125cm (49.2in), overall length 430cm 169.3in), overall width 150cm (59.1in), overall height 180cm (70.9in).

PERFORMANCE
Max speed mph 53mph (85kph); 39.8kg/kW (29.2 kg/bhp); av fuel consumption 28mpg (10 l/100km) manufacturer's fig.

Right: Nobody could call a Wanderer of the 1920s rakish. A certain stolid charm yes, but racy – never. The company was progressive however, and in 1926 adopted a conveyor belt car assembly system. It had also begun to make components in chill-cast aluminium (silumin). This 6/30 shows evidence of the new electro-plating facility at the factory.

WANDERER
6/30

A 4755

NSU 5/30 Avus Sportwagen 1926

The four-cylinder side valve 1.2-litre engine was sufficiently strong to allow it to be tuned to develop 22.1kW at 3100rpm, surprisingly high for this period. Drive to the rear wheels was through a four-speed gearbox, but despite the top speed of around 78mph, the 5/30 driver had to rely on rear wheel brakes alone.

Accordingly it was natural for NSU to further its reputation by taking part in motor sport, which it did with some vigour starting with the Prince Henry Trials in which its cars acquitted themselves well against much larger-engined opposition.

The 75 mph victory of the 5/15 in the 1923 Avusrennen at Berlin was specially noteworthy. A team of three factory cars finished within 42 seconds of one another after an hour's racing in a fine display of speed and reliability. A 1.5-litre supercharged prototype scored again in 1925.

BODY
Two-seater racing car; weight 510kg (1122lb).

ENGINE
4 cylinders, in line; front; 68.0x90.0 mm, 1230cc; 22.1kW (30bhp) @ 3100rpm; 18.0 kW/l (24.4bhp/l).

ENGINE STRUCTURE
Side valve; 2 valves per cylinder; 1 gear driven side camshaft; cast iron cylinder head and block; 3 bearing crankshaft; single carburettor; water cooled.

TRANSMISSION
Rear wheel drive; separate 4 speed gearbox; hypoid bevel final drive.

CHASSIS DETAILS
Separate steel chassis, aluminium bodywork; front suspension, dead front axle, semi-elliptic springs; rear suspension, live axle, semi-elliptic springs; rear wheel drum brakes; 710x100 tyres.

DIMENSIONS
Wheelbase 265.0cm (104.3in).

PERFORMANCE
Maximum speed 78mph (125kph), 23.1kg/kW (17.0kg/bhp).

Right: **The 1926 German Grand Prix team of NSUs. They took the first four places in the small car class. Klöble's winning speed for the 400 kms was 128.8kph (80mph).**

HORCH 306 13/65 1927

Unveiled at the 1927 Berlin Motor Show, the 13/65 quickly attracted large crowds. The 306 was the first of the Horch 8 series of cars with a new twin overhead camshaft engine designed by Horch's chief engineer, Paul Daimler, son of Gottlieb Daimler, one of the founders of the German motor industry. In every respect the limousine was a massive motor vehicle, weighing 1800kg; the cabriolet ran on a 29cm shorter wheelbase, but with the same track.

All models used straightforward semi-elliptic suspension, and the mechanically-operated drum brakes were assisted by a vacuum servo. A smaller, short-stroke version of the engine, with a capacity of 3132cc and output of 45.6kW, was used in the slightly less expensive 12/60 303.

BODY
4 door saloon/cabriolet; weight 1800kg (3960lb).

ENGINE
8 cylinders, in line; front; 67.5x118.0mm, 3328cc; compr 5.4:1; 48.5kW (65bhp) @ 3200rpm; 14.5kW/l (19.5 bhp/l).

ENGINE STRUCTURE
Ohv; 2 valves per cylinder; 2 gear driven overhead camshafts; cast iron cylinder head and block; 5 bearing crankshaft; Solex 40 MCV carburettor; water cooled.

TRANSMISSION
Rear wheel drive; 4 speed gearbox; spiral bevel final drive, 5.11.

CHASSIS DETAILS
Separate U-section chassis; steel bodywork; front suspension, dead axle, semi-elliptic springs; rear suspension, live axle, underslung semi-elliptic springs; drum brakes; Bosch-Dewandre vacuum servo; worm steering; 100.0l

(22.0 Imp gal) (26.4 US gal) fuel tank; 6.50x20 tyres.

DIMENSIONS
Wheelbase 345.0cm (135.8in), front track 142.5cm (56.1in), rear track 141.4cm (55.7in), turning circle 14.5m (47.9ft), overall length 470.0cm (185.0in), overall width 176.5cm (69.5in), overall height 190.0cm (74.8in).

PERFORMANCE
Maximum speed 62mph (100kph); 37.1kg/kW (27.7kg/bhp); average fuel consumption 16.6mpg (17.0l/100km).

Left: Daimler's magnificent Twin-cam head with gear drive at the rear.
Right: Horch advertised Germany's first production 8-cylinder.

AUDI R1 1928

After the complexity of the Type K and M, with their linered aluminium alloy blocks, Audi returned to more basic engineering for the Type R. The initial used was from Rickenbacker, whose engine technology Audi was now using under licence. The design was kept simple, with side valves, just five crankshaft bearings and a three-speed gearbox. There was nothing new about the chassis, either, which was thoroughly conventional, with mechanically-operated Perrot-Bendix drum brakes and semi-elliptic springs.

Sales, however, hardly prospered, with just 150 being sold in the first year. Later the Type R was renamed the Imperator, with a two-door roadster body which would not have looked out of place in Chicago.

Audi's declining fortunes had led to a takeover by the Zschopauer Motorenwerke JS Rasmussen AG. Jörgen Skafte Rasmussen, the founder of DKW was elected to the supervisary board and effectively took charge. He bought the design and the engine plant from the defunct American Rickenbacker company which ceased making cars in 1927.

BODY
4 door saloon; 4 seats; weight 2300kg (5060lb).

ENGINE
8 cylinders, in line; front; 80.0x122.6mm, 4870cc; 74.6kW (100bhp) @ 2700rpm; 15.3kW/l (20.5bhp/l).

ENGINE STRUCTURE
Side valve; 2 valves per cylinder; 1 gear driven camshaft; cast iron cylinder head and block; 5 bearing crankshaft; Zenith carburettors; water cooled.

TRANSMISSION
Rear wheel drive; 3 speed gearbox; spiral bevel final drive, 5.20.

CHASSIS DETAILS
Box-section chassis; steel body; front suspension, beam axle, semi-elliptic springs; rear suspension, live axle, underslung semi-elliptic springs; hydraulic dampers; drum brakes; worm steering; 70.0l (15.4 US gal) (18.5 US gal) fuel tank; 7.00x20 tyres.

DIMENSIONS
Wheelbase 362.0cm (142.5in), front track 145.0cm (57.1in), rear track 145.0cm (57.0in).

PERFORMANCE
Maximum speed 75mph (120kph); 0.8kg/kW (23.0kg/bhp).

Right: Still number 1. A 1928 Audi with mascot design claim.

HORCH Type 350 1928

Horch's main shareholder Dr Strauss recruited Stoewer engineer Fritz Fiedler (later to gain fame with BMW) to deal with technical problems in Paul Daimler's twin-cam straight-eight engine. New production techniques enabled it to reduce prices by over one-third as the luxury car market slumped.

Innenansicht der Horch 8 - Weymann - Limousine

BODY
4 door saloon/cabriolet; 4 seats; weight 1400kg (3080lb).

ENGINE
8 cylinders, in line; front; 73.1x118.0mm, 3950cc; compr 5.4:1; 60kW (80bhp) @ 3200rpm; 15.2kW/l (20.2bhp/l).

ENGINE STRUCTURE
Ohv; 2 valves per cylinder; 2 overhead camshafts, bevel gear drive; cast iron cylinder head and block; 5 bearing crankshaft; Solex 35MHOV carburettor; water cooled.

TRANSMISSION
Rear wheel drive; 4 speed gearbox; spiral bevel final drive; 5.11; 5.33 or 5.55 option.

CHASSIS DETAILS
Pressed steel U-section chassis; steel bodywork; front suspension semi-elliptic springs; rear suspension, underslung semi-elliptic springs; drum brakes; Bosch/Dewandre vacuum servo;

worm steering; 90.0l (19.8 Imp gal) (23.8 US gal) fuel tank.

DIMENSIONS
Wheelbase 345.0cm (135.8 in), front track 142.5cm (56.1in), rear track 141.4cm (55.7in), turning circle 13.5m (44.6ft), overall length 500.0cm (196.9 in), overall width 176.5cm (69.5in), overall height 190.0cm (74.8in).

PERFORMANCE
Maximum speed 62mph (100kph); 23.3kg/kW (17.5kg/bhp); average fuel consumption 18.8 mpg (15.0 l/100km) manufacturer's fig.

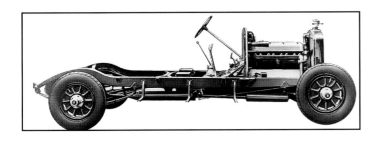

HORCH Type 375 18/20 1928

This was the second of the Horch 8 models, again with Paul Daimler responsible for the design of the engine. For the 375 he went back to a simpler valve gear layout, with just a single gear-driven overhead camshaft. But he did use the same basic block.

Buyers had the choice between a massive and imposing limousine and a rather smaller cabriolet. There was also the option of a 5.11 or 5.33 final drive ratio, the latter giving rather better acceleration. There were few changes in the straightforward chassis, which used semi-elliptic springs and servo-assisted mechanically-operated drum brakes.

BODY
4 door saloon/cabriolet; weight 2200kg (4840lb).

ENGINE
8 cylinders, in line; front; 73.0x118.0mm, 3950cc; compr 5.4:1; 59.7kW (80bhp) @ 3200rpm; 15.1kW/l (20.2bhp/l).

ENGINE STRUCTURE
Ohv; 2 valves per cylinder; 1 spur gear driven overhead camshaft; cast iron cylinder head and block; 5 bearing crankshaft; Solex 40MOV carburettor; water cooled.

TRANSMISSION
Rear wheel drive; 4 speed gearbox; spiral bevel final drive, 5.11 or 5.33.

CHASSIS DETAILS
Separate box-section chassis; steel bodywork; front suspension, dead axle, semi-elliptic suspension; rear suspension, live axle, underslung semi-elliptic suspension; drum brakes; Bosch-Dewandre vacuum sero; ZF-Gemmer worm steering; 90.0l (19.8 Imp gal) (23.8 US gal) fuel tank; 6.50x20 tyres.

DIMENSIONS
Wheelbase 345.0cm (135.8in), front track 142.5cm (56.1in), rear track 141.4cm (55.7in), turning circle 13.5m (44.6ft), overall length 500.0cm (196.9in), overall width 176.5cm (69.5in), overall height 190.0cm (74.8in).

PERFORMANCE
Maximum speed 62mph (100kph); 36.9kg/kW (27.5kg/bhp); average fuel consumption 14.9mpg (19.0l/100km).

Left and right: **Winged emblem used on 8 cylinder cars created by Professor Hadank to exemplify precision of new machine tools.**

DKW P-15 1928

During and immediately after the First World War DKW built few small cars, its main business remaining deeply involved with motor cycles. It returned to the automobile business in 1928, with the P-15, the first in a long line of production two-stroke cars. Wood had long been used in coachbuilding to form the frame over which metal panels were fastened. DKW went a step further, using wood panels to form the simple cabriolet body for its new model.

The rear wheel drive P-15 used a simple semi-elliptic suspension layout, with mechanically-operated drum brakes on all four wheels. Rather less refined was the three-speed Prometheus gearbox, which, with the limited power and torque available, needed skill to use without creating terrible noises.

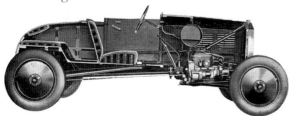

BODY
2 door cabriolet; 2 seats; weight 530kg (1166lb).
ENGINE
2 cylinders, in line; front; 74.0x68.0mm, 584cc; comp 5.5:1; 11.2kW (15bhp) @ 3500rpm; 19.2kW/l (25.7bhp/l).
ENGINE STRUCTURE
Ported two stroke; cast iron cylinder head and block; 3 bearing crankshaft; Meco M2N carburettor; water cooled.
TRANSMISSION
Rear wheel drive; 3 speed gearbox; spiral bevel final drive, 5.50.
CHASSIS DETAILS
Separate chassis; plywood body; front suspension, beam axle, transverse semi-elliptic spring; rear suspension, live axle, transverse semi-elliptic spring; drum brakes; worm steering; 20.0l (4.4 Imp gal) (5.3 US gal) fuel tank; 3.50 or 4.00x26 tyres.

DIMENSIONS
Wheelbase 259.0cm (101.9in), front track 110.0cm (42.3in), rear track 110.0cm (42.3in), overall length 360.0cm (141.7in), overall width 135.0cm (53.1in), overall height 160.0cm (63.0in).
PERFORMANCE
Maximum speed 50mph (80kph); 47.3kg/kW (35.3kg/bhp).

Left and right: **Gravity-feed fuel supply, two stroke engine, fabric-covered wooden body were recipe for minimal motoring in the 1920s, one stage up from motorcycle and sidecar. Sophisticated for a small car of the time it had a differential which some cyclecars did not, and a neat metal engine cover with cooling louvres.**

132

Using the same chassis as the 1926 W10, Wanderer installed its new 2.0 litre 30kW four cylinder overhead valve engine in its 1929 model. But inflation was seriously affecting the German economy, so the new model was built down to a price which would make it more acceptable to potential buyers.

The four-seater open version of the 6/30 form of the W10 in 1928 cost 6,250 Marks, while in the following year the 8/40, with its larger engine and greater performance, was being offered for just 6,000 Marks. In addition to the open car, there were also two and four-door saloon versions.

BODY
4 door saloon, 2 door convertible; 4 seats; weight 875kg (1925lb).

ENGINE
4 cylinders, in line; front; 72.0x120.0mm, 1940cc; compr 5.3:1; 30kW (40bhp) @ 2800rpm; 15.5kW/l (20.6bhp/l; 112.7Nm (11.5mkp) @ 2000rpm.

ENGINE STRUCTURE
Ohv; 2 valves per cylinder; 1 gear driven camshaft; cast iron cylinder head and block; 3 bearing crankshaft; Pallas SA11 carburettor; water cooled.

TRANSMISSION
Rear wheel drive; 3 speed gearbox; spiral bevel final drive, 5.33.

CHASSIS DETAILS
Separate box section chassis; steel bodywork; front and rear suspension, semi-elliptic springs; friction dampers; 4 wheel drum brakes, rod operated; 45.0l (9.9 Imp gal) (11.9 US gal) fuel tank; 730x130 tyres.

DIMENSIONS
Wheelbase 280.0cm (109.4in), front track 125.0cm (49.2in), rear track 125.0cm (49.2in), overall length 430.0cm (169.3in), overall width 150.0cm (59.1in), overall height 180.0cm (70.9in).

PERFORMANCE
Maximum speed 59mph (95kph); 29.2kg/kW (21.9kg/bhp); average fuel consumption 25.7mpg (11l/100km).

Right: Advertisement for the W10/2 shows Hirth, Varta and Bosch amongst component suppliers. Open tourers still popular in 1929.

WANDERER-OFFENER TOURENWAGEN,
TYPE W 10/2, 8/40 PS

MOTOR, GETRIEBE, HINTERACHSE, VORDERACHSE, LENKUNG

Motor, Fabrikat, Type	Wanderer, W 10/2
Anzahl der Zylinder	4
Bohrung	72 mm
Hub	120 mm
Verdichtungsverhältnis	
bei Benzin	—
bei Benzol	—
bei Gemisch Benzin-Benzol	1 : 5,3
Hubraum	1940 cm³
Arbeitsweise	Viertakt
Drehzahl normal	2800 Umdr./min.
Drehzahl maximal	4300 Umdr./min.
Gebremste Dauerleistung	38 PS
Gebremste Spitzenleistung	42 PS
Größtes Drehmoment des Motors	11,5 mkg bei 2000 Umdr./min.
Gußform der Zylinder	Block
Zylinder-Werkstoff	Grauguß
Zylinderkopf	abnehmbar
Ventilanordnung	Einl. hängend; Ausl. hängend
Zahl der Nockenwellen	1
Nockenwellenanordnung	im Kurbelgehäuse
Nockenwellenantrieb	Zahnkette
Kurbelgehäuse-Werkstoff	Aluminium
Kurbelwellenlagerung	Gehäuseoberteil mit Lagerdeckel
Zahl der Kurbelwellenhauptlager	3
Art der Kurbelwellenhauptlager	Gleitlager
Pleuelstangen-Werkstoff	Stahl
Kolben-Werkstoff	Aluminium-Speziallegierung
Kolbenbolzenanordnung	schwimmend mit Pilzen
Aufhängung des Motors	mit Hilfsrahmen
Schmierung des Motors	Druckumlauf, mit Zahnradpumpe
Ölreiniger, Fabrikat, Type	Hirth
Zündung	Magnetzündung
Fabrikat, Type	Bosch, FF 4, R 99.
Zündfolge	1 : 4 : 2
Zündverstellung	automatisch
Lichtmaschine, Fabrikat, Type	Bosch, J 60/1200/6, 12 Volt
Leistung	60 Watt bei 900 Umdr./min.
Anlasser, Fabrikat, Type	Bosch, BNL 0,6/6 R 1 Z 7, 12 Volt
Batterie, Fabrikat, Type	Varta, 6 Volt
Kapazität	70 Ampèrestunden

WANDERER 10/50 W11 1928

This was Wanderer's biggest car ever. The six cylinder 2.5-litre engine featured an overhead valve layout, with the camshaft shaft driven from the front of the crankshaft. Yet it retained a three-speed gearbox and low overall gearing. Where the W11 did break new ground was in the hydraulic operation of its drum brakes.

On the basic chassis buyers were offered a wide range of body styles including open, roadster cabriolet and saloon styles. The Pullman Limousine had a longer wheelbase – 317cm against the standard 292cm – and tipped the scales at 1350kg. Most models just managed to reach 60mph, while fuel consumption was around 19mpg.

In 1930 the W11 appeared as a sporting version known as the W11S with a 2995 cc engine, a lowered cross-braced chassis, and a Maybach two-speed back axle. This had the effect of an overdrive and the extension of the wheelbase to 12ft 2in allowed the fitting of glamorous sports cabriolet bodywork by Gläser of Dresden. Its top speed was around 80mph.

BODY
4 door open, saloon; 4 seats; weight 1050kg (2310lb).

ENGINE
6 cylinders, in line; front; 72.0x104.0mm, 2540cc; comp 5.3:1; 37.3kW (50bhp) @ 3400rpm; 14.7kW/l (19.7bhp/l); 142Nm (14.5mkp) @ 2000rpm.

ENGINE STRUCTURE
Ohv; 2 valves per cylinder; 1 overhead camshaft; cast iron cylinder head and block; 5 bearing crankshaft; Pallas sidedraught carburettor; water cooled.

TRANSMISSION
Rear wheel drive; 3 speed Wanderer gearbox; spiral bevel final drive, 5.77.

CHASSIS DETAILS
Separate box section chassis; steel bodywork; front and rear suspensions semi-elliptic springs; friction dampers; drum brakes front and rear, hydraulically operated; single braking circuit; 45.0l (9.9Imp gal) (11.9 US gal) fuel tank; 6.00x30 tyres.

DIMENSIONS
Wheelbase 292.0cm (115.0in), front track 142.0cm (55.9in), rear track 142.0cm (55.9in), overall length 430.0cm (169.3in), overall width 172.0cm (67.7in), overall height 185.0cm (72.8in).

PERFORMANCE
Maximum speed 60mph (90kph); 61.9kg/kW (46.2 kg/ bhp); average fuel consumption 18.8mpg (15.0l/100km).

Right: **High straight waistline and good proportions characteristic of late 1920s German body design on Wanderer 11.**

NSU 6/30 1928

Despite the increasingly serious financial situation in Germany at the time, with inflation running out of control, NSU went ahead with its six-cylinder 6/30 models. The new 1.6 litre engine developed 22.1kW, but the car remained faithful to a three-speed gearbox.

Also in 1928 NSU produced the 7/34, and both models were effectively the last designed until the outbreak of the Second World War. The 6/30 was available either as a saloon or a 2+2 roadster, with a dickey seat tucked away in the tail, and the factory also produced a version with a Roots supercharger in an effort to overcome the restrictions imposed by side valves.

NSU had not learned financial prudence however, building a new plant at Heilbronn. No sooner was it complete than it had to be sold to Fiat, and the old NSU company broke away from car manufacturing, leaving motorcycles to rule the roost.

BODY
4 door roadster, limousine, 4 seats; weight 750kg (1650lb).

ENGINE
6 cylinders, in line; front; 60.8x 90.0mm, 1567cc; 22.1kW (30bhp) @ 3000rpm; 14.1kW/l (19.1bhp/l).

ENGINE STRUCTURE
Side valve; 2 valves per cylinder; 1 gear-driven side camshaft; cast iron cylinder head and block; 5 bearing crankshaft; single carburettor; water cooled.

TRANSMISSION
Rear wheel drive; 3 speed gearbox; hypoid bevel final drive.

CHASSIS DETAILS
Separate U-section steel chassis, steel bodywork; front suspension, dead axle, semi-elliptic springs; rear suspension, live axle, semi-elliptic springs; drum brakes.

DIMENSIONS
Wheelbase 281.5cm (110.8in), front track 125.0cm (49.2in), rear track 125.0cm (49.2in), overall length 406.0cm (159.8 in), overall width 155.0cm (61.0in)

PERFORMANCE
33.9kg/kW (25.0kg/bhp).

Right: Last in line. Henceforward NSUs would be NSU-Fiats, the company title changing in 1930 to NSU-Automobil AG.

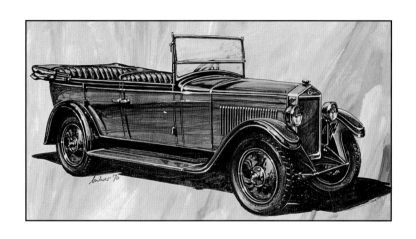

NSU 7/34 1928

The larger of the six-cylinder cars launched in 1928 was produced when NSU was in a serious financial situation. In 1930, agreement was reached for Fiat to acquire its car manufacturing business, including the new factory at Heilbronn. The proceeds of the sale went not to NSU however but the German government. As part of the deal, 1000 7/34 models were rebadged as NSU-Fiats and run as taxis in Germany. NSU was later bought back from Fiat and in due course became a member of the modern Auto Union group.

In 1933 Dr Ferdinand Porsche was commissioned to design a new model, the Type 32 (q.v.), and although the project was abandoned, it became the basis for the first Volkswagen. As Fiat had all rights to NSU car production, it was realised that if the Type 32 had gone ahead, the Italian company would have built and sold it as a Fiat, and it was abandoned. NSU's motorcycle business, which was not included in the deal with Fiat, thrived, and as car production slumped to 2,175 in 1930 motorcycle numbers went up. But the Weimar Republic's borrowing caught up with it and motorcycle output too suffered in 1931.

BODY
4 door saloon, 4 seats; weight 1200kg (2640lb).

ENGINE
6 cylinders, in line; front; 62.0x99.0mm, 1,781cc; 25kW (34 bhp) @ 3200rpm; 14.0 kW/l (19.1bhp/l).

ENGINE STRUCTURE
Side valve; 2 valves per cylinder; single gear-driven camshaft; cast iron cylinder head and block; water cooled.

TRANSMISSION
Rear wheel drive; 3 speed gearbox; hypoid bevel final drive.

CHASSIS DETAILS
Separate steel chassis, steel bodywork; drum brakes; worm and roller steering; 35l (7.7 Imp Gal) (9.2 US gal) fuel tank; 5.00x28 tyres.

DIMENSIONS
Wheelbase 281.5 (110.6 in), front track 125.0cm (49.2in), rear track 125.0cm (49.2in), overall length 406.0cm (159.8 in); overall width 155.0cm (61.0in).

PERFORMANCE
48.0kg/kW (35.3kg/bhp).

Right: A consignment of Heilbronn-built NSU-Fiat taxis line up for delivery to Berlin. Their upright radiators and heavy-duty bumpers became features of city traffic.

AUDI Type S ZWICKAU 1929

Audi went through a lean period in the late 1920s, with new model annual sales barely reaching four figures. The eight cylinder engine, made under licence from Rickenbacker, was refined by reducing capacity from the original 4.9 to 4.4 litres, and stiffening the crankshaft by increasing the number of main bearings from five to nine. However, with its massive Pullman limousine bodywork, the Type S was a heavy car, so that with just 52.2kW, performance was hardly impressive. But progress was helped by the fact that this model did at least have a four-speed gearbox.

The large-car market was still hampered by government policy which continued to regard cars as luxury items. Taxation policies discouraged their use. In 1922 heavy burdens were imposed and although doctors paid no tax on cars under 8hp, others paid 100 Marks annual licence for a 6hp, 200 Marks up to 10hp, and 300 Marks up to 12hp. By 1929 currency reform improved matters, but the number of car manufacturers had fallen from 71 in 1924 to only 19.

BODY
4 door saloon; 4 seats; weight 2100kg (4620lb).

ENGINE
8 cylinders, in line; front; 76.2x120.6mm, 4371cc; 52.2kW (70bhp) @ 2700rpm; 11.9kW/l (16.0bhp/l).

ENGINE STRUCTURE
Side valve; 2 valves per cylinder; 1 gear driven camshaft; cast iron cylinder head and block; 9 bearing crankshaft; 2 Zenith carburettors; water cooled.

TRANSMISSION
Rear wheel drive; 4 speed gearbox with overdrive; spiral bevel final drive, 4.25.

CHASSIS DETAILS
Box-section chassis; steel body; front suspension, beam axle, semi-elliptic springs; rear suspension, live axle, underslung semi-elliptic springs; drum brakes; single hydraulic circuit; worm steering; 70.0l (15.4 US gal) (18.5 US gal) fuel tank.

DIMENSIONS
Wheelbase 350.0cm (137.8in), front track 140.0cm (55.1in), rear track 148.0cm (58.3in), overall length 496.5cm (195.5in), overall width 178.0cm (70.1in), overall height 187.0cm (73.6in).

PERFORMANCE
Maximum speed 68mph (110kph); 40.2 kg/kW (50.0kg/bhp).

Right: Audi takes shape. Archetypal 930s chassis frame with deep side-members and half elliptic springs on front and rear axles. Photograph shows underslung rear axle, and massive low propellor shaft to spiral bevel final drive. Engine 8-cylinder Rickenbacker.

DKW P-15 Roadster 1929

Encouraged by the success of the cabriolet version of its new P-15, DKW added a roadster version a year later. The same plywood panelling system was used for the main bodywork, but even with more fabric in the hood the new model was some 70kg lighter. This was not sufficient to make any great difference in top speed, which remained at 80kph, thanks to the bluff aerodynamics. The two-stroke engine was relatively unsophisticated, drawing the petrol-oil mix into the cylinders via the crankcase, through ports in the cylinder walls.

Rasmussen's resolve to remain a small-car manufacturer assured prosperity for DKW. He was able not only to survive the worst years of the 1920s, but he even expanded the company which by 1928 was also the world's largest motorcycle manufacturer.

BODY
Roadster; 2 doors; 2 seats; weight 600kg (1320lb).

ENGINE
2 cylinders, in line; front; 74.0x68.0mm, 584cc; compr 5.5:1; 11.2kW (15bhp) @ 3500rpm; 19.2kW/l (25.7bhp/l).

ENGINE STRUCTURE
Ported two-stroke; cast iron cylinder head and block; 3 bearing crankshaft; Meco M2N carburettor; water cooled.

TRANSMISSION
Rear wheel drive; 3 speed gearbox; spiral bevel final drive, 5.50.

CHASSIS DETAILS
Separate chassis; plywood body; front suspension, beam axle, transverse semi-elliptic spring; rear suspension, live axle, transverse semi-elliptic spring; drum brakes; worm steering; 20.0l (4.4 Imp gal) (5.3 US gal) fuel tank; 3.50 or 4.00x26 tyres.

DIMENSIONS
Wheelbase 259.0cm (101.9in), front track 110.0cm (42.3in), rear track 110.0cm (42.3in), overall length 360.0cm (141.7in), overall width 135.0cm (53.1in), overall height 170.0cm (66.9in).

PERFORMANCE
Maximum speed 50mph (80kph); 53.6kg/kW (40.0kg/bhp).

Right: DKW sports cars had competition success to back up their pert appearance. They even racked up international speed records for 500cc supercharged cars at the Montlhéry track in France.

In the wake of the two larger 2.0 litre W10 and 2.5 litre W11 models, Wanderer returned to the smaller-engined thinking it had employed before the 1914-1918 War. The 1.5 litre long-stroke engine was the same as the one first seen in the 1926 W10, with the same 22.4kW output and three-speed Wanderer-made gearbox. The rod-operated drum brakes were also carried over from the earlier W10 model. But with the heavy two- or four-door saloon Reuter bodywork, performance was limited.

The two Gläser open-bodied cabriolet versions were rather lighter, at just 875kg. Although both bodies had a very upright stance, these Wanderer models had a more civilised appearance than some of their predecessors.

BODY
2/4 door saloon and tourer; weight 1150kg (2530lb).

ENGINE
4 cylinders, in line; front; 67.0x110.0mm, 1551cc; compr 5.3:1; 22.4kW (30bhp) @ 2800rpm; 14.4kW/l (19.3bhp/l).

ENGINE STRUCTURE
Side valve; 2 valves per cylinder; 1 gear driven side camshaft with pushrods; cast iron cylinder head and block; 3 bearing crankshaft; Pallas SA11 carburettor; water cooled.

TRANSMISSION
Rear wheel drive; 3 speed Wanderer gearbox; spiral bevel final drive, 5.33.

CHASSIS DETAILS
Separate box-section chassis; steel bodywork; Front and rear suspension, semi-elliptic springs; friction dampers; 4 wheel drum brakes, rod operated; cam and peg steering; 45.0l (9.9 Imp gal)

(11.9 US gal) fuel tank; 730x130 tyres.

DIMENSIONS
Wheelbase 280.0cm (110.2in), front track 125.0cm (49.2in), rear track 125.0cm (49.2in), overall length 430.0cm (169.3in), overall width 150.0cm (59.0in), overall height 180.0 (70.9in).

PERFORMANCE
Maximum speed 53mph (85kph); 51.3 kg/kW (38.3kg/bhp); average fuel consumption 35mpg (8 l/100km) manufacturer's fig.

Right: The media campaign to launch the amalgamation of four world-class makes into a single model programme emphasised the wide span of the market covered by the individual marque names.

4 WERKE VON WELTRUF

AUDI · DKW · HORCH · WANDERER

111/170
DEMAR

EINHEITLICHES TYPENPROGRAMM

AUDI Type SS Zwickau 1930

Since the initials SS held no particular significance, it seemed logical that the new version of the Type S should be the Type SS. The engine was essentially unchanged, except that the cylinder bores were increased to raise capacity from 4.4 to 5.1 litres, with a corresponding increase in power from 52.2 to 74.6kW. The increase in power meant the new model was now able to have an overdrive gear to give longer-legged cruising. The chassis remained relatively simple, with semi-elliptic springs for both axles, and hydraulically-operated drum brakes.

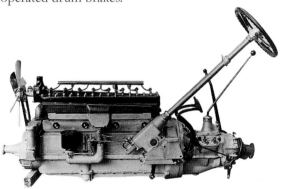

BODY
Saloon; 4 doors; 4 seats; weight 2100kg (4620lb).

ENGINE
8 cylinders, in line; front; 82.6x120.6mm, 5130cc; 74.6kW (100bhp) @ 3000rpm; 14.5kW/l (18.8bhp/l).

ENGINE STRUCTURE
Side valve; 2 valves per cylinder; 1 gear driven camshaft; cast iron cylinder head and block; 9 bearing crankshaft; 2 Zenith carburettors; water cooled.

TRANSMISSION
Rear wheel drive; 4 speed gearbox with overdrive; spiral bevel final drive, 4.25.

CHASSIS DETAILS
Box-section chassis; steel body; front suspension, beam axle, semi-elliptic springs; rear suspension, live axle, underslung semi-elliptic springs; drum brakes; single hydraulic circuit; worm steering; 70.0l (15.4 Imp gal) (18.5 US gal) fuel tank.

DIMENSIONS
Wheelbase 350cm (137.8in), front track140cm (55.1in), rear track 148cm (58.3in), length 496.5cm (195.5in), width 178cm (70.1in), height 187cm (73.6in).

PERFORMANCE
Maximum speed 68mph (110kph); 28.2kg/kW (21.0kg/bhp).

Left: **Choke and hand-throttle controls on the steering wheel led from bottom of the column to intake side of engine. Casting for clutch housing encased steering box and drop-arm.**
Right: **SS Zwickau Doctor's Coupe. Snug lines of body style traditionally popular with members of the medical profession. Small-volume interior was quick to warm up on cold winter call-outs.**

HORCH Type 400 1930

The US influence was reflected in the body styling of the Type 400, although underneath the chassis remained much as before, with a simple semi-elliptic suspension layout and mechanically-operated brakes. But now the driver was at least getting some help with the steering, which used the ZF-Ross system, with a hydraulic ram acting in conjunction with the standard ZF cam and peg system. The lower weight allowed the Type 400 to use a three-speed gearbox, although this now had synchromesh on second and top gears. Although no torque figures are quoted, the long stroke of the Paul Daimler-designed engine suggests that there would be more than sufficient to compensate for the absence of a fourth gear.

BODY
4 door saloon; 2 door cabriolet; 4 seats; weight 1350kg (2970lb)

ENGINE
8 cylinders, in line; front; 73.0x118.8mm, 3950cc; compr 5.4:1; 60kW (80bhp) @ 3200rpm.

ENGINE STRUCTURE
Ohv; 2 valves per cylinder; double overhead camshaft, bevel drive; cast iron cylinder head and block; 5 bearing crankshaft; Solex MHOV carburettor; water cooled.

TRANSMISSION
Rear wheel drive; 3 speed gearbox; spiral bevel final drive; 4.90.

CHASSIS DETAILS
Box section chassis; steel bodywork; front suspension, semi-elliptic springs; rear suspension, underslung semi-elliptic springs; drum brakes; cam and peg steering; PAS; 75.0l (16.5 Imp gal) (19.8 US gal) fuel tank;

6.50x20 tyres.

DIMENSIONS
Wheelbase 316.0cm (124.4in), front track 143.4cm (56.5in), rear track 147.7cm (58.2in), turning circle 13.5m (44.6ft), overall length 472.0cm (185.8in), overall width 175.0cm (68.9in), overall height 176.0cm (69.3in).

PERFORMANCE
Maximum speed 62mph (100kph); 22.5kg/kW (16.9kg/bhp); average fuel consumption 16.6mpg (17.0 l/100km) manufacturer's fig.

Right: **The sheer bulk of the Type 400 two-door cabriolet can be judged from the way the lady's shoulders barely reach the window line. Even those standing on the pavement are almost overwhelmed by its size.**

HORCH Type 500B 1930

Although Paul Daimler's short but innovative time with Horch was at an end, his influence showed through on the new engine for the 500B. It retained the single overhead camshaft layout. with the crankshaft now running in 10 main bearings to further improve smoothness. Driving was assisted by the use of a ZF-Aphon pre-selector gearbox, which gave owners the choice of normal or overdrive ratios, with final drive ratios to suit.

The chassis design remained conservative, but with the massive limousine coachwork on top of it, handling was probably not high on the driver's list of priorities. In addition to the limousine there was a six-seater touring model or a Pullman cabriolet.

Horch cars were still finding a ready market outside Germany. The company had export offices in Holland and Switzerland. Yet the world economic collapse of 1929 took its toll. Production was curtailed and the factory was closed for a time in the winter of 1930.

BODY
4 door saloon, touring, cabriolet; 4 seats; weight 2250kg (4950lb).

ENGINE
8 cylinders, in line; front; 87.0x104.0mm, 4944cc; compr 5.2:1; 74.6kW (100bhp) @ 3400rpm; 15.2kw/l (20.2bhp/l).

ENGINE STRUCTURE
Ohv; 2 valves per cylinder; single gear driven overhead camshaft; 10 bearing crankshaft; Solex 32 JFFP carburettor; water cooled.

TRANSMISSION
Rear wheel drive; 4.speed ZF Aphon; spiral bevel final drive, 4.90 without overdrive, 5.45 with overdrive.

CHASSIS DETAILS
Separate box section chassis; steel bodywork; front suspension, dead axle, semi-elliptic springs; rear suspension, live axle, semi-elliptic springs; drum brakes; ZF Gemmer or Ross worm steering; PAS; 100.0l (21.2 Imp gal) (26.4 US gal) fuel tank; 7.00x17 tyres.

DIMENSIONS
Wheelbase 375.0cm (147.6in), front track 147.0cm (57.9in), rear track 150.0cm (59.1in), turning circle 16.5m (54.5ft), overall length 550.0cm (216.5in), overall width 182.0cm (71.7in), overall height 172.0cm (67.7in).

PERFORMANCE
Maximum speed 75mph (120kph); 30.2kg/kW (22.5kg/ bhp); average fuel consumption 11.7mpg (24.0 l/100km).

Right: Autobahn cruiser. A big car for Germany's new motor roads the eight cylinder Horch had an imposing appearance.

DKW 4=8 V4 1930

After the simplicity of the twin-cylinder engine in the P-15, DKW went to the opposite end of the scale with the 4=8. The model's name was meant to persuade customers that a four-cylinder V4 would be as smooth as an in-line eight. The V4 layout was already unusual for a two stroke, but now its complexity was added to by making the cylinder block in effect a V6 with two additional 'slave' cylinders. These were used to pump the petrol-oil mixture into the working cylinders through the crankcase, rather than relying on suction alone. The system appeared to work, with the output of the 980cc engine, a relatively vigorous 18.6kW. Drive to the rear wheels was through a 3-speed non-synchromesh gearbox.

In 1931 the 4=8 was given hydraulic brakes. The original upright two-door saloon was later joined by a two-door cabriolet and rather grandly named cabriolet limousine. A smaller-capacity version of the engine, with 15kW was available in a cabriolet only. The two-door coach-body car sold for 2985 Reichsmarks. In 1930 DKW also announced its first front wheel drive car.

BODY
2 door saloon; 4 seats; weight 780kg (1760lb).

ENGINE
4 cylinders, in 90deg vee; 68.0x68.0mm, 980cc; compr 4.8:1; 18.6kW (25bhp) @ 3200rpm; 18.2kW/l (24.5bhp/l); 64Nm (6.5mkp) @ 2200rpm.

ENGINE STRUCTURE
Ported two stroke; cast iron cylinder heads and block; 2 bearing crankshaft; Zenith carburettor; water cooled.

TRANSMISSION
Rear wheel drive; 3 speed gearbox; spiral bevel final drive, 5.25.

CHASSIS DETAILS
Separate steel chassis; front suspension, dead axle, semi-elliptic springs; rear suspension, live axle, semi-elliptic springs; drum brakes; worm steering; 30.0l (6.6 Imp gal) (7.9 US gal) fuel tank; 4.40x26 tyres.

DIMENSIONS
Wheelbase 280cm (110.2in), front track 110cm (43.3in), rear track 120cm (47.2in), overall length 360cm (141.7in), overall width 145cm (57.1in), overall height 162cm (63.8in).

PERFORMANCE
Maximum speed 56mph (90kph); 41.9kg/kW (31.2kg/bhp); average fuel consumption 40.3 mpg (7.0 l/100km).

Below: Novel V4

The Dresden was to the last and smallest Audi to use a version of the licence-built Rickenbacker engine, this time with just six cylinders. The design was modest, with the side-valve layout making engine maintenance easy. Similarly the chassis made use of uncomplicated semi-elliptic suspension, with hydraulically-operated drum brakes. An unusual feature was the overdrive facility on the four-speed gearbox, stepping up top gear to give easy cruising. The Type T came as a four-door saloon or two-door cabriolet.

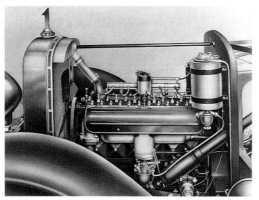

BODY
4 door saloon; 4 seats; 1310kg (2882lb).

ENGINE
6 cylinders, in line; front; 82.5x129.7mm, 3838cc; 52.2kW (70bhp) @ 2820rpm; 13.6kW/l (18.2bhp/l).

ENGINE STRUCTURE
Side valve; 2 valves per cylinder; 1 gear driven side camshaft; cast iron cylinder head and block; 7 bearing crankshaft; water cooled.

TRANSMISSION
Rear wheel drive; 4-speed gearbox plus overdrive; spiral bevel final drive, 5.1.

CHASSIS DETAILS
Separate box-section chassis; steel body; front suspension, dead axle, semi-elliptic springs; rear axle, live axle, semi-elliptic springs; drum brakes; single hydraulic circuit; worm steering.

DIMENSIONS
Wheelbase 310.0cm (122.1in), front track 140.0cm ((55.1in) rear track 140.0cm (55.1in).

PERFORMANCE
Maximum speed 62mph (100kph); 25.1kg/kW (18.7kg/bhp).

Left: Induction side of six cylinder engine.
Right: Heavy coachwork., artillery wheels, side-mounted spare wheels, upright stance; the epitome of luxury travel for upper-middle class in 1930s.

4517

AUDI Type P 5/30 1931

With the German economy in turmoil, Audi was desperate to add a smaller, lower-priced model to off-set the slump in sales of its larger Type T Dresden and Type SS Zwickau cars. Auto Union had yet to be formed, so Audi was able to look outside Germany for its engine. This was a simple 1.1-litre side valve Peugeot unit complete with its own three-speed gearbox. Rather than investing in a new chassis, Audi simply bought-in the chassis and suspension from DKW's 4=8 drive rear wheel drive model.

As well as the two-door saloon, the 5/30 was offered in cabriolet form, with either two or four seats. Production of the model lasted for just one year, Audi later returning to its larger-engine model policy.

Promoted with vigour by DKW founder and now principal shareholder, Rasmussen, the P-type's failure convinced him that only an industry-wide initiative could save the day and he launched the movement that led to the formation of Auto Union.

BODY
2 door saloon; 4 seats; weight 780kg (1716lb).

ENGINE
4 cylinders, in line; front; 63.0x90.0mm, 1122cc; 22.4kW (30bhp) @ 3200rpm; 20.0kW/l (26.7bhp/l).

ENGINE STRUCTURE
Side valve; 2 valves per cylinder; 1 gear driven side camshaft; cast iron cylinder head and block; 3 bearing crankshaft; water cooled.

TRANSMISSION
Rear wheel drive; 4 speed gearbox.

CHASSIS DETAILS
Separate chassis; steel bodywork. Front suspension transverse semi-elliptic spring; rear suspension, live axle, transverse semi-elliptic spring; drum brakes; single hydraulic circuit; worm steering. 30.0l (6.7 Imp gal) (7.9 US gal) fuel tank;

4.50x18 tyres.

DIMENSIONS
Wheelbase 270.0cm (106.3in), front track 112.0cm (44.1in), rear track 112.0 (44.1in), overall length 368.0cm (144.9in), overall width 140.0cm (55.1in), height 165.0cm (65.0in).

PERFORMANCE
Maximum speed 56mph (90kph); 34.8kg/kW (26.0kg/bhp); average fuel consumption 28 mpg (10l/100km).

Right: **Proud family with Audi still number '1' on the upright radiator. The 'P' was not a success and soon the figure '1' would be replaced by the famous four-ringed symbol of 'vorsprung durch technik'.**

HORCH Type 600-670 V12 1931

The V12 may have been an engineering triumph but, like Jaguar's V12 after the 1970s' first oil crisis, it could not have come at a worse time. It may have been a technical success but it was a sales disaster. The 600 was built as a Pullman limousine on a 375cm wheelbase and the 670 as a handsome cabriolet weighing 200kg less on a 345cm wheelbase.

The new engine was not quite the largest Horch ever made (that distinction went to the 8.7-litre of 1907) but it was the most powerful thus far. Laid out in a 60 degree vee, the side valves were operated from a central chain-driven camsaft but despite the enormous swept volume of the engine it was relatively slow-revving and feeble for heavy bodywork with a laden weight getting on for two tons.

The 600's long wheelbase provided ample room for passengers who could relax at fast cruising speeds thanks to the ZF Aphon's schnellgang (overdrive) top gear. Yet despite its imposing appearance the 670 attracted a mere 54 customers during its three-year span, and the 600 only 27.

BODY
2/4 door cabriolet; 4 door saloon; 4 seats; 1700kg (3740lb).

ENGINE
12 cylinders, in 60deg V; front; 80.0x100.0mm, 6021cc; compr 5.2:1; 90kW (120bhp) @ 3200rpm; 14.9kw/l (19.9bhp/l).

ENGINE STRUCTURE
Side valve; 2 valves per cylinder; chain driven central camshaft; cast iron cylinder heads and block; 7 bearing crankshaft; Solex 32 JFFP or Stromberg D-3 carburettor; water cooled.

TRANSMISSION
Rear wheel drive; 4 speed ZF Aphon gearbox; spiral bevel final drive, 5.10 (600), 5.35 (670);

CHASSIS DETAILS
Separate box section chassis; steel bodywork; front suspension, semi-elliptic springs; rear suspension underslung semi-elliptic springs; hydraulic dampers; drum brakes, single hydraulic circuit; PAS; 100.0l (22.0 Imp gal) 26.4 US gal) fuel tank; 7.00/7.50x17 tyres.

DIMENSIONS
Wheelbase 345.0cm (135.8in), front track 147.0cm (57.9in), rear track 150.0cm (59.1in), overall length 540.0cm (212.6in), overall width 182.0cm (71.7in), overall height 165.0cm (65.0in).

PERFORMANCE
Maximum speed 87mph (140kph); 18.9kg/kW (14.7kg/bhp); average fuel consumption 10.9mpg (26.0l/100km) manufacturer's fig.

Right: imposing car, imposing factory.
V12 engines outside the Horch-Werke.

DKW FA (F-1) 1931

This was to be the 'stepping stone' model for DKW that encompassed the move from conventional rear wheel drive to front wheel drive, Front Antrieb, so was known as the FA. The F-1 title came later. The little twin-cylinder engine (below) lay behind the three-speed gearbox, which was adjacent to the front axle. There was a separate chassis, with the cabriolet body being made in plywood; the larger four-seater saloon had the make's first steel bodywork from Ambi Budd.

The limiting factor on front wheel drive was the universal joint needed to accommodate its steering movement. The usual type of joint could operate over only a limited angular range, which meant that the FA/F-1 had a very large turning circle and, at anything other than slight steering movement, rather jerky progress.

BODY

2 door roadster, 2 seats; also cabriolet and steel saloon, 4 seats; weight 450kg (990lb).

ENGINE

2 cylinders; transverse; front; 68.0x68.0mm, 490cc; compr 5.5:1; 11.2kW (15bhp) @ 3500rpm; 22.9kW/l (30.6bhp/l).

ENGINE STRUCTURE

Ported two stroke; cast iron cylinder head and block; 3 bearing crankshaft; Solex FH 26 carburettor; water cooled.

TRANSMISSION

Front wheel drive; multi-plate oil-filled clutch; 3 speed gearbox; spur gear final drive, 3.05:1.

CHASSIS DETAILS

Steel ladder-type chassis; plywood body (cabriolet), steel body (saloon); ifs, transverse springs; irs, transverse springs; drum brakes; worm steering; 25.0l (5.53 Imp gal) (6.6 US gal) fuel tank; 3.50x19 tyres.

DIMENSIONS

Wheelbase 240.0cm (94.5in), front track 110.0cm (43.3in), rear track 110.0cm (43.3in), turning circle 12m (40.0ft), overall length 310.0cm (122.1in), overall width 130.0cm (51.2in), overall height 125.0cm (49.2in).

PERFORMANCE

Maximum speed 47mph (75kph); 40.2kg/kW (30.0kg/bhp); average fuel consumption 35.3mpg (8.0l/100km).

The decline of Saxony's motor industry seemed to be epitomised by the Wanderer Type 8, a stillborn design of great brilliance which seemed to lead nowhere. Yet it established an automotive dynasty and formed the basis for an industrial recovery that lasted throughout the second half of the twentieth century.

Most of its details were kept in the mind or the notebooks of its creator, Dr Ferdinand Porsche. As a result, very little of its technical specification was ever recorded, and only one car was ever built.

The straight-eight ohc engine had bore and stroke dimensions of 72x100mm, giving a capacity of 3,257cc. A cruciform section chassis was used, with independent rear suspension, using a swing axle layout. The Type 8's wheelbase was 3200mm (126in) , while the track was 1420mm (60in). The two-door fastback streamlined bodywork had the classic Wanderer grille, with the headlamps semi-faired into the front wings. The spare wheel was stowed

near-vertically in the rear panel, covered by a hinged circular flap.

The Type 8 was very much Dr Porsche's personal project. In an interview in 1992 his son Ferry recalled that he remembered the Type 8 well, often being driven around in it by his father. Alas he had no idea what became of the car. The Type 8 followed logically enough on the Type 7, which was the 2.0 litre Wanderer also designed by the Porsche consultancy, and which went into production (qv p160). The Type 8 was devised with a Roots-type supercharger which could be cut-in to provide extra boost for overtaking.

The plan was abandoned following the merger of Audi, Horch, Wanderer, and DKW into Auto Union. Wanderer was positioned between DKW's popular small cars and Audi's premium quality upper middle class cars. Horch kept its traditional quality upper-crust image but crucially it had eight and twelve cylinder cars already in production, so Dr Porsche's

Type 8 straight-eight was already surplus to requirements.

Its historical significance lay in its aerodynamic shape, which followed research by the Austrian Paul Jaray, who studied Zeppelins (too long and narrow, those he designed were teardrop-shaped) and designed a car with a drag coefficient of 0.245 – still a respectable value 70 years later, even though it was high and narrow. Its deeply curved windscreen, built-in headlights, pointed tail and faired-in wheels were keenly debated. Jaray's example was followed in the 1930s most convincingly by Alfa Romeo and BMW at Le Mans. One little low-drag Adler managed 100mph on only 55bhp. Audi also worked on Jaray principles, anticipating the latter-day firm's commitment to low drag coefficients.

Jaray designed bodies that were streamlined underneath, and had their widest point one-third of the way back, although he had to compromise to achieve rear-seat headroom. The higher the speed the greater the benefit of efficient aerodynamics. Fuel consumption improved, full-width bodies gave more space, and aerodynamics became no longer a question of style; it was a science which made cars more efficient and quieter.

Ferdinand Porsche exploited Jaray's streamlining in the Wanderer Type 8, extended it to his next car, the radial-engined Type 12 which he designed for Zündapp, on principles he would apply to one of his greatest creations, the Volkswagen. They were principles that would hold good in the 1980s for his grandson, Ferdinand Piëch and the cars he created for Audi.

Left: Jaray's aerodynamic study for Audi.
Right: The small closely-knit team in the new Porsche design consultancy included Ferdinand Porsche, by the drawing board, Ferry Porsche on right, and staff member Leopold Jänschke. The engine is an air-cooled boxer-motor.

HORCH Type 850 1932

The complexities of the twin overhead camshaft straight eight engine were dropped in favour of a simpler design. The new 5.0 unit used a less complicated overhead valve layout, operated by pushrods from a block-mounted gear-driven camshaft. With the new engine came two new versions of the ZF Aphon pre-selector gearbox, both with a choice of two final drive ratios. The standard box had direct top gear drive, the second had overdrive for more relaxed high-speed cruising. Refinement was helped with ZF-Ross power steering, and servo assistance for the hydraulic drum brakes. The front suspension too was new, using twin transverse semi-elliptic springs acting as upper wishbones. At the rear, a rudimentary layout of semi-elliptic springs was retained.

The US influence continued, with both the Pullman limousine and cabriolet carrying their spare wheels upright in the front wings.

BODY
4 door saloon/cabriolet; 4 seats; weight 1800kg (3960lb).

ENGINE
8 cylinders, in line; front; 87.0x104.0mm, 4944cc; compr 5.8:1; 75kW (100bhp) @ 3400rpm; 15.2kW/l (20.2bhp/l).

ENGINE STRUCTURE
Ohv; 2 valves per cylinder; 1 side camshaft, gear driven, pushrods; cast iron cylinder head and block; 10 crankshaft bearings; Solex 35JFF carburettor; water cooled.

TRANSMISSION
Rear wheel drive; 4 speed gearbox; spiral bevel final drive; 3.60/3.90 direct drive, 5.30/4.90 overdrive.

CHASSIS DETAILS
Box section chassis; steel bodywork; independent front suspension, twin transverse semi-elliptic springs; rear suspension, underslung semi-elliptic springs;

drum brakes; vacuum power assistance; cam and peg steering; PAS; 95.0l (20.9 Imp gal) (25.1 US gal) fuel tank; 7.00/7.50x17 tyres.

DIMENSIONS
Wheelbase 375.0cm (147.6in), front track 147.0cm (58.9in), rear track 150.0cm (59.1in), turning circle 16.5m (54.4ft), overall length 550.0cm (216.5in), overall width 182.0cm (71.7in), overall height 177.0cm (69/7in).

PERFORMANCE
Maximum speed 78mph (125kph); 24.0kg/kW (18.0kg/ bhp); average fuel consumption 17.7 mpg (16.0 l/100km) manufacturer's fig.

Left and right: **Top of the range. The stylish Horch roadster was most expensive of Auto Union range.**

DKW 1001 Rear-drive Sonderklasse 1932

DKW was not yet quite prepared to commit itself wholly to front wheel drive, so the 1001 stayed with the well-established technology of rear wheel drive. The V4 engine, with its unusual pair of 'slave' cylinders used to pump mixture under pressure into the working cylinders, was one of the more powerful 1.0-litre units on the market at the time. On the downside, this system did mean a heavy fuel consumption, with the 1001 averaging little more than 23 mpg on its mixture of petrol and oil. The trail of blue smoke and distinctive smell were characteristic of two-stroke DKW engines of the time.

Once again the plywood body, covered in artificial leather cloth, was used. Progress however was being made, because the new model now had hydraulic rather than mechanically operated drum brakes.

BODY
Cabriolet; 4 doors; 4 seats; weight 980kg (2156lb).

ENGINE
4 cylinders, in 90deg vee; front; 68.0x69.5mm, 990cc; compr 5.9:1; 19.4kW (26bhp) @ 3500rpm; 19.6kW/l (26.3bhp/l).

ENGINE STRUCTURE
Ported two stroke; cast iron cylinder heads and block; Solex FH 26S carburettor; 2 bearing crankshaft; water cooled.

TRANSMISSION
Rear wheel drive; 4 speed gearbox; spiral bevel final drive, 4.90.

CHASSIS DETAILS
Separate steel chassis; plywood body; front suspension, dead axle, semi-elliptic spring; rear suspension, live axle, transverse semi-elliptic spring; drum brakes; single hydraulic circuit; worm steering; 35.0l (7.7 Imp gal) (9.2 US gal) fuel tank; 5.00x17 tyres.

DIMENSIONS
Wheelbase 285.0cm (122.2in), front track 125.0cm (49.2in), rear track 125.0cm (49.2in), overall length 415.0cm (163.4in), overall width 152.0cm (59.8in), overall height 156.0cm (61.4in).

PERFORMANCE
Maximum speed 53mph (85kph); 50.5kg/kW (37.8kg/bhp); average fuel consumption 23.5mpg (12.0l/100km) manufacturer's fig.

Left: Basic instruments, springy gear lever, opening windscreen familiar features of 1930s motoring.
Right: Auto Union four-ring symbol makes its appearance on spare wheel cover.

Ferdinand Porsche's engineering innovations were in demand throughout the German motor industry, but there were still a couple of years to go before his most magnificent creation, the first of the V16 Auto Unions. The engine he designed for Wanderer's W15 had a cast aluminium alloy block with wet steel cylinder liners, but a conventional cast iron head carrying the overhead valves. The engine is also notable for having a relatively short stroke for the period. The chassis remained with semi-elliptic springs, but in 1933, the mechanical brake operation was replaced by a hydraulic system.

Design work started the week before Christmas, 1930, and the finished drawings were delivered to Wanderer at Chemnitz on 1 April 1931, complete with parts list. The first big contract won by Porsche, it was undertaken before the new design consultancy moved into its proper Stuttgart office. It should have been designated Porsche Type 1, but since the proprietor did not want outsiders to know he had no other work yet, he began numbering at 7.

The four-door saloon cost 5,250 Marks, and the four seat cabriolet 6,250 Marks.

BODY
4 door saloon; 4 seats; weight 1230kg (2706lb).

ENGINE
6 cylinders, in line; front; 65.0x85.0mm, 1690cc; compr 5.6:1; 26.1kW (35bhp) @ 3400rpm; 15.4kW/l (20.7bhp/l).

ENGINE STRUCTURE
Ohv; 2 valves per cylinder; 1 gear driven side camshaft; cast iron cylinder head, aluminium alloy block, with steel liners; 5 bearings; Solex Type 30 carburettor, water cooled.

TRANSMISSION
rear wheel drive; 4 speed gearbox; spiral bevel final drive, 5.00.

CHASSIS DETAILS
U-section chassis; steel body; front suspension, beam axle, semi-elliptic springs; rear suspension, live axle, semi-elliptic springs; drum brakes; worm steering; 42.0l (9.2 Imp gal) (11.0 US gal) fuel tank; 5.00x18 tyres.

DIMENSIONS
Wheelbase 300.0cm (118.1in), front track 130.0cm (51.2in), rear track 125.0cm (49.2in), overall length 450.0cm (177.2in), overall width 157.0cm (61.8in), overall height 169.0cm (66.5in).

PERFORMANCE
Maximum speed 56mph (90kph); 47.1kg/kW (35.1kg/bhp); average fuel consumption 24mpg (12.0l/100km).

Right: There was space for a cabin trunk when the rear luggage grid and spare wheel mount was folded out. Cabriolet had front-hinged doors, a "modern" safety innovation.

AUDI FRONT 1933-1938

A significant model in Audi's history because it was the first to feature front wheel drive, the Front had the engine behind rather than in front of the gearbox. The 2.3 ohv six cylinder was a Porsche-Wanderer design, driving through a four-speed non-synchromesh gearbox.

To accommodate the new front wheel drive layout, the Type 225 used lower wishbones with a transverse upper semi-elliptic spring. With the front wheels now doing both the steering and driving, the ZF cam and peg was assisted by a US-licensed power system. The model had a separate chassis and was available with an assortment of bodies, including an Ambi-Budd four-door sport limousine, a larger six-light saloon and a four-light cabriolet by Gläser.

There were three models from 1933 to 1938; a 2.0 litre of 40bhp, the 225 a 2.25 litre with 50bhp, and probably the best a 55bhp version of the 225, all quality productions from the former Horch factory.

BODY
4 door saloon, 2 door sports cabriolet, special roadster; weight 1350kg (2970lb).

ENGINE
6 cylinders, in line, front; 71.0x95.0mm; 2257cc; compr 6.1:1; 41kW (55bhp) @ 3300rpm; 18.2kW/l (24.4bhp/l).

ENGINE STRUCTURE
Ohv; 2 valves per cylinder; 1 side camshaft, bevel drive; pushrods; cast iron cylinder head and block; 7 bearing crankshaft; Solex 30JFF carburettor; water cooled.

TRANSMISSION
Front wheel drive; 4 speed; spiral bevel final drive, 5.25.

CHASSIS DETAILS
Box section backbone chassis; steel bodywork; independent front suspension, lower wishbones, upper transverse semi-elliptic spring; independent rear suspension, swing axle, transverse semi-elliptic spring;

mechanically operated drum brakes; cam and peg steering; PAS; 50.0l (11.0 Imp gal) (13.2 US gal) fuel tank; 6.00x16 tyres.

DIMENSIONS
Wheelbase 310.0cm (122.0in); front track 135.0cm (53.2in), rear track 140.0cm (55.1in), turning circle 12.5m (41.3ft), overall length 450.0cm (177.2in), overall width 165.0cm (65.0in), overall height 157.5cm (61.8in).

PERFORMANCE
Maximum speed 65mph (105kph); 32.9kg/kW (24.6kg/bhp); average fuel consumption 23.4mpg (13.0 l/100km) manufacturer's fig.

Far right: Audi's front wheel drive masterpiece pre-dated Citroën.
Left: Engine had Wanderer logo on sump. Bulky drive-shaft joints gave large turning circle.

DKW F-2 Reichsklasse 1933

Soon after the launch of its first front wheel drive car, DKW added a second. It had the same engine, now of DKW's traditional 584cc and producing 13.4kW (18bhp), again with a three-speed gearbox, still without the benefit of synchromesh. There was a refinement though to the plywood-based body, which was still carried on the separate steel chassis. Rather than being simply painted, it was now covered in an artificial leathercloth, giving a novel appearance. The body styles for the F-2 were limited to a cabriolet and a saloon.

As with its first production model in 1928, DKW placed the fuel tank high up on the engine bay bulkhead, with the petrol-oil mixture being fed to the carburettor by gravity. The F-1 and F-2 introduced in the 1930s were almost identical except for engine size.

BODY

2 door cabriolet, roadster; 4 seats; weight 450kg (990lb).

ENGINE

2 cylinders; transverse; front; 74.0x68.0mm, 584cc; compr 5.5:1; 13.4kW (18bhp) @ 3500rpm; 22.9kW/l (30.8bhp/l).

ENGINE STRUCTURE

Ported two stroke; cast iron cylinder head and block; 3 bearing crankshaft; Solex FH 26 carburettor; water cooled.

TRANSMISSION

Front wheel drive; multi-plate oil-filled clutch; 3 speed gearbox; spur gear final drive, 3.05:1.

CHASSIS DETAILS

Steel ladder-type chassis; plywood body (cabriolet), steel body (saloon); independent front suspension, transverse springs; independent rear suspension, transverse springs; drum brakes; worm steering; 25.0l (5.53 Imp gal) (6.6 US gal) fuel tank; 3.50x19 tyres.

DIMENSIONS

Wheelbase 240cm (94.5in), front track 110cm (43.3in), rear track 110cm (43.3in), turning circle 12m (40.0ft), overall length 310cm (122.1in), overall width 130cm (51.2in), overall height 125cm (49.2in).

PERFORMANCE

Maximum speed 50mph (80kph); 33.6kg/kW (25kg/bhp); average fuel consumption 35mpg (8.1l/100km).

Left: **Backbone chassis, double transverse leaf springs were basis for Auto Union's most prolific model.**

By 1933 Horch's situation was becoming grave. Large cars were not selling well in the wake of the world depression. One of the factory V12s was being used to drive to Berlin every Friday to collect cash from the previous week's car sales to pay the wages, so it was just as well that, led by Rasmussen's DKW and under an initiative of the banks of Saxony, the Auto Union had been formed from Audi, DKW, Horch, and Wanderer. The makes would remain largely as brands instead of wholly autonomous manufacturers, and each was to keep its market niche.

Horch had concentrated on large capacity straight six or eight cylinder engines, producing its 6.0 litre V12 for the Type 600-670 in 1931. In 1933 it decided on a more rational approach, using a V8 that was effectively two-thirds of the V12, with the angle between the banks opened out from 60 degrees to 66 degrees. Its capacity was 3517cc and its unusual valve gear led to debate whether it should be described as side valve or overhead valve.

A camshaft in the middle of the vee operated the valves through rockers so that the stems lay horizontally.

BODY
4 door saloon; 5 seats; weight 2030kg (4466lb).

ENGINE
8 cylinders in 66deg V; front; 78.0x92.0mm, 3517cc; compr 6.0:1; 60kW (75bhp) @ 3600rpm; 17.1kW/l (21.3bhp/l).

ENGINE STRUCTURE
Side overhead valve; 2 valves per cylinder; 1 chain driven centre camshaft; cast iron cylinder head and block; 3 bearing crankshaft; Solex carburettor; water cooled.

TRANSMISSION
rear wheel drive; 4 speed ZF Aphon 32 JFFP gearbox; spiral bevel final drive, 3.75.

CHASSIS DETAILS
Separate chassis, with various body styles in steel; drum brakes; single hydraulic circuit; ZF-Ross cam and peg steering; PAS; 75.0l (16.5 Imp gal) (19.9 US gal) fuel tank; 6.50x17in tyres.

DIMENSIONS
Wheelbase 310.0cm (122.0in), front track 144.0cm (56.7in), rear track 150.0 (59.1in), turning circle 13.5m (44.6ft), overall length 505.0cm (198.8in), overall width 178.0cm (70.1in), overall height 165.0cm (65.0in).

PERFORMANCE
Maximum 75speed mph (120kph), 33.8kg/kW (27.1kg/bhp); average fuel consumption 14.1 mpg (20.0l/100km) factory fig.

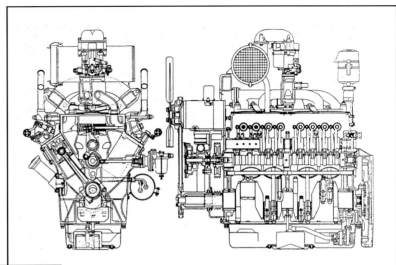

While they were not exactly overhead in relation to the pistons in the 66 degree cylinder bores, the valves were not exactly at the side either. The first 3.0-litre (3004cc) for the Type 830 gave 70bhp. In 1934 it went up to 3250cc and in 1935 to 3517cc and 75bhp. By 1939 it was 3823cc and the 930V gave 92bhp.

The V8's chassis engineering was more conventional in the beginning, except for the ZF Aphon synchromesh gearbox. The car had beam axles front and rear with half-elliptic springs, but underwent a transformation after only a year with

independent front suspension by wishbones and coil springs, and a De Dion arrangement at the rear. The cranked De Dion tube was suspended by a semi-elliptic leaf spring.

The 1939 car exhibited at the Berlin motor show followed the vogue for aerodynamics. It was a four door pillarless saloon with many modern luxury features. Only a handful were made and only one survived. A total of 9443 Type 830s were produced between February 1933 and April 1940, and 2058 Type 930Vs after its introduction at the beginning of 1937.

WANDERER W20 and W21 1933

The Porsche-designed aluminium wet-liner Wanderer engine was an off-the-peg initiative intended at first for Daimler-Benz, but later sold to both Wanderer and Steyr. During the year following its introduction, Wanderer added the W20, a 2.0-litre version of the pushrod ohv 1.7-litre six. Smooth-running with a seven-bearing crankshaft there was clearly scope for development since it was not a very vigorous performer. Cylinder bore was increased from 65mm to 70mm, power was increased to 40bhp and most of the chassis and running gear were carried over from the W15.

The W21 featured the 35bhp 1692cc engine in a much improved chassis with independent rear suspension by swing-axles, and a transverse semi-elliptic leaf spring. It also had hydraulic brakes and ZF-Ross power assisted steering. Confusingly the W21 title used up to 1934 became W23, then in 1936 W35 even though the design remained largely unaltered.

The larger-engined car had stylish bodywork designed under Auto Union by Horch, which provided Wanderer with the means to compete against the newly successful small Mercedes-Benz models.

BODY
4 door saloon, cabriolet; weight 920kg (2024lb).

ENGINE
6 cylinders, in line; front; 70.0x85.0mm. 1963cc; compr 5.6:1; 29.8kW (40bhp) @ 3400rpm; 14.8kW/l (20.5bhp/l).

ENGINE STRUCTURE
Ohv; 2 valves per cylinder; 1 spur gear driven camshaft; aluminium cylinder head and block; 7 bearing crankshaft; Solex 30 carburettor; water cooled.

TRANSMISSION
Rear wheel drive; 4 speed gearbox, spiral bevel final drive, 5.00.

CHASSIS DETAILS
Separate U-section chassis; steel bodywork; front suspension, dead axle, semi-elliptic springs; rear suspension, live axle, semi-elliptic springs; drum brakes, worm steering; 42.0l (9.2 Imp gal) (11.1 US gal) fuel tank; 5.00x18 tyres.

DIMENSIONS
Wheelbase 300.0cm (118.1in), front track 130.0cm (51.2in), rear track 125.0cm (49.2in), overall length 450.0cm (177.2in), overall width 157.0cm (61.8in), overall height 169.0cm (66.5in).

PERFORMANCE
Maximum speed 59mph (95kph); 30.8kg/kW (23.0kg/bhp); average fuel consumption 23.5mpg (12.0 l/100km) manufacturer's fig.

Right: Open and closed bodies were available for the mid 1930s Wanderers following the Auto Union amalgamation. Louvred bonnet, flowing wings and free-standing headlamps lent a rakish air to a perfectly conventional car of modest performance.

DKW F-4 1934

Once more the original twin-cylinder two stroke engine was used for the latest front wheel drive design. There was, however, a major change in the transmission, which now had a 2.0:1 chain step-down transfer between the engine and gearbox, which allowed a higher final drive ratio to be used. But in every other way the F-4 stayed with what was now becoming established DKW practice as far as body construction was concerned.

On the separate U-section chassis the F-4 continued to use plywood construction trimmed in leathercloth. A year after production started, a more upmarket cabriolet limousine was added.

Sales of the larger cars dwindled while exports of the popular front-drive twin cylinder cars equipped with a free-wheel gearbox flourished. The Reichsklasse 601 was a development of the front-drive DKWs launched under Auto Union.

BODY
Cabriolet/ saloon; 2 doors; 4 seats; weight 850kg (1870lb).

ENGINE
2 cylinders, in line; front; 74.0x68.0mm, 584cc; compr 5.5:1; 13.4kW (18bhp) @ 3500rpm; 22.9kW/l (30.8bhp/l).

ENGINE STRUCTURE
Ported two stroke; cast iron cylinder head and block; 3 bearing crankshaft; Solex FH 26 carburettor; water cooled.

TRANSMISSION
Front wheel drive; 3 speed gearbox; 2.0 transfer ratio; spur gear final drive, 3.05.

CHASSIS DETAILS
Separate U-section steel chassis; independent front suspension, tranverse semi-elliptic spring; independent rear suspension, transverse semi-elliptic spring; drum brakes; worm steering; 25.0l (5.5 Imp gal) (6.6 US gal) fuel tank; 4.00x19 tyres.

DIMENSIONS
Wheelbase 240.0cm (94.5in), front track 110.0cm (43.3in), rear track 110.0cm (43.3in), overall length 340.0cm (133.9in), overall width 130.0cm (52.4in), overall height 136.0cm (53.5in).

PERFORMANCE
Maximum speed 51mph (82kph); 63.4kg/kW (47.2kg/bhp); average fuel consumption 33mpg (8.6l/100km).

Right: Classic transverse leaf springing for front wheel drive DKWs. Twin cylinder engine at rear, final drive casing in centre front. Outboard drive shaft joints limited steering lock.

DKW F-5 701 Meisterklasse 1934

After eight years the original motorcycle 584cc twin cylinder two-stroke engine was replaced by something more efficient. Unusally for the time, it had square bore and stroke dimensions implying relatively high piston speeds but improved performance.

Internally a new cross-scavenging system was used for the first time, ensuring that more of the exhaust from the previous stroke was cleared before the new charge entered the crankcase. The transmission remained much as before, with a 2.0:1 chain transfer to the three-speed gearbox. A freewheel was added. The worm steering and mechanically operated drum brakes were also carried over. The separate chassis and leathercloth plywood body construction was retained, and the 701 was marketed as a cabriolet and saloon.

Expensive, overweight, and underpowered, the long wheelbase, longer and wider, Meisterklasse was a failure as a mini Horch but something of a saleroom success nevertheless, with 200,000 made between 1935 and 1938. There was also a Meisterklasse Luxus with wire wheels instead of discs and a coachbuilt cabriolet body by Hornig.

BODY
Cabriolet / saloon; 2 doors; 4 seats; weight 750kg (1540lb).

ENGINE
2 cylinders, in line; front; 76.0x76.0mm, 684cc; compr 5.8:1; 14.9kW (20bhp) @ 3500rpm; 21.8kW/l (29.2bhp/l); 57Nm (5.8mkp) @ 2300rpm.

ENGINE STRUCTURE
Ported two stroke with cross-scavenging; cast iron cylinder head and block; 3 bearing crankshaft; Solex 26 BLF carburettor; water cooled.

TRANSMISSION
Front wheel drive; 3 speed gearbox; 2.0 transfer ratio; spur gear final drive, 3.05.

CHASSIS DETAILS
Separate U-section steel chassis; independent front suspension, tranverse semi-elliptic spring; rear suspension dead axle, transverse semi-elliptic spring; drum brakes; worm steering; 28.0l (6.2 Imp gal) (7.4 US gal) fuel tank; 4.00 (4.5)x17 tyres.

DIMENSIONS
Wheelbase 261.0cm (102.7in), front track 110.0cm (43.3in), rear track 122.0cm (48.0in), turning circle 12.0m (39.6ft), overall length 398.5cm (156.9in), overall width 148.0cm (58.3in), overall height 150.0cm (59.1in).

PERFORMANCE
Maximum speed 53mph (85kph); 47.0kg/kW (35.0kg/bhp); average fuel consumption 35mpg (8.07l/100km).

Right: **Motor show exhibit Meisterklasse Luxus with the Horch look. Weight penalty of 200 lbs affected accceleration.**

DKW Schwebeklasse 1934

Although this was to be DKW's final rear wheel drive model, the Schwebeklasse was important because it heralded the 'new look' which was to become a hallmark of the marque. In place of the upright lines, the new model had a more flowing appearance with curved bonnet and sloping back.

    The cabriolet was interesting because the two doors closed onto full frames, with the tops forming a cant rail against which the flat, single-piece roll-back hood could rest. The tough and thirsty V4 engine, with its twin slave cylinders, was given a final boost in power in 1935. An additional Solex carburettor was fitted increasing its output to 22.2kW.

The four-speed non-synchromesh transmission and hydraulic drum brakes were carried over from the 1932 Sonderklasse.

BODY
2 door cabriolet/saloon; weight 1000kg (2200lb).

ENGINE
4 cylinders in 90deg vee; front; 68.0x68.5mm, 990cc; compr 5.8:1; 19.4kW (26bhp) @ 3500rpm; 19.6kW/l (26.3bhp/l).

ENGINE STRUCTURE
Ported two stroke; cast iron cylinder heads and block; 2 bearing crankshaft; Solex FH26 carburettor; water cooled.

TRANSMISSION
Rear wheel drive; 4 speed Prometheus gearbox; spiral bevel final drive, 4.90.

CHASSIS DETAILS
Separate U-section chassis; plywood bodywork; front suspension, dead axle, transverse semi-elliptic spring; rear suspension, live axle, transverse semi-elliptic spring; drum brakes; single hydraulic circuit; worm steering; 35.0l (7.7 Imp gal) (9.5 US gal) fuel tank; 5.00x17 tyres.

DIMENSIONS
Wheelbase 285cm (112.2in), front track 130cm (51.2in), rear track 125cm (49.2in), length 430cm (169.3in), width 159cm (65.6in), height 156cm (61.4in).

PERFORMANCE
Max speed 53mph (85kph); 51.5kg/kW (38.5 kg/bhp); av. fuel cons. 22.6mpg (12.5 l/ 100km) manufacturer.

Right: **Röntgenbild (X-ray picture) of DKW Schwebeklasse demonstrates stable characteristics of high-mounted transverse leaf-spring on right against the body-roll expected of a car with a low-mounted spring on left.**

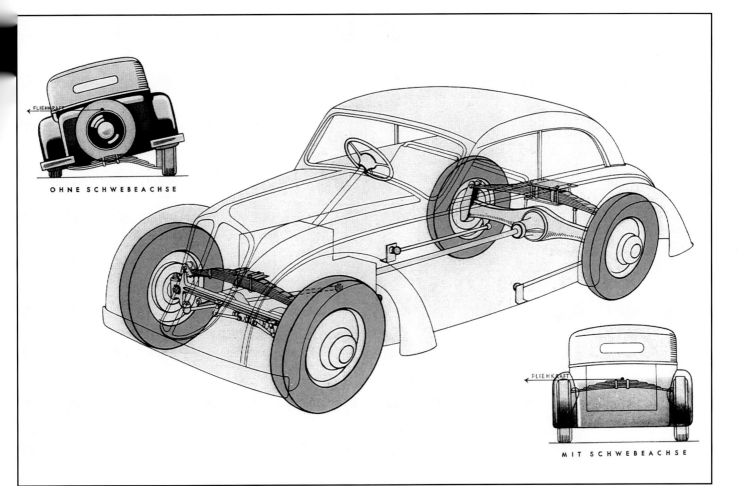

OHNE SCHWEBEACHSE

FLIEHKRAFT

FLIEHKRAFT

MIT SCHWEBEACHSE

DKW F-5 Reichsklasse 1934

DKW unexpectedly dropped its larger twin-cylinder engine, retaining the smaller 584cc unit. But now it used the cross-scavenging system first seen on the larger twin, which gave more efficient exhaust extraction and better cylinder filling. Like the rear wheel drive V4-engined Schwebeklasse launched the same year, the F-5 had a similar body shape, with the door and rear window frames forming guides for the roll-back hood. The front suspension was independent with twin transverse leaf springs. At the rear the dead axle and single tranverse semi-elliptic spring layout was retained. The rest of the chassis was much as before, with worm steering and mechanically-operated drum brakes. The three-speed gearbox, with its transfer chain drive from the engine, was once again retained.

BODY
Cabriolet; 2 doors; 4 seats; weight 850kg (1870lb).

ENGINE
2 cylinders, in line; front; 74.0x68.0mm, 584cc; compr 5.9; 13.4kW (18bhp) @ 3500rpm; 22.9kW/l (21.2bhp/l).

ENGINE STRUCTURE
Ported two stroke; cast iron cylinder head and block; 2 bearing crankshaft; Solex 26 BFL carburettor; water cooled.

TRANSMISSION
Front wheel drive; 3 speed gearbox, 2.0:1 chain transfer; spur gear final drive, 3.26.

CHASSIS DETAILS
Separate U-section chassis; plywood body; independent front suspension, twin transverse semi-elliptic springs; rear suspension, dead axle, transverse semi-elliptic spring; drum brakes; worm steering; 28.0l (6.1 Imp gal) (7.4 US gal) fuel tank;

4.00x19 tyres.

DIMENSIONS
Wheelbase 240.0cm (94.5in), front track 111.0cm (43.7in), rear track 122.0cm (48.0in), turning circle 12.0m (39.6ft), overall length 345.0cm (138.8in), overall width 145.0cm (57.1in), overall height 144.0cm (56.7in).

PERFORMANCE
Maximum speed 50mph (80kph); 63.4kg/kW (47.2kg/bhp); average fuel consumption 40.4mpg (7.0l/100km) manufacturers fig.

Right and left: The German addiction to open cars with large pram hoods was carried though to the smallest models. Wire wheels were bolt-on and the cabriolet bodies by Horch gave the cars a straight-eight appearance.

AUTO UNION A-type 1934

Auto Union set up a competition department at the old Horch plant in Zwickau, and took over a design, the "P-wagen", which had been started as a private venture at the recently-established consultancy of Dr Ing hc Ferdinand Porsche and his partner Adolf Rosenberger. Porsche had been in charge of design at Austro-Daimler from 1906-1923, and in 1924 was responsible for a supercharged four cylinder 2.0-litre Mercedes.

   With astonishing prescience he drew up a single-seater racing car anticipating the layout of the modern grand prix car by 25 years, with the engine behind the driver and ahead of the rear wheels. The rearwards engine location was held responsible for the car's quirky handling and it earned a reputation for being difficult to drive, but such problems as it had were more likely a result of the swing-axle independent rear suspension.Porsche wanted the largest-capacity engine possible within the limitation of 750kg imposed by the 1934-1937 regulations, so he drew up a relatively slow-revving lightly stressed V16 with a narrow 45 degrees between the cylinder banks and

BODY
Single-seater racing car; weight 825kg (1815lb). (750kg Formula excluded wheels, fuel, oil, tyres, water.).

ENGINE
16 cylinders, in 45deg V; mid; 68.0x75.0mm, 4358cc; compr 7.0:1; 220kW (295bhp) @ 4500rpm; 51.5kW/l (67.7bhp/l); 529Nm (54.0mkp) @ 2700rpm.

ENGINE STRUCTURE
Ohv; 2 valves per cylinder; one overhead gear driven camshaft; silicon aluminium cylinder heads and block with wet liners; 10 bearing crankshaft; water cooled;Solex carburettor, plus Roots-type supercharger, 0.59 bar 10lb.sq.in.max boost; water cooled.

TRANSMISSION
Rear wheel drive; 5 speed gearbox; spiral bevel final drive. Optional ratios 3.0 or 3.3.

CHASSIS DETAILS
Tubular steel chassis, 75mm dia main frames; independent front suspension, trailing arms; torsion bars; independent rear suspension, swing axles; transverse semi-elliptic spring; friction dampers; drum brakes; two master cylinder hydraulic circuit; worm steering; 210.0l (46.2 Imp gal) (55.4 US gal) fuel tank; 5.25x17 front; 6.50x19 rear tyres.

DIMENSIONS
Wheelbase 280.0cm (110.2in), front track 139.0cm (54.7in), rear track139.0cm (54.7in), overall length 450.0cm (177.2in), overall width 166.0cm (65.4in) overall height 116.0cm (45.7in).

PERFORMANCE
Maximum speed 174mph (280kph); 3.75kg/kW (2.80kg/bhp).

engine weight down. In another ploy to reduce weight, the sides of the cockpit were made from the doped linen used in Count Zeppelin's airships. Aluminium was used for the cowlings over the engine and the nose of the car..

There were no restrictions on the type of fuel that could be used, so Auto Union employed an alcohol-based mix, of which the fuel tank had to hold sufficient for a 3.5mpg fuel consumption and only one refuelling stop during the specified race distance of 500km (311 miles. The weight of some 46 gallons (around 400lbs [181kg]) amidships did not alter the car's handling characteristics as the tank emptied.

The Auto Union made its first appearance on 6 March 1934 when Hans Stuck broke three world records on the AVUS track in Berlin. During the ensuing season it was successful in the German, Swiss, and Czechoslovak Grands Prix, and was second in the Italian. The racing Auto Union could have formed the basis of a road-going super-sports car. Dr Porsche designed a three-seat closed coupe with the driver in a central seat which pre-dated the McLaren F1 by sixty years.

Above: Hans Stuck urges the A-Type Auto Union to victory in the 1934 German Grand Prix at the Nürburgring. A crowd of 200,000 watched Caracciola's Mercedes-Benz challenge the Auto Union only to fail with a broken engine.

Far right: Dr Porsche on right watches as one of his Auto Unions comes to a stop after a record attempt on one of Germany's arrow-straight autobahns. Driver protected by wind-cheating cockpit cowl.

Although NSU had sold its car side to Fiat in 1930, with the Italian company having all rights to any cars made under the NSU name, in 1933 NSU Germany asked Dr Ferdinand Porsche to design a new model neglecting the possibility that Fiat would have title to it if it ever went into production. When Porsche produced his first drawings in January 1934, the design was revolutionary. A steel backbone platform carried the flat-four air cooled engine at the rear, driving the rear wheels through an integral four-speed gearbox. The engine's modest 20bhp was developed at just 2600rpm.

Independent suspension was used all round, with torsion bars. Three prototypes of the Porsche 32 (its in-house design number) were built. Drauz of Heilbron built two, with wooden frames and canvas body, and the third was bodied in steel by Reutter of Stuttgart. Even though Porsche had yet to be asked to design the Volkswagen, the NSU Volksauto had all the ingredients for the car that was to become the Beetle. When testing was well under way, NSU discovered that sales of its motorcycles were picking up, so the Volksauto project was abandoned.

BODY
2 door saloon, 4 seats; weight 750kg (1650lb).
ENGINE
4 cylinders, horizontally-opposed; rear; 80.0x72.0mm, 1470cc; 14.7 kW(20bhp) @ 2600rpm; 10.0 kW/l (13.6bhp/l).
ENGINE STRUCTURE
Ohv; 2 valves per cylinder; 1 gear driven central camshaft; aluminium cylinder head and barrels, cast iron crankcase; 3 bearing crankshaft; single carburettor; air cooled
TRANSMISSION
Rear wheel drive; 4 speed gearbox; spiral bevel final drive
CHASSIS DETAILS
Steel platform chassis; steel or wood and canvas body; independent front suspension, trailing arms, torsion bars; independent rear suspension, swing axles, torsion bars; drum brakes, single hydraulic circuit;

5.25 or 5.75x16 tyres.
DIMENSIONS
Wheelbase 260.0cm (102.4in).
PERFORMANCE
Maximum speed 65mph (105km/h); 51.0 kg/kW (37.5kg/bhp).

Right: Porsche did not proceed with his radical Zündapp which was proposed with either a radial engine or a novel opposed-piston design. Its 30hp engine produced a lively 70mph but after three prototypes it was abandoned. NSU commissioned a similar project but it too was discontinued.

WANDERER W50 1935

Logically this model should have been the W22, coming between the W21 and W23. There were few technical novelties as far as the engine design went, with overhead valves operated through pushrods from a block mounted camshaft. Even at this relatively late stage the four-speed gearbox still lacked synchromesh on any ratio, calling for a skilful driver to avoid nasty noises when changing up or down. On the other hand, it did have power-assisted steering using the rather basic system made by ZF under licence from Ross in the Unites States.

Two saloon models were available, in four or six-light form, plus a pair of Gläser-bodied cabriolets, all with independent suspension front and rear.

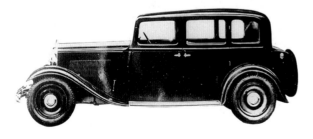

BODY
4 door saloon, 2/4 door cabriolet; 4 seats; weight 1275kg (2805lb).

ENGINE
6 cylinders, in line; front; 71.0x95.0mm, 2257cc; compr 6.1:1; 37.3kW (50bhp) @ 3000rpm; 16.5kW/l (22.1bhp/l).

ENGINE STRUCTURE
Ohv; 2 valves per cylinders; 1 gear driven side camshaft; cast iron cylinder head and block; 7 bearing crankshaft; Solex 30 JFF carburettor; water cooled.

TRANSMISSION
Rear wheel drive; 4 speed; spiral bevel final drive; 4.90.

CHASSIS DETAILS
U-section chassis; steel bodywork; independent front suspension, double wishbones; independent rear suspension, swing axle, transverse semi-elliptic spring; drum brakes; single hydraulic circuit; ZF-Ross cam and peg steering; PAS; 53.0l (11.7 Imp gal) (14.0 US gal) fuel tank; 5.25x17 tyres.

DIMENSIONS
Wheelbase 300cm (118in), front track 135cm (53.1in), rear track 135cm (53.1in), turning circle12m (39.6ft), length 450cm (177.2in), width 167cm (65.7in), height 165cm (65.0in).

PERFORMANCE
Max. speed 65mph (105kph); 34.2kg/kW (25.5kg/bhp); av. fuel consumption 20.2 mpg (14.0 l/100km) manufacturer's fig.

What a difference a year makes. The 1935 W50 (*left*) **was still staid and upright with a bluff front and an add-on luggage trunk at the back. The following year** (*right*) **it had the style and status of a Mercedes. Contemporary Rovers adopted a similar shape.**

AUTO UNION B Type 1935

Lessons learned during the first season were quickly incorporated into the car for 1935, although the basic design remained essentially unaltered.

Engine capacity was increased to 4951cc, with both the compression ratio and supercharger boost pressure increased. A Hirth-type crankshaft, using separate main and big-end bearings plus webs, pressed together to form a single unit was used, with roller rather than plain main bearings. This in turn allowed the engine to run at a sustained 4700rpm, the extra power enabling first gear to be blanked off. In place of the conventional exhaust system, the Type B had 16 separate curved stub exhaust pipes pointing skywards.

The chassis of the A-type had cracked during races, allowing coolant to leak out. The diameter of the main tubes was increased to 105mm and separate plumbing was used between engine and radiator. As well as shortening the wheelbase and increasing track, the Type B had torsion bars at the rear, located within the rear chassis tubes. With all-aluminium bodywork, the new model was some 20kg lighter than the first one. Worries about the car's handling persisted.

BODY
Single seater racing car; weight 805kg (1771lb).

ENGINE
12 cylinders in 45deg V; mid; 72.5x75.0mm, 4951cc; compr 8.95:1; 280kW (375bhp) @ 4800rpm; 56.6kW/l (67.7bhp/l); 647.5Nm (66mkp) @ 3000rpm.

ENGINE STRUCTURE
Ohv; 2 valves per cylinder; one overhead gear driven camshaft; aluminium cylinder head and block with steel wet liners; 10 bearing crankshaft; Solex carburettor, plus Roots-type supercharger, 0.74 bar max boost; water cooled.

TRANSMISSION
rear wheel drive; 4 speed gear box; spiral bevel final drive.

CHASSIS DETAILS
Tubular steel chassis, 105mm dia main frames; independent front suspension, trailing arms; torsion bars; independent rear suspension, swing axles; transverse semi-elliptic spring; friction dampers; Lockheed drum brakes; separate hydraulic circuits front and rear; worm steering; 210.0l (46.2 Imp gal) (855.4 US gal) fuel tank; 5.25x19 front; 7.00x19 rear tyres.

DIMENSIONS
Wheelbase 291cm (114.6in), front track 142cm (55.9in) rear track 142cm (55.9in), length 392cm (154.3in), width 169cm (66.5in), height 102cm (40.1in).

PERFORMANCE
Maximum speed 183mph (295kph), 2.9kg/kW (2.14kg/bhp).

Right: **Auto Union was committed to the mid-engine, but despite the best efforts of former motorcycle racer Bernd Rosemeyer it won only at Tunis, Pescara, Monza and Brno.**

AUTO UNION C-type 1936

Throughout its three-year span the key to success in the 750kg Formula was to have as powerful an engine as could be contrived within the constraints of light weight design. In 1936 the V16 engine was enlarged to just over 6.0 litres, and together with its new limited slip differential turned the tables on the Mercedes-Benz team which had been triumphant in 1935.

It was a year of glory for the popular Bernd Rosemeyer who won the Eifelrennen and the German Grand Prix at the Nürburgring, the Coppa Acerbo at Pescara, the Swiss Grand Prix at Berne where he had a bitter duel with the more experienced Rudolf Caracciola (Mercedes-Benz), and the Italian Grand Prix at Monza. At 27 he was European champion and idolised in Germany although it was months before he and Caracciola could forget their animosity about Berne.

Efforts were again made to improve the the car's tricky handling, so it was a matter of some relief when Mercedes-Benz withdrew part-way through the year to concentrate on getting ready for 1937 under its new engineer Rudolph Uhlenhaut and team manager Alfred Neubauer. Auto Union could field a team which

BODY
Single seater racing car; weight 824kg (1813lb).

ENGINE
16 cylinders in 45deg vee; mid; 75.0x85.0mm, 6005cc; compr 9.2:1; 388kW (520bhp) @ 5000rpm; 64.6kW/l (86.6bhp/l); 853Nm (87mkp) @ 2500rpm.

ENGINE STRUCTURE
Ohv; 2 valves per cylinder; 1 gear-driven camshaft; aluminium cylinder heads and block, steel wet liners; 10 bearing crankshaft; Solex carburettor; Roots-type supercharger, 0.94bar max boost; water cooled.

TRANSMISSION
Rear wheel drive; 4 or 5 speed gearbox; limited slip diff, spiral bevel final drive.

CHASSIS DETAILS
Tubular steel chassis, 105mm dia main frames; ifs, trailing arms; torsion bars; independent rear suspension, swing axles; torsion bars; friction dampers; Lockheed drum brakes; single hydraulic circuit; worm steering; 225l (49.5 Imp gal) (59.4 US gal) fuel tank; 5.50x19 front; 7.00x19 or 7.00x22 rear tyres.

DIMENSIONS
Wheelbase 291cm (114.6in), front track 142cm (55.9in) rear track 142cm (55.9in), length 392cm (154.3in), width 169cm (66.5in), overall height 102cm (40.1in).

PERFORMANCE
Maximum 211mph (340kph); 21kg/kW (1.58kg/bhp).

included the veteran Italian Achille Varzi, the elegent Hans Stuck, and the new Rudolf Hasse to compete with the redoubtable Nuvolari in the Scuderia Ferrari Alfa Romeos.

The mighty V16 yielded an imposing 520bhp, making it one of the most powerful racing cars of its era. It could exceed 200mph and do 180mph in race trim, but just as the P-Wagen (named after Dr Porsche) attained its apotheosis, its designer was tempted away to design a front-engined Mercedes-Benz, and the 750kg Formula came to an end. The glowing reputation of the four-ringed symbol had been branded for ever on a titanic era of motor racing.

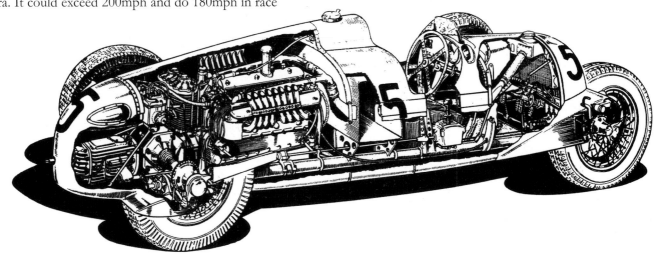

Right: 4 speed gearbox gate on right of C-type cockpit. The single dog-leg to the left is for reverse. The 5 speeder had a double dog-leg with a slot for 1st.

Below: Record car streamlining. Cowled wheels and tear-drop profile suspension arms demonstrate Auto Union's obsessive attention to detail.

HORCH 108 1937

Graceful is not a word that comes to mind for the Type 108. This was a strictly utilitarian vehicle built for the German Military, with a good cross-country ability. The short overhangs front and rear enabled the Type 108 to tackle ditch and bank without becoming bogged down. The spare wheels were carried in recesses between the front and rear doors.

Two 4wd systems were available, one full time, the second with selectable front drive being added to the full-time rear wheel drive. A feature of the Type 108 was the very short bonnet, with louvres across the top as well as along the flanks.

Horch supplied military vehicles for the Kaiser's army from 1914, then to the Reichswehr from 1926-1928, and finally to the Wehrmacht. In the first half of 1939 the German military took nearly a quarter of all new car sales and a third of all new motorcycles.

BODY
4 door open cross-country vehicle, 6 seats; weight 3950kg (8690lb).

ENGINE
8 cylinders, in vee; front; 78.0x100.0 mm, 3823cc; 60kW (81bhp) @ 3600rpm.

ENGINE STRUCTURE
2 valves per cylinder; cast iron cylinder head and block; water cooled.

TRANSMISSION
All-wheel drive; 5 speed gearbox.

CHASSIS DETAILS
Separate steel chassis; steel bodywork; front suspension, semi-elliptic springs; rear suspension, semi-elliptic springs; drum brakes, single hydraulic circuit; worm and roller steering; 210x 18 tyres.

DIMENSIONS
Wheelbase 395.0cm (155.5in), front track 164.6cm (64.8in), rear track 164.6cm (64.8in)

PERFORMANCE
Maximum speed 53mph (84km/h), 65.8kg/kW (48.8kg/bhp).

Right: The 66 degree 3.5-litre Horch V8 was a powerful mainstay of German military transport. This prototype 108 artillery tractor and its similar personnel carriers provided the basis for many armoured and soft-skinned vehicle types.

HORCH Type 901 1937

Where the Type 108 was a general-use field car, the Type 901 was very much more of a comfortable staff car, but still with a short front and rear overhang to allow it access over rough country.

The V8 engine drove through a four-speed gearbox, with a low-ratio transfer box for off-road use, when the speed was limited to just 19mph. Again, the spare wheels were carried in recesses on the sides of the vehicles, which meant that the doors had to be very narrow. Weather protection was limited to a fold-back hood, with no provision for side screens.

The 901 was primarily a personnel carrier with a wide range of gear ratios available in its Prometheus and ZF non-synchromesh gearboxes for off-road versatility (see right) and on-road speed.

BODY
4 door cabriolet, 4 seats; weight 2700kg (5940lb).

ENGINE
8 cylinders in vee; front; 78.0x92.0 mm, 3517cc; 59kW (80bhp) @ 3600rpm; 16.8kW/l (22.8bhp/l).

ENGINE STRUCTURE
Ohv; 2 valves per cylinder; 1 chain-driven camshaft; cast iron cylinder head and block; water cooled

TRANSMISSION
All wheel drive; 4- speed gearbox, plus two-ratio transfer box; hypoid bevel final drives.

CHASSIS DETAILS
Separate steel chasssis, steel bodywork; front suspension, semi-elliptic springs; rear suspension, semi-elliptic springs; drum brakes, single hydraulic circuit; worm and roller steering; 190 x 18 tyres.

DIMENSIONS
Wheelbase 310.0cm (122.0in), front track 153.2cm (60.3in), rear track 153.2cm (60.3in)

PERFORMANCE
Maximum speed 60mph on road, 19mph off road (95km/h and 50km/h) 45.8kg/kW (33.8kg/bhp).

HORCH 830R Kubelwagen 1937

Kubel translates as an open bucket – which in the case of the Type 830R meant that there were no doors to get in the way. There was, however, a simple hood to give the driver and passengers some protection against the weather. Cross country ability was limited, with just two wheel drive, but as a precaution, a spade was strapped to the rear wing in case progress was halted.

There was a smaller-engined version of the Type 830R, with a 3.0 litre V8, developing 62bhp/46kW. Both versions used the ZF Aphon four-speed gearbox. The production run was short, with the last being built in 1937.

The 830 also became the basis for a number of special bodies which included ambulances, fire engines, and police vehicles. Car production ceased in 1940, and Auto Union turned to light delivery and commercial trucks as well as military vehicles along with Opel, Ford, and VW, until 1945.

BODY
Open; 4 seats; weight 1820kg (4004lb).
ENGINE
8 cylinders in vee; front; 78.0x85.0 mm, 3250cc; 51kW (70bhp) @ 3250rpm; 15.7kW/l (21.5 bhp/l)
ENGINE STRUCTURE
Ohv; 2 valves per cylinder; 1 chain driven central camshaft; cast iron cylinder head and block; water cooled.
TRANSMISSION
Rear wheel drive; 5 speed gearbox, spiral bevel final drive.
CHASSIS DETAILS
Separate steel chassis, steel body; front suspension, semi-elliptic springs; rear suspension, semi-elliptic springs; drum brakes, single hydraulic circuit; worm and roller steering; 6.00x20 tyres.
DIMENSIONS
Wheelbase 320.0cm (126.0in), front track 145.6cm (57.3in), rear track 151.6cm (59.7in)
PERFORMANCE
Maximum speed 68mph (110kph), 35.7kg/kW (26.0kg/bhp).

Right: In its basic form the Kubelwagen had no doors and only the most basic furnishings.

WANDERER W23 1937

The engine Porsche designed for Wanderer had an aluminium cylinder block with cast iron wet cylinder liners and, although not a very striking performer, it was well-made and refined.

Porsche also designed a 3.5-litre straight-eight with a clutched supercharger, with which Wanderer intended to challenge Mercedes-Benz, but by the time Rasmussen took over the emphasis was on survival rather than innovation and the project was abandoned. The new W23 and W24 were still expected to challenge Mercedes-Benz although not at so exalted a level. The side-valve engine was relatively feeble, although the car's chassis was good, with independent suspension at the front and DKW's 'floating axle' at the back.

Besides the customary saloon and cabriolet, by 1939 Wanderer offered a fully-timbered estate car called the Farmerwagen, and also a long wheelbase W26 with an extra 250cm between the wheels (accompanied by a weight penalty of 80kg) suitable for six-seat saloon or cabriolet bodywork. It was a slow car with a top speed of only 65mph and a ponderous turning circle of 47ft between kerbs.

BODY
4 door saloon/cabriolet; 4 seats; 1390kg (3058lb).

ENGINE
6 cylinders, in line; front; 75.0x100.0mm, 2651cc; compr 6.4:1; 46.3kW (62bhp) @ 3500rpm; 17.5kW/l (23.4bhp/l).

ENGINE STRUCTURE
Side valve; 2 valves per cylinder; 1 chain driven side camshaft; aluminium cylinder block with cast iron wet liners; 4 bearing crankshaft; Solex 35 BFRH carburettor; water cooled.

TRANSMISSION
Rear wheel drive; 4 speed gearbox, spiral bevel final drive, 4.10 or 4.50.

CHASSIS DETAILS
Box section chassis; steel bodywork; independent front suspension, double wishbones; independent rear suspension, swing axle, transverse semi-elliptic spring; hydraulic dampers; drum brakes; single hydraulic circuit; ZF-Ross cam and peg steering; PAS; 60.0l (13.2 Imp gal) (15.9 US gal) fuel tank; 5.25x17in tyres.

DIMENSIONS
Wheelbase 290.0cm (114.2in), front track 142.0cm (55.9in), rear track 145.0cm (57.1in), turning circle 12.0m (39.6ft), overall length 460.0cm (181.1in), overall width 170.0cm (66.9in), overall height 165.0cm (65.0in).

PERFORMANCE
Maximum speed 71mph (115kph); 30.0kg/kW (22.4kg/bhp); average fuel consumption 18.8mpg (15.0 l/100km).

Right: Upright, respectable, middle-weight, middle-class, the Wanderer was a step up from DKW, with a hint of Detroit in its rounded grille and flowing wings.

The formation of the Auto Union meant that each manufacturer was starting to make use of the others' components. Wanderer stayed 'in house' for the W24's engine, which was simply a four-cylinder version of the larger W23's. But rather than design a new chassis, Wanderer, like Audi, brought in the DKW Sonderklasse chassis, with its independent front suspension, using wishbones and a single transverse semi-elliptic spring.

The bodywork for both the two and four door saloons and the four door cabriolet was all made by coachbuilder Reutter. The W23 and 24, and the supercharged S25K, were the last cars to be made before the Wanderer name vanished.

The cars had been advertised as upper middle-class Saxon which was probably a true aspiration. The styling grew indistinct with American overtones in the 'fencer's mask' grille and flowing lines. Other members of the Auto Union survived in eastern Germany after the war but Wanderer had reached the end of the road.

BODY
4 door saloon; 4 seats; 1140kg (2508lb).

ENGINE
4 cylinders, in line; front; 75.0x100.0mm, 1767cc; compr 6.4:1; 31.3kW (42bhp) @ 3500rpm; 17.7kW/l (23.8bhp/l).

ENGINE STRUCTURE
Side valve; 2 valves per cylinder; 1 chain-driven side camshaft; cast iron cylinder head and block; 3 bearing crankshaft; Solex BFRH carburettor; water cooled.

TRANSMISSION
rear wheel drive; 4 speed; spiral bevel final drive, 4.22 or 4.50.

CHASSIS DETAILS
U-section chassis; steel body; independent front suspension, wishbones and transverse semi-elliptic spring; rear suspension, live axle, transverse semi-elliptic springs; drum brakes, single hydraulic circuit; ZF-Ross worm steering; 43.0l (9.5 Imp Gal) (11.4 US gal) fuel tank; 5.00x17 tyres.

DIMENSIONS
Wheelbase 260.0cm (102.4in), front track130.0cm (51.2in), rear track 133.0cm (52.4in), turning circle 11.5m (49.5ft), overall length 430.0cm (169.3in), overall width 161.5cm (63.6in), overall height 165.0cm (65.0in).

PERFORMANCE
Maximum speed 65mph (105kph); 36.4kg/kW (27.1kg/bhp); average fuel consumption 26mpg (11.0l/100km).

Right: **Smallest Wanderer, the 1939 W24 still carried the winged 'W' of its 1887 bicycle beside the four rings of Auto Union.**

WANDERER W25K 1937

While the supercharged Auto Union racing cars were gathering glory on the race tracks of Europe and breaking speed records, Wanderer seized the opportunity to produce the W25 K, for Kompresser. With the Roots-type blower turning at 2.3 times engine speed, or 9200rpm when the Porsche-designed six cylinder engine was developing its maximum 63kW, the W25 K had a maximum speed of 90mph. Stopping power was provided by hydraulically-operated drum brakes.

Two models were produced, a two-door sports and two-door cabriolet, the latter weighing 70kg more. Production made it into three figures only in 1936-37, when 149 were built. The following year only 72 were made, while in the last year of production, 1938, sales collapsed to 37.

Reliability was the W25K's real problem. Driving fast along the autobahn could be exciting at over 90mph but not for long. The non-synchromesh gearbox was also frail and although the last sports Wanderer looked like a thoroughbred it could not last the course.

BODY
2 door open sports car; 2 seats; weight 1000kg (2200lb).

ENGINE
6 cylinders, in line, front; 70.0x85,0mm, 1962cc; compr 6.4:1; 63kW (85bhp) @ 4000rpm. 32.3kW/l (43.6bhp/l).

ENGINE STRUCTURE
Ohv; 2 valves per cylinder; chain driven side camshaft, pushrods and rockers;aluminium cylinder head; aluminium block with chrome-plated cast iron liners; 7 bearing crankshaft; Solex 32 FFUS carburettor and Roots-type supercharger; water cooled.

TRANSMISSION
Rear wheel drive; 4 speed gearbox; spiral bevel final drive, 3.60.

CHASSIS DETAILS
Separate box section chassis; steel bodywork; independent front suspension, wishbones and transverse semi-elliptic spring; rear suspension,beam axle, transverse semi-elliptic spring; drum brakes; single hydraulic circuit; ZF-Ross steering; 80.0l (17.6 Imp gal) (21.1 US gal) fuel tank; 5.25x17 tyres.

DIMENSIONS
Wheelbase 265.0cm (104.3in), front track 132.5cm (52.2in), rear track 133.0cm (52.4in), turning circle 12.4m (41.0ft), overall length 422.0cm (166.1in), overall width 168.0cm (66.1in), overall height 140.0cm (55.1in).

PERFORMANCE
Maximum speed 90mph (145kph); 15.9kg/kW (11.8kg/bhp); average fuel consumption 23.5 mpg (12.0l/100km) estimated fig.

Right: Sweeping lines and flush tail enclosing spare wheel epitomised 1930s roadster.

AUTO UNION Record Cars 1937

Not content with dominating grand prix racing, Germany was determined to be supreme in record-breaking. It was an intense and ultimately tragic contest between Auto Union and Mercedes-Benz. The cars that emerged from Zwickau for Bernd Rosemeyer to drive were brawny V-16s of 6.3 litres and 4.4 litres with strikingly beautiful streamlined bodies.

The sprint cars were short, the high-speed cars had an extra 160cm added to provide aerodynamic stability over a 16km stretch of the Frankfurt-Darmstadt autobahn recently completed with record-breaking in mind. During the 1937 *Rekordwoche* in late October, Rosemeyer set a new record for the mile at 252.47mph (406.29kph) in the 6.3 litre car and broke 13 other international flying and standing-start records.

His Mercedes-Benz rivals abandoned their attempts when their car suffered from aerodynamic lift at over 230mph, yet even Rosemeyer was visibly shaken after holding the car at 211mph on a narrow ribbon of highway for ten miles.

Three months later Rosemeyer tried to improve his times. His car's bodywork was modified in search of more speed, but it proved susceptible to cross-winds, and the brave and popular driver was killed when he struck the abutments to a bridge. Hitler sent a personal telegram to his widow and forbade further record bids on the fatal 16kms.

BODY
Record breaking cars (two made with different engine capacities); weight 910kg (2002lb).

ENGINE
77.0x85.0mm, 6330cc; 406.6kW (545bhp) @ 5000rpm; 64.2kW/l (86.1bhp/l) @ 2600rpm.

ENGINE STRUCTURE
Ohv; 2 valves per cylinder; one gear driven ohc; aluminium cylinder heads and block, wet liners; 10 bearing crankshaft; Solex carburettor; Roots-type supercharger, 0.93bar max boost; water cooled.

TRANSMISSION
Rear wheel drive; 4 speed gearbox; spiral bevel final drive.

CHASSIS DETAILS
Tubular molybdenum steel chassis, 105mm diameter main frames; ifs, trailing arms; torsion bars; independent rear suspension, swing axles; torsion bars; friction dampers; Lockheed drum brakes; single hydraulic circuit; worm steering; 210.0l (46.2 Imp gal) (55.4 US gal) fuel tank; 7.00x24 tyres.

DIMENSIONS
Wheelbase 291cm (114.6in), front track142cm (55.9in), rear track 142cm (55.9in), length 552cm (217.3in), width 183.5cm (72.2in), height 106cm (41.7in).

PERFORMANCE
Max speed 253.7mph (408.3kph); 2.2kg/kW (1.7kg/bhp).

Auto Union used
its open-wheel, short
wheelbase mountain-
climb versions of the
grand prix racers,
with no front brakes,
for the 1937 sprint
record attempts.

Right: Rosemeyer races
a streamlined record
car in the 1937 Avus
Grand Prix in Berlin.

Above right:
Rosemeyer consults
with Professor Eberan
von Eberhorst
(in glasses) before
the record attempt.

Using the same cross-scavenging twin-cylinder engine, the F-8 was a larger version of the F-5, with longer wheelbase and slightly wider track. It was this same chassis which would form the basis of the F-80, the first DKW to be produced after World War II. For the F-8 the usual artificial leather-clad plywood body was used, again with the smoother lines which were first seen on the 1934 V4 Schwebeklasse; as with all models to this time it had just two doors.

There was no change in the output of the engine, while the same three-speed gearbox, with the 2.0:1 step down chain-driven transfer system was used. The drum brakes and worm steering also remained as before. Two versions in addition to the soft-top cabriolet were a saloon and fixed head coupe.

BODY
Cabriolet/saloon; 2 doors; weight 870kg (1914lb).

ENGINE
2 cylinders, in line; front; 74.0x68.0mm, 584cc; compr 5.9:1; 13.4kW (18bhp) @ 3500rpm; 22.9kW/l (30.8bhp/l).

ENGINE STRUCTURE
Ported two stroke; cast iron cylinder head and block; 2 bearing crankshaft; Solex 30BFLH/55 carburettor; water cooled.

TRANSMISSION
Front wheel drive; 3 speed gearbox, with 2.0:1 chain driven transfer; spur gear final drive, 3.26.

CHASSIS DETAILS
Separate U-section chassis; plywood bodywork; independent front suspension, single semi-elliptic spring, lower links; rear suspension, dead axle, single transverse semi-elliptic suspension, drum brakes; worm steering; 32.2l (7.0 Imp gal) (8.4 US gal) fuel tank; 4.00x19 tyres.

DIMENSIONS
Wheelbase 261.0cm (102.7in), front track 115cm (45.3in), rear track 125.0cm (49.2in), turning circle 12.0m (39.4ft), overall length 389.5cm (153.3in), overall width 148.0cm (58.3in), overall height 150.0cm (59.0in).

PERFORMANCE
Maximum speed 50mph (80kph); 64.9kg/kW (48.3kg/bhp); average fuel consumption 40.4mpg (7.0 l/100km) manufacturer's fig.

Left and right: **Substantial cabriolet hood and winding windows gave the open Reichklasse cars all-weather ability.**

AUDI Type 920 1938

When Auto Union was formed, DKW was the most prolific manufacturer and needed more capacity, so Audi manufacture was transferred to the Horch plant at Chemnitz which became the group's headquarters, and DKW took over the works at Zwickau. Auto Union was also able to keep its costs down by an exchange of ideas and components, so Audi was able to use an almost ready-made Horch 3.2 litre engine for its rear wheel drive 920 succeeding the Audi Front in 1939. It was a welcome relief after the dull and over-large Rickenbacker-engined models to launch a six-cylinder version of the splendid Horch ohc straight-eight.

The running gear and bodywork were derived from a Wanderer model, betraying some US influence with a divided windscreen and rounded radiator shell. The up-market 920 was joined by a cheaper 920B which had a more austere air, less brightwork, and was sold only as a saloon. By 1938 the group's business was booming, with 30% of the German motorcycle market and nearly a quarter of the car market with sales of 52,000 cars, 40,000 of which were DKWs.

BODY
4 door saloon and cabriolet; 4 seats; weight 1395kg (3069lb).

ENGINE
6 cylinders, in line; front; 87.0x92.0mm; 3281cc; compr 6.0:1; 56kW (75bhp) @ 3000rpm; 17.1kW/l (22.9bhp/l); 206Nm (21.0mkp) @ 2000rpm.

ENGINE STRUCTURE
Ohv; 2 valves per cylinder; 1 gear driven side camshaft, pushrods; cast iron cylinder head and block; 8 bearing crankshaft; Solex 35 MMOVS carburettor, water cooled.

TRANSMISSION
Rear wheel drive; 4 speed gearbox; spiral bevel final drive; 3.80.

CHASSIS DETAILS
Box section chassis; steel bodywork; independent front suspension, lower wishbones, upper transverse semi-elliptic spring; independent rear suspension, swing axle, transverse semi-elliptic spring; drum brakes; single hydraulic circuit; cam and peg steering; PAS; 70.0l (15.4 Imp gal) (18.5 US gal) fuel tank; 6.00x16 tyres.

DIMENSIONS
Wheelbase 310.0cm (122.0in), front track 143.5cm (56.5in), rear track 146.5cm (57.7in), turning circle 11.5m (38.0ft), overall length 490.0cm (192.9in), overall width 172.0cm (67.7in), overall height 162.0cm (63.8in).

PERFORMANCE
Maximum speed 81mph (130kph); acceleration 0-100kph (62mph) sec 30.0sec; 24.9kg/kW (18.6kg/bhp); average fuel consumption 20.2mpg (14.0l/100km) manufacturer's fig.

Right: Audi was late moving to unitary construction. 1938 chassis reveals weight and cost economies.

HORCH Type 951 1938

While Wanderer concentrated on the medium-sized range, Horch models seemed to become larger with each successive design. The 5.0-litre engine had a gear driven single overhead camshaft, while the long crankshaft ran in no fewer than 10 main bearings to ensure smoothness at high speeds.

The standard 951 models used the ZF-Aphon gearbox, with the choice of direct of overdrive ratios. The larger, six-seater 951A saloon and tourer were fitted with a manual-change four-speed ZF gearbox, with an overdrive ratio on top. Styling of the saloons once again reflected the transatlantic influence, while the imposing tourer had the distinctive folded hood sitting proud behind the rear seats.

BODY
4 door saloon/cabriolet; 4 seats; weight 1470kg (3234lb).

ENGINE
8 cylinders, in line; front; 87.0x104.0mm, 4944cc; compr 6.1:1; 90.0kW (120bhp) @ 3600rpm; 18.2kW/l (24.3kW/l).

ENGINE STRUCTURE
Ohv; 2 valves per cylinder; single gear driven overhead camshaft; cast iron cylinder head and block; 10 bearing crankshaft; Solex 35 JFF carburettor; water cooled.

TRANSMISSION
Rear wheel drive; 4 speed pre-selector gearbox; spiral bevel final drive; 3.6 or 3.9; overdrive gearbox available.

CHASSIS
Box-section chassis; steel bodywork; independent front suspension, twin transverse semi-elliptic springs; rear suspension, underslung semi-elliptic springs; hydraulic dampers; drum brakes, single hydraulic circuit; ZF-Ross cam and peg steering; PAS; 95.0l (20.9 Imp gal) (25.1 USgal) fuel tank; 7.50x17 tyres.

DIMENSIONS
Wheelbase 375.0cm (147.6in), front track 151.0cm (59.4in), rear track 151.6cm (59.7in), turning circle16.5m (54.5ft), overall length 564.0cm (222.0in), overall width 184.0cm (72.4in), overall height 174.0cm (68.5in).

PERFORMANCE
Maximum speed 81mph (130kph); 16.3kg/kW (12.3kg/bhp); average fuel consumption 166mpg (17.0l/100km).

The last model made by Horch was in many ways the ultimate expession of motoring in the late 1930s. The straight eight engine had a single, shaft-driven overhead camshaft, and gave a useful 90kW at, for the time, a relatively rapid 3600rpm. Owners had the choice of two final drive ratios – the higher giving the more relaxed cruising, while the lower would provide swifter acceleration.

The Sport Cabriolet was a massive and impressive vehicle, with a vee-shaped windscreen and the spare wheel carried in the front right hand wing. The body was finished in two-tone paint, with the dark flowing wings, bonnet top and door cappings picked out against the flat sides of the coachwork.

BODY
2 door sports cabriolet; 4 seats; weight 1700kg (3740lb).
ENGINE
8 cylinders, in line; front; 87.0x104mm, 4944cc; compr 6.10:1; 90kW (120bhp) @ 3600rpm; 1.82kW/l (24.3kW/l).
ENGINE STRUCTURE
Ohv; 2 valves per cylinder; 1 shaft-driven ohc; cast iron cylinder head and block; 7 bearing crankshaft; Solex 35 JFF carburettor; water cooled.
TRANSMISSION
Rear wheel drive; 4 speed gearbox; spiral bevel final drive, 3.90 standard, 4.17 option;
CHASSIS DETAILS
Separate box section chassis; steel bodywork; rear suspension; live axle, semi-elliptic springs; hydraulic dampers; drum brakes; single hydraulic circuit; 95.0l (20.1 Imp gal) (25.1 US gal) fuel tank; 7.00x17 tyres.

DIMENSIONS
Wheelbase 345.0cm (135.8in), front track 151.0cm (59.5in), rear track 151.6cm (59.7in), turning circle 14.5m (47.9ft), overall length 535.0cm (210.6in), overall width 183.0cm (72.1in), overall height 158.0cm (62.2in).
PERFORMANCE
Maximum speed 84mph (135kph), 18.9kg/kW (14.2kg bhp); average fuel consumption 12.8mpg (22.0l/100km).

Left and right: Horch 855 special roadster of 1938-1939. **Top priced Auto Union at 22,000 Reichsmarks, it had 15cm shorter wheelbase than the 853A but more presence.**

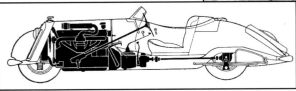

DKW F-8 Meisterklasse 1938

The F-8 was important because the chassis was to be the basis of the DKW F-89, the first model built after the end of World War II. It was also the last time the twin-cylinder engine, launched in 1928, was to be used.

In the F-8, although the bore was opened slightly to raise the swept volume to 589cc, power remained unchanged. The same transmission was employed, but instead of the worm steering, the F-8 had rack and pinion steering. The front suspension, with a single transverse upper semi-elliptic spring and lower locating links, was carried over from the F-7. In 1939 Meisterklasse and Luxus versions were added, with bigger 692cc, 15kW (20.1bhp) engines; these were to remain in production until 1942. The F-8 was produced in Eastern Germany as the IFA F8 after the war until 1955.

A significant feature of the two models was the freewheel in the transmission which eliminated drive-line snatch that occurred on the overrun. It also provided an agreable luxury for drivers who longed for the simplification of clutchless gearshifts.

BODY

Cabriolet/saloon; 2 doors; weight 700kg (1540lb).

ENGINE

2 cylinders, in line; front; 74.0x68.5mm, 589cc; compr 5.91; 13.4kW (18bhp) @ 3500rpm; 22.8kW/l (30.6bhp/l).

ENGINE STRUCTURE

Ported two stroke; cast iron cylinder head and block; 2 bearing crankshaft; Solex 30 BFLH carburettor; water cooled.

TRANSMISSION

Front wheel drive; 3 speed gearbox with 2.0:2 chain driven transfer; spur gear final drive, 3.26.

CHASSIS DETAILS

Separate U-section chassis; plywood bodywork; independent front suspension, single transverse semi-elliptic springs, lower links; rear suspension, dead axle, transverse semi-elliptic spring; drum brakes; rack and pinion steering; 32.0l (7.0 Imp gal) (8.5 US gal) fuel tank; 4.00x19 tyres.

DIMENSIONS

Wheelbase 260.0cm (102.4in), front track 119.0cm (46.9in), rear track 125.0cm (49.2in), turning circle 12.0m (39.6ft), overall length 390.0cm (153.9in), overall width 149.0cm (58.7in), overall height 148.0cm (58.3in).

PERFORMANCE

Maximum speed 50mph (80kph); 52.2kg/kW (38.9kg/bhp); average fuel consumption 40.3mpg (7.0l/100km) manufacturer.

Right: The curved 'mini-Wanderer' grille was used on the open – sports, cabriolet – versions of the F5 on. The rest all had flat grilles.

AUTO UNION D-type 1938

Dr Ferdinand Porsche left Auto Union to concentrate on the Volkswagen project and ironically design a rival racing car for Mercedes-Benz, but his engineering disciplines lived on in the Type D.

Its designer was the formidable Professor Robert Eberan van Eberhorst who was responsible for a new 45deg V12 engine with three camshafts, one in each cylinder head for the exhaust valves, plus a central one for the inlet valves. A higher supercharger pressure was used, running at a maximum of 1.2 bar. Depending on the circuit, the Type D ran either with a pair of twin-choke Solex carburettors or a single SU instrument.

Later 1939 D-types *(this page and opposite)* **had 2-stage superchargers and gave 485bhp (362kW). Müller wins French GP with modified body car.**

BODY
Single seater racing car; weight 850kg (1870lb); 45.5:54.5 front:rear distribution.

ENGINE
12 cylinders in 45deg vee; mid; 65.0x75.0mm, 2985cc; compr 10.0:1; 313kW (420bhp) @ 7000rpm; 104.9kW/l (162bhp/l); 549Nm (56mkp) @ 4000rpm.

ENGINE STRUCTURE
Ohv; 2 valves per cylinder; 3 gear driven camshafts; aluminium cylinder heads and block, wet liners; fabricated Hirth crankshaft, 7 bearings, roller big-end bearings; 2 Solex or 1 SU carburettor; Roots-type supercharger, 1.2 bar max boost; water cooled; dry sump lubrication; fuel 30% methanol, 30% ethanol, 20% benzole.

TRANSMISSION
Rear wheel drive; 5 speed gearbox; spiral bevel final drive.

CHASSIS DETAILS
Tubular chrome molybdenum steel chassis, 105mm dia main frames 65mm dia cross tubes; independent front suspension, trailing arms; torsion bars; independent rear suspension, twin link; de Dion tube; torsion bars. Hydraulic lever-type dampers front & rear; Lockheed drum brakes dual circuit; triple thread cam steering; 285.0l (62.7 Imp gal) (75.2 US gal) fuel tank; 5.50x19 front, 7.00x19 or 7.00x22 rear. Frame weight 51kg.

DIMENSIONS
Wheelbase 285.0cm (112.2in), front track 139.0cm (54.7in), rear track 139.0cm (54.7in), overall length 420.0cm (165.4in), overall width 166.0cm (65.4in), overall height 106.0cm (41.7in).

PERFORMANCE
Maximum speed 205mph (330kph), 2.72kg/kW (1.75kg/bhp).

AUTO UNION D-type 1938 (cont)

Transmission was through a five speed gearbox, with synchromesh on the top four. Trailing arm front suspension was kept, and the D-type used a de Dion layout to give better wheel angle control. For the first time hydraulic dampers were used at both ends, although as a belt-and-braces measure friction dampers were retained at the rear. With the fuel tanks now flanking him, the driver sat further back. Alas Bernd Rosemeyer died in a record attempt in January 1938.

Smaller and more compact, the D-type's side fuel tanks and smoother profile gave it a decidedly modern air that would scarcely have looked out of place in the 1960s. When it first appeared in 1938 the story according to an elderly von Eberhorst goes, there were the usual 8 stub exhausts on either side – but only 6 of the 8 were issuing any exhaust. By the time rival teams noticed the new car had a light, responsive 12 cylinder engine, it was a race winner in the hands of the great Nuvolari, who won with a two-stage blower car, the race that marked the end of an unforgettable era of motor racing, taking the chequered flag in the Yugoslav Grand Prix at Belgrade on 3 September 1939.

Aerodynamics featured strongly in two Auto Union models at this time – the big Horch 930 and the smaller DKW F-9. The F-9's rounded styling meant that the new 900cc three-cylinder two-stroke engine which was launched at the same time could give a top speed of around 68mph on the new *Autobahnen*.

Suspension too was new, with the high-mounted transverse semi-elliptic spring at the rear serving as an anti-roll stabiliser. The original engine used a conventional ignition distributor, but when it eventually went into production, it used three interrupters on the nose of the crankshaft.

BODY
2 door saloon; 4 seats; weight 870kg (1914lb).

ENGINE
3 cylinders, in line, front; 70.0x78.0 mm, 900 cc; compr 6.25:1; 28kW (38bhp) @ 3600rpm; 25.2kW/l (34.2bhp/l)

ENGINE STRUCTURE
Ported two stroke; cast iron cylinder head and block; Solex carburettor; 4 bearing crankshaft; water cooled.

TRANSMISSION
Front wheel drive; 4 speed gearbox; hypoid bevel final drive.

CHASSIS DETAILS
Steel chasssis, steel bodywork; independent front suspension, twin transverse semi-elliptic springs; rear suspension, dead axle, single transverse semi-elliptic spring; drum brakes, single hydraulic circuit; rack and pinion steering; 30.0l (6.6Imp gal) (7.9 US gal) fuel tank; 5.00x16 tyres.

DIMENSIONS
Wheelbase 235.0cm (92.5in), front track 119.5cm (47.0in), rear track 126.0cm (49.6in), overall length 420.0cm (165.4 in), overall width 153.0cm (60.2in), overall height 145.0cm (57.1in).

PERFORMANCE
Maximum speed 68mph (110 kph), 31.1kg/kW (22.9kg/bhp); average fuel consumption 33.2mpg (8.51l/100km) manufacturer's fig.

Right and left: Aerodynamics was becoming an exact science by 1939 and the sleek lines of the F-9 would be echoed for the best part of twenty years.

NSU Half-tracked Kettenrad Motorcycle 1940

The Second World War created a number of curious vehicles. Launched in 1940, the Kettenrad (track/wheel) or, officially, Sd.Kfz.2 was designed as a small go-anywhere workhorse.

Power was supplied by a 1.5 litre four-cylinder Opel Olympia engine, mounted back to front. Drive to the front sprockets of the tracks was through a three-speed gearbox, with a two-stage transfer, with six ratios running from 4.23 (high top) to 60.6 (low first). Top speed was 50mph at 3000rpm in top gear. Small steering corrections were done by the driver (rider?) moving the front wheel with the handlebars. More major movements of the handlebars actuated a differential braking system in the appropriate hydraulic array in the tracks. There were seats for two rear-facing passengers behind the driver.

The Kettenrad was first used during the invasion of Crete and served in the Western Desert and Europe.

BODY
Open; 3 seats; weight 1560kg (3120lb).

ENGINE
4 cylinders, in line; mid; 80.0x74.0mm, 1478cc; compr 6.0:1; 27kW (36bhp); 18.3kW/l (24.4bhp/l).

ENGINE STRUCTURE
Ohv; 2 valve per cylinder; 1 gear chain driven side camshaft; cast iron cylinder head, cast iron block; Solex Fallstrom-Gelande carburettor; water cooled.

TRANSMISSION
Drive to tracks through front sprocket; 3-speed all indirect gearbox, with two-speed transfer box.

CHASSIS DETAILS
Steel unitary body; coil spring front suspension; coil spring track suspension; drum brakes, separate hydraulic circuits linked to steering; handlebar steering, actuating appropriate track braking at increased angles; 42.0l (9.2 Imp gal) (11.0 US gal) fuel tank; 3.50x19 front tyre.

DIMENSIONS
Track 100.0cm (39.3in), overall length 300.0cm (118/1in), overall width 100.0cm (39.3in), overall height 120.0cm (47.2in).

PERFORMANCE
Maximum speed 50mph (80kph), 57.7kg/kW (43kg/bhp).

Right: Highly manoeuvrable, with good pulling power with its crawler tracks, the Kettenrad was the Wehrmacht's smallest vehicle. At the end of the war the American army took over the NSU factory which restarted civilian production in 1945.

With its former factory in Saxony now under Soviet control in East Germany and building the IFA F8, DKW needed to get back into production in West Germany.

The solution was to look back to pre-war days and combine its former F-9 streamlined body with the twin-cylinder F-8 engine. The F-8 had been called the Meisterklasse (master class), so the new car, the F-89, was named the New Meisterklassse.

The lines of the unusual body, with its curving slopes front and rear, were to become a DKW feature in the following years. The vertical twin two-stroke was placed transversely, driving through a non-synchromesh three-speed gearbox on the saloon, with the Universal estate having four speeds. Cooling was by water, relying on thermosyphon rather than a pump for circulation. The front suspension used wishbones and transverse leaf spring, while at the rear a simple dead axle was carried on a transverse leaf spring.

BODY
Saloon; 2 doors; 4 seats; weight 860kg (1892lb).

ENGINE
2 cylinders, in line; front; 76.0x76.0mm, 684cc; compr 6.25.:1; 17kW (25bhp) @ 4200rpm; 24.9kW/l (36.5bhp/l).

ENGINE STRUCTURE
Ported two stroke; cast iron cylinder head and block; 3 bearing crankshaft; Solex PBJ carburettor; water cooled.

TRANSMISSION
Front wheel drive; 3 speed gearbox non-synchromesh; spur gear final drive, 5.72.

CHASSIS DETAILS
Box section chassis, with steel bodywork; independent front suspension, wishbones and transverse semi-elliptic spring; rear suspension, beam axle, transverse semi-elliptic spring; hydraulic dampers; drum brakes; single braking circuit; rack and pinion steering; 32.0l (7.0 Imp gal) (8.4 US gal) fuel tank; 5.50x16 tyres, 3.5in rim width.

DIMENSIONS
Wheelbase 235.0cm (92.5in), front track119.0cm (46.8in), rear track 125.0cm (49.2in), turning circle 11.7m 38.6ft), overall length 420.0cm (165.4in), overall width 160.0cm (63.0in), overall height 145.0cm (57.1in).

PERFORMANCE
Maximum speed 62mph (100kph); acceleration 0-100kph (62mph) 55.0sec; 50.6kg/kW (34.4kg/bhp); average fuel consumption 35mpg (8.1l/100km) estimated fig.

DKW F-91 Sonderklasse 1953

DKW's advanced F-9 prototype, developed in 1939, was a far cry from the rather upright designs of the period. The sloping bonnet line, faired-in headlamps and curved roof and boot shapes appeared in the F-89 when production was resumed after WW2. The F-9 had a three-cylinder two stroke engine and it was this that formed the basis of the power unit used in the F-91.

With very few internal moving parts – crankshaft and three sets of pistons and connecting rods – the compact engine was able to sit ahead of the front axle line, with the three-speed gearbox behind it. A four-speed box, with the same 4.72 final drive ratio, later became standard.

The smooth lines of the DKW became familiar in West Germany – as did the cloud of blue exhaust smoke from the petrol and oil mixture which usually followed them. The F-91 was made as a two-door saloon, convertible, and three-door estate.

BODY
2 door saloon; 3 door estate; 4 seats; 890kg (1958lb).

ENGINE
3 cylinders, in line; front; 71.0x76.0mm, 896cc; compr 6.5:1; 25W (34bhp) @ 4000rpm; 27.9kW/l (37.9bhp/l); 63Nm (6.4mkp) @ 2000rpm.

ENGINE STRUCTURE
Ported two stroke; cast iron cylinder head and block; 4 bearing crankshaft; Solex 40 PBIC carburettor; water cooled.

TRANSMISSION
Front wheel drive; 3 speed gearbox; spiral bevel final drive, 4.72.

CHASSIS DETAILS
Separate chassis frame; steel bodywork; independent front suspension, lower wishbones, transverse semi-elliptic spring; rear suspension, dead axle, control arms, transverse semi-elliptic spring; drum brakes, single hydraulic circuit, rack and pinion steering; 32.0l (7.0 Imp gal) (8.5 US gal) fuel tank; 5.50x16 tyres.

DIMENSIONS
Wheelbase 230.0cm (90.6in), front track 119.0cm (46.9in), rear track 125.0cm (49.2in), turning circle 11.7m (38.6ft), overall length 420.0cm (165.4in), overall width 160.0cm (63.0in), overall height 145.0cm (57.1in).

PERFORMANCE
Maximum speed 75mph (120kph); acceleration 0-100kph (62mph) 34.0sec; 35.6kg/kW (26.2kg/bhp); average fuel consumption 28.2mpg (10.0 l/100km).

Right: The forward engine mounting disposed the occupants within the wheelbase and endowed the modern DKW with useful luggage capacity.

SCHLENZIG

DKW tried to create an impression that the three cylinder two-stroke really was as smooth as an in-line four-stroke six. In theory it might have been – the firing impulses per crankshaft revolution were the same, but three cylinders did not quite equal six and few people were convinced.

The engine was a development of the unit seen originally in the F-91. Extracting more power from a ported two stroke, where the mixture is fed through the crankcase to ports in the cylinder walls, was a trade-off between smoothness and tractability. The 3=6 remained faithful to a three-speed gearbox, and in 1957 buyers were offered the luxury of the Saxomat clutchless system, which like so many of similar pattern was not a success.

The 3=6 was unusual for the period as not only a two-door saloon, but also a grandly named long wheelbase 'limousine' and a Universal estate car. The limousine's wheelbase and overall length was stretched by 10cm to give more leg room in the back.

F-93 3=6:
BODY
Saloon/estate; 2 doors; 4 seats; weight 930kg (2046lb).

ENGINE
3 cylinders, in line; front; 71.0x76.0mm, 896cc; compr 6.5:1; 29kW (38bhp) @ 4200rpm; 32.4kW/l (42.4bhp/l); 71Nm (7.25mkp) @ 3000rpm.

ENGINE STRUCTURE
Ported two stroke; cast iron cylinder head and block; 4 bearing crankshaft; Solex 40JCB carburettor; water cooled.

TRANSMISSION
Fwd; 3 speed; spiral bevel final drive; Saxomat clutchless system

option from 1957.
CHASSIS DETAILS
Separate chassis frame; steel bodywork; ifs, wishbones, transverse semi-elliptic spring; rear suspension, dead axle, locating arms, transverse semi-elliptic spring; drum brakes; single hydraulic circuit; rack & pinion; 45.0l (9.9 Imp gal) (11.8 US gal) fuel tank; 5.60x15 tyres.

DIMENSIONS
Wheelbase 235.0cm (92.5in), front track 129.0cm (50.8in), rear track 135.0cm (53.1in), turning circle 11.6m (38.3in), overall length 422.5cm (166.3in), overall width 169.5cm (66.7in), overall height 146.5 (56.7in).

PERFORMANCE
Maximum speed 76mph (123kph); acceleration 0-100kph (62mph) 29.0sec; 32.1kg/kW (24.5kg/bhp); average fuel consumption 28.3mpg (10.0 l/100km) manufacturer's fig.

Following the establishment of an Auto Union DKW competitions department in 1953 (one manager and three mechanics in Düsseldorf), Sonderklasse cars did well in motor sport. They won the Austrian Alpine Rally and a class in the Monte Carlo Rally, and Walter Schlüter won the 1954 European Touring car Championship. In the following ten years Auto Union DKW won 100 championship titles and 150 races. Tuning firms such as A M Mantzel claimed power outputs of

100bhp from the three-cylinder engine. In a symbolic return to Monza in 1956 a specially-bodied Sonderklasse set 1100cc records over 4000 miles (87.5mph), 48 hours (87.6mph), 5000 miles (86.6mph), 10,000km, and 72 hours(86.7mph) driven by G Ahrens, H Meier, G Teiler, and R Barbay. The body was commissioned by Günther Ahrens from Dannenhauser & Stauss of Stuttgart, and a limited edition of 230 of the well proportioned little cars was built by Massholder of Heidelberg, and Schenk in Stuttgart.

DKW F-91/4 Munga 1955

When the German armed forces were re-established after WWII, DKW was commissioned to design a new, small general purpose off-roader. With only the small three-cylinder two stroke engine to work with, the F-91/4 started to take shape. The same layout mechanically as the cars was retained, with the radiator behind the engine. The normal front wheel drive gearbox mounted behind the engine sowed the seeds of the quattro idea, because it was relatively easy to take a drive to the rear wheels from the output shaft. A step-down transfer box provided low ratios for heavy going. In 1958 the original 896cc engine was replaced by the more powerful 33kW 980cc unit, which also provided more torque.

The name Munga was an acronym for Mehrzweck Universal Geländefahrzeug mit Allradantrieb (multi-purpose universal land-vehicle with four wheel drive). A total of 50,000 were built before being replaced by the Audi-designed but VW-badged Ilitis in 1977.

BODY
Open cross-country; 4 seats; weight 1450kg (3190lb).

ENGINE
3 cylinders, in line; front; 71.0x78.0mm, 896cc; compr 6.5:1; 28kW (38bhp) @ 4200rpm; 25.1kW/l (34.1bhp/l); 71Nm (7.25mkp) @ 3000rpm.

ENGINE STRUCTURE
Ported two stroke; cast iron cylinder head and block; 4 bearing crankshaft; Zenith 32NDIX carburettor; water cooled.

TRANSMISSION
4 wheel drive; 4 speed; spiral bevel final drives; 6.333; 1.604:1 transfer ratio.

CHASSIS DETAILS
Separate chasssis; steel bodywork; independent suspension front and rear, lower wishbones, transverse semi-elliptic springs; drum brakes; single hydraulic circuit; rack and pinion steering; 45.0l (9.9 Imp gal) (11.9 US gal) fuel tank; 6.00x16 tyres.

DIMENSIONS
Wheelbase 200.0cm (78.7in), front track 120.6cm (47.5in), rear track 120.6cm (47.5in), ground clearance 24.0cm (9.5in), turning circle 11.25m (37.1 ft), overall length 345.0cm (135.8in), overall width 181.0cm (71.3in), overall height 173.5cm (68.3 in).

PERFORMANCE
Max speed 60.1mph (98kph), 51.7kg/kW (38.1kg/bhp); av. fuel consump 21.7-16.6mpg (13-17 l/100km) manfacturer's fig..

DKW "Junior" 1957 & 1959; F-12 1963

With its larger cars established in the European market, DKW moved into the smaller sectors. A twin-cylinder, 700cc prototype version of the Junior was unveiled at the Frankfurt Show in September 1957. Production at Ingolstadt started in 1959, with the Junior powered by a scaled-down version of the three cylinder two-stroke engine used in the larger models.

A de luxe version, with a 796cc engine also developing 34bhp but with increased torque and slightly better performance, came later. Production ran until 1962, when 118,968 cars had been built.

The F12, which went into production in 1963, was longer, with a bigger luggage boot, an engine of 890cc 53.6kW (40bhp), and disc brakes.

BODY
Saloon; 2 doors; 4 seats; weight 700kg (1540lb).

ENGINE
3 cylinders, in line; front; 68.0x68.0mm, 741cc; compr 8.0:1; 25.4kW (34bhp) @ 4300rpm; 34.3kW/l (45.9bhp/l); 63Nm (6.5mkp) @ 2500rpm.

ENGINE STRUCTURE
Ported two stroke; aluminium cylinder head; cast iron block; 4 bearing crankshaft; Solex 40JCB carburettor; water cooled.

TRANSMISSION
Front wheel drive; 4 speed; spiral bevel final drive, 3.875.

CHASSIS DETAILS
Steel chassis; steel bodywork; ifs, double wishbones, torsion bars; rear suspension, dead axle, Panhard rod, torsion bars; telescopic dampers; drum brakes, single hydraulic circuit; rack and pinion steeting; 32.0l (7.1 Imp gal) (8.5 US gal) fuel tank;

5.20x12 tyres.

DIMENSIONS
Wheelbase 217.5cm (85.6in), front track 157.5cm (62.0in), rear track 143.0cm (56.3in), turning circle 10.7m (34.0ft), overall length 396.6cm (145.5in).

PERFORMANCE
Maximum speed 71mph (114kph); acceleration 0-100kmh (62mph) 31sec; 27.6kg/kW (20.6kg/bhp); average fuel consumption 31.4mpg (9.0l/ 100km) manufacturer's fig.

Left: **Simple instruments and wood-effect facia of DKW Junior. Tidy styling shows US influence.**

240

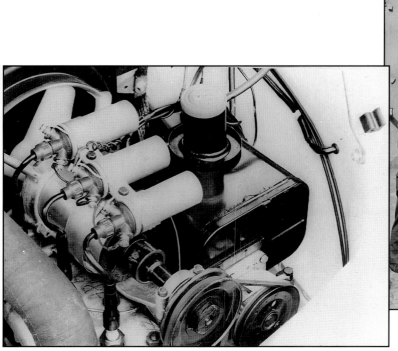

NSU Prinz I 1958

For 13 years following the end of WW2, NSU concentrated on motorcycles. It had been 29 years since the last car to bear the NSU name was produced before the company was briefly owned by Fiat.

The Prinz 1 was a tiny 2+2 saloon, with a vertical twin engine drawing on the company's extensive motorcycle technology, at the rear. There was a step-down transfer gear between engine and the four-speed gearbox as well as the more usual reduction gear in the differential. The 583cc engine started out with just 20bhp, but went to 23 bhp in 1959, and later 30.

The Prinz was an engaging little car, its small wheels and nimble handling contemporary with the Mini whose arrival eclipsed the small NSU, which struggled with swing-axles and 60% of its weight in the back to keep up. The ride was firm and cornering free from body roll. Luggage space in the front was adequate rather than generous, the rounded body restricting headroom in the back.

BODY
2 door saloon; 4 seats; weight 510kg (1122lb).

ENGINE
2 cylinders, in line; rear; 75.0x66.0mm, 583cc; compr 6.8:1; 14.7kW (20bhp) @ 4000rpm; 25.2kW/l (34.3bhp/l); 41Nm (4.3mkp) @ 2250rpm.

ENGINE STRUCTURE
Ohv; 2 valves per cylinder; Ultramax eccentric strap drive; aluminium alloy cylinder head and block; 2 bearing crankshaft; Bing 7/26 carburettor; air cooled.

TRANSMISSION
Rear wheel drive; four-speed gearbox, helical spur final drive, 4.2:1 total

CHASSIS DETAILS
Steel unitary construction; independent front suspension, wishbones, coil springs; independent rear suspension, swing axle and coil spring; telescopic dampers; drum brakes; single hydraulic circuit; 25.0l (5.5Imp gal) (6.6 US gal) fuel tank.

DIMENSIONS
Wheelbase 200.0cm (78.7in), front track 120.0 cm (47.2 in), rear track 120.0cm. (47.2 in), overall length 314.5cm (123.8in), overall width 142.0cm (55.9in), overall height 137.0cm (53.9in).

PERFORMANCE
Maximum speed 66mph (105kph); acceleration 0-100kph (62mph) 53.0sec; 34.7kg/kW (25.5 kg/bhp); average fuel consumption 40.4mpg manufacturer's fig.

Right: Body styling analogous with contemporary bubble cars gave the first Prinz a rotund appearance.

DKW AUTO UNION 1000 1958

The revival of the Auto Union name came with the DKW Auto Union 1000 in 1958. The three cylinder, two-stroke theme was retained, at 980cc the largest engine of its kind made by the firm. The layout too was familiar, with the short engine hung out ahead of the front axle line, with the gearbox in unit with the final drive. To keep as much weight as possible within the wheelbase, the radiator was located at the rear of the engine bay, with the fan driven by a shaft from a belt drive at the front of the engine. The ported two-stroke design, with a separate coil for each cylinder, required a mix of petrol and oil in the fuel tank.

BODY
Saloon; 2 doors; 4 seats; weight 897kg (1974lb).

ENGINE
3 cylinders, in line; front; 74.0x76.0mm, 980cc. compr 7.25:1; 33.3kW (44.6bhp) @ 4500rpm; 34kW/l (45.5bhp/l); 83Nm (8.5mkp) @ 2250rpm.

ENGINE STRUCTURE
Ported two stroke; cast iron cylinder head and block; Bing carburettor; water cooled.

TRANSMISSION
Front wheel drive; 4 speed gearbox with freewheel; spiral bevel final drive, 3.87.

CHASSIS DETAILS
Separate chassis, with steel bodywork; independent front suspension, lower wishbones, upper transverse semi-elliptic spring; rear suspension, dead axle, transverse semi-elliptic spring; telescopic dampers; drum brakes, single braking circuit; rack and pinion steering; 44.6l (9.8 Imp gal) (11.8 US gal) fuel tank; 5.60x15 tyres, 3.5in rim width.

DIMENSIONS
Wheelbase 235.0cm (92.5in), front track 129.0cm (50.8in), rear track 135.1cm (53.2in), ground clearance 10.1cm (7.5in), turning circle 11.2m (36.9ft), overall length 422.7cm (166.4in), overall width169.7cm (66.8in), overall height 146.8cm (57.8in).

PERFORMANCE
Maximum speed 80mph (129kph); 29.9kph (18.6mph) @ 1000rpm; acceleration 0-100kph (62mph) 24.2sec; standing quarter mile 22.5sec; 26.9kg/kW (20.1kg.bhp); average fuel consumption 28mpg (10.1l/100km) test fig.

Shortly after the 1000 saloon came the pretty-looking coupe 1000SP. Wheelbase and track were similar to the saloon's but the coupe was three inches shorter. The long doors opened almost to 90deg to give good access, but the rear seats were little more than a padded shelf designed more to carry luggage than passengers.

Without any valve timing, extracting more power from a two-stroke engine had to be done by carefully altering the porting in the cylinders and increasing the compression ratio, which tended to make the engine slightly less tractable. Peak torque was developed at 3000rpm against the saloon's 2250rpm. The same gearing was used, along with the steering column gearchange and bottom-hinged pedal layout. As with the 1000 saloon, the freewheel was automatically locked out when reverse was selected, giving some engine braking going backwards.

With styling influenced by the Ford Thunderbird, the little Auto Union quickly became a popular fashion accessory even if it never gained recognition as a serious sports car.

BODY
2 door coupe; 2+2 seats; weight 874kg (1924lb).

ENGINE
3 cylinders, in line; 74.0x76.0mm, 980cc; compr 8.0:1; 41kW (55bhp) @ 4500rpm; 41.8kW/l (56.1bhp/l); 88Nm (9.0mkp) @ 3000rpm.

ENGINE STRUCTURE
Ported two stroke; cast iron cylinder head and block; Bing carburettor; water cooled.

TRANSMISSION
Front wheel drive; 4 speed gearbox with freewheel; spiral bevel final drive, 3.87.

CHASSIS DETAILS
Separate chassis with steel bodywork; independent front suspension, lower wishbones, upper transverse semi-elliptic springs; rear suspension dead axle, transverse semi-elliptic spring; telescopic dampers; drum brakes; single braking circuit;

rack and pinion steering; 50.0l (11.0 Imp gal) (13.2 US gal) fuel tank; 155x15 tyres, 3.5in rim width.

DIMENSIONS
Wheelbase 234.0cm (92.5in), front track 129.0cm (50.8in), rear track 135.1cm (53.2in), ground clearance 20.0cm (7.9in), turning circle 11.8m (39ft), overall length 414.0cm (163.0in), overall width 142.2cm (56.0in), overall height 109.2cm (43.0in).

PERFORMANCE
Maximum speed 82mph (132kph); 29.9kph (18.6mph) @ 1000rpm; acceleration 0-100kph (62mph) 24.2sec; 21.3kg/kW (15.9kg/bhp); average fuel consumption 24.9mpg (11.3l/100km) test fig.

NSU Sport Prinz 1958

All the NSU models launched since the end of WW2 had in-house body designs which did not really match the lively performance provided by the tiny rear-mounted twin-cylinder engine, so the choice of Italian coachbuilder Bertone to create the Sport Prinz was a major step. The result was one of the best-looking small cars of the period. NSU was quite candid that it was just a two-seater with space in the back for a couple of children or, more probably, extra luggage.

The claimed top speed was around 134kph (84mph), but the firm's publicists were reluctant to be drawn on how long it took to reach 100kph. At something close to half a minute the performance could scarcely be regarded as swift. Equipment was reasonable, including a rev counter and a rather ineffectual heating system using air ducted from the engine.

Air cooling brought problems of noise and a poor heater but despite the rear engine the handling was not strongly biased towards over- or under-steer. Fuel consumption increased sharply at high speeds.

BODY
Two-door, 2+2 coupe; weight 517kg (1137lb).

ENGINE
2 cylinders, in line; transverse rear; 76.0x 66.0mm, 598cc; compr 7.2:1; 22.3kW (30bhp) @ 5500rpm; 37.3 kW/l (50.2bhp/l).

ENGINE STRUCTURE
Ohv; 2 valves per cylinder; single eccentric drive to camshaft; aluminium cylinder head, aluminium block; Solex 34PCi downdraught carburettor; air cooled.

TRANSMISSION
Rear wheel drive; 4 speed gearbox; helical spur final drive.

CHASSIS DETAILS
Steel unitary construction; independent front suspension, coil springs; independent rear suspension, swing axles, coil springs; telescopic dampers; drum brakes; single hydraulic circuit; rack and pinion steering; 25.0l (5.5 Imp gal) (6.6 US gal) fuel tank; 4.40x12 tyres.

DIMENSIONS
Wheelbase 200.0cm (78.7in), front track 120.0cm (47.2in), rear track 120.0cm (47.2in), overall length 362.0cm (142.5 in), overall width 145.0cm (57.1in), overall height 124.5cm (49.0in).

PERFORMANCE
Maximum speed 78mph (125kph); acceleration 0-60mph 27.8sec; average fuel consumption 46mpg; 23.2kg/kW (17.2kg/bhp).

Right: **Sheep in wolf's clothing. The scaled-down lines of the Sport Prinz suggested a turn of speed it did not possess.**

NSU Prinz 4 1961

The small-car theme continued, with the Prinz 4 showing distinct signs of having its styling influenced by the much larger Chevrolet Corvair, which was also rear engined and air cooled.

The little 598cc vertical twin cylinder engine sat in line with the drive shafts, driving through a four speed all-synchromesh gearbox. The engine design owed a good deal to NSU's motor cycle business, with the overhead camshaft driven by eccentrics rather than chain, a system seen on Bentleys of the mid-1920s. The combination of swing axles and a fan-cooled rear engine, no matter how light, resulted in some doubtful handling at the limit. However, the Prinz 4 had auxiliary air springs at the back which helped keep the suspension in order. The low gearing meant that at maximum speed the engine was reaching a somewhat frenzied 6300rpm.

Two cylinder engines were no match for smooth-running four cylinders in the 1960s, and air cooling proved to have more drawbacks than merit. Yet the Prinz 4 enjoyed a long run, lasting 12 years without a major change.

BODY
2 door saloon; 4 seats; weight 616kg (1232lb).

ENGINE
2 cylinders, in line; rear; 76.0x66.0mm, 598cc; compr 7.5:1; 22kW (30bhp) @ 5500rpm; 36.7kW/l (50.2bhp/l); 44Nm (4.5mkp) @ 3250rpm.

ENGINE STRUCTURE
Ohv; 2 valves per cylinder; eccentric strap driven ohc; aluminium alloy cylinder head and block; 3 bearing crankshaft; Solex 34PC1 carburettor; air cooled.

TRANSMISSION
Rear wheel drive; 4 speed gearbox; helical spur final drive; 4.80.

CHASSIS DETAILS
Steel unitary construction; independent front suspension, wishbones, coil springs; independent rear suspension; swing axles, coil springs, auxiliary air springs; telescopic dampers; drum brakes, finned alloy drums; single braking circuit; rack and pionion steering; 36.6l (8.0 Imp gal) (9.6 US gal) fuel tank; 4.80x12 tyres, 3.5in rim width.

DIMENSIONS
Wheelbase 203.9cm (80.3in), front track122.9cm (48.4in), rear track 120.7cm (47.5in), ground clearance 17.8cm (7.0in), turning circle 8.2m (27ft), overall length 344.2cm (135.5in), overall width 148.6cm (58.5in), overall height 161.3cm (63.5in).

PERFORMANCE
Maximum speed 124kph (77mph)mph; standing quarter mile 23.6sec; 28.0kg/kW (20.5kg/bhp); average fuel consumption 37.4mpg (7.5l/100km) test fig.

DKW F-102 1964

After the distinctive curves of previous DKW and Auto Union models, the styling of the F-102 came as something of a conservative shock. The upright conventional body style, with a flat grille and crisp straight lines, hinted at the changes to come, because this was to be the very last DKW.

Two years after it was launched, the same body but now with a four cylinder, four-stroke engine, would bring back the Audi name. The F-102 showed the way forward to the Audi's engine position, hung out ahead of the front axle line. As with previous DKWs, the F-102 remained faithful to the three-cylinder two stroke unit and four speed gearbox with freewheel and steering column change. Although the smaller two stroke, with fewer moving parts, was lighter than a similar four-stroke, by placing the radiator behind the engine, a better weight distribution was obtained. Also as in other DKW models, each sparking plus was served by a single coil, eliminating the need for a high-tension distributor. Production begain in January 1964, and 53,053 were built before the DKW two-stroke was consigned to history.

BODY
2/door saloon; 4 seats; weight 910kg (2002lb).

ENGINE
3 cylinders, in line; front; 81.0x76.0mm, 1175cc; compr 7.25:1; 45kW (60bhp) @ 4500rpm; 38.3kW/l (51.1bhp/l); 103Nm (10.5mkp) @ 2200rpm.

ENGINE STRUCTURE
Ported two stroke; aluminium cylinder head; cast iron block; 4 crankshaft bearings; Solex 45CIB carburettor; water cooled.

TRANSMISSION
Front wheel drive; 4 speed gearbox, with freewheel; spiral bevel final drive, 4.125.

CHASSIS DETAILS
Steel unitary construction; independent front suspension, wishbones, torsion bars; rear suspension, dead axle, trailing arms, Panhard rod, torsion bars; telescopic dampers; discs front, drums rear; single braking circuit; rack and pinion steering; 53.0l (11.7 Imp gal) (14.0 US gal) fuel tank; 6.00/13 tyres, 4.0in rim width.

DIMENSIONS
Wheelbase 248.0cm (97.6in), front track 133.0cm (52.4in), rear track 133.0cm (52.4in), ground clearance 21.0cm (8.3in), turning circle 10.7m (35.3ft), overall length 428.0cm (168.5in), overall width 162.0cm (63.8in), overall height 146.0cm ((57.5in).

PERFORMANCE
Maximum speed 84mph (135kph); 29.9kph (18.6mph) @ 1000rpm; 20.2kg/kW (15.2kg/bhp); average fuel consumption 29.7mpg (9.5l/100km).

NSU Prinz 1000 1964; NSU TT 1965

Although the basic rear engine design was retained, the Prinz 1000 benefited from a longer wheelbase and better passenger space. Even more significant was the break from motor cycle engine technology. The twin cylinder was abandoned for a four-cylinder engine with a conventional chain drive for its overhead camshaft. The same transverse layout was used as with the twin-cylinder models, driving the end-on gearbox through a 2.05:1 reduction gear. On the output side of the gearbox, another shaft took the drive back to the helical spur gear final drive unit on the centre line of the car. All these gears added a good deal to the overall noise levels, which were not helped by the low mass of the alloy engine. Once more the four speed gearbox was all synchromesh, but the Prinz 1000 stayed with drum brakes and the swing axle rear suspension layout.

The Corvair appearance continued, the standard Prinz 1000 having oval headlamps. The badging and frontal trim were changed in 1967. The low weight compensated for the lack of power, giving the Prinz 1000 a fair turn of speed. It had a fine all-synchromesh gearbox but a firm ride and quirky handling.

Prinz 1000 1964:

BODY
Saloon; 2 doors; 4 seats; weight 645kg (1419lb).

ENGINE
4 cylinders, in line; rear; 69.0x66.6mm, 996cc; compr 7.7:1; 32.1kW (43bhp) @ 5500rpm; 32.2kW/l (43.2bhp/l); 70Nm (7.0mkp) @ 2500rpm.

ENGINE STRUCTURE
Ohv; 2 valves per cylinder; 1 chain driven ohc; aluminium cylinder head, iron cylinder barrels; Solex 34PC1 carburettor; air cooled.

TRANSMISSION
Rear wheel drive; 4 speed gearbox; spiral bevel final drive; 3.78.

CHASSIS DETAILS
Steel unitary construction; ifs, wishbones, coil springs; irs, swing axles, semi-trailing wishbones; coil springs; front anti-roll bar; telescopic dampers; drum brakes, single braking circuit; rack and pinion steering; 36.8l (8.1 Imp gal) (9.2 US gal); 5.50x12 tyres, 4.5in rim width.

DIMENSIONS
Wheelbase 224.8cm (88.5in); front track 149.9cm (59.0in); rear track 137.2cm (54.0in); ground clearance 10.1cm (7.5in); turning circle 8.0m (26.5ft); overall length 379.2cm (149.3in); overall width 149.6cm (58.9in), overall height 136.4cm (53.7in).

PERFORMANCE
Maximum speed 80mph (129kph); acceleration 0-100kph (62mph) 21.5sec; standing quarter mile 21.2sec; 20.1kg/kW (15.0kg/bhp); average fuel consumption 33.1mpg (8.5l/ 100km) test fig.

Far right: In 1965 a sports version of the Prinz 1000 was introduced. It was called 1000 TT although the enlarged engine was actually 1085cc. Power output was 41kW (55bhp), maximum speed 150kph (93mph) and it accelerated from 0-100kph in 14.8sec. The TT had disc brakes, four headlamps, a rev counter and sports seats. In 1967 the engine was further enlarged to 1177cc, giving 48.4kW (65bhp) and the car was then known as 1200 TT.

Until the arrival of the Wankel engine, the reciprocating engine, with a crankshaft translating the piston movement into rotary motion, had been almost unchallenged. Dr Felix Wankel's ingenious engine, with a trochoid rotor moving in an opened-out figure-of-eight casing, was seen as an alternative.

Its compact size and smooth high speed running were obvious advantages. The few moving parts, with no valve gear, should have kept wear to the minimum. NSU's little open Spider was perhaps an unusual choice for the world's first Wankel-engined model. The rear-mounted single rotor engine drove through a four-speed gearbox. Ignition was provided by a single sparking plug, with a twin-choke Solex carburettor supplying mixture.

NSU claimed that the engine capacity was just 500cc, but the German tax authorities proclaimed it to be 1500cc on account of its three-lobe rotor, and more in keeping with the 50bhp power output. Wind noise at speed was loud, and it did not take long for the Wankel engine's shortcomings to become apparent, with rapid rotor tip seal wear, and poor low-speed running.

BODY

2 door convertible; 2 seats; weight 770kg (1540lb).

ENGINE

Single rotor, three-chamber Wankel; rear; 1500cc; 37.5kW (50bhp) @ 5000rpm; 25.0kW/l (33kW/l); 70.6Nm (7.2mkp) @ 2500rpm;

ENGINE STRUCTURE

Ported induction and exhaust controlled by rotor position; cast iron rotor and rotor casing; 2 bearings; Solex HHD 18.32 twin choke carburettor; water cooled.

TRANSMISSION

rear wheel drive; 4 speed gearbox; spiral bevel final drive, 4.43.

CHASSIS DETAILS

Steel integral construction; separate tubular subframes front and rear; independent front suspension;wishbones; coil springs; independent rear suspension; semi-trailing arms; coil springs; front anti-roll bar; telescopic dampers; disc front, drum rear brakes; single braking circuit; rack and pinion steering; 35.0l (7.7 Imp gal) (9.2 US gal); 5.00x12 tyres, 4.0in rim width.

DIMENSIONS

Wheelbase 203cm (80.0in), front track 124.5cm (49.0in), rear track 122.7cm (48.3in), ground clearance 14.5cm (5.7in), turning circle 9.2m (30.5ft), overall length 357.6cm (140.8in), overall width 151.9cm (59.8in), overall height 126.5cm (49.8in).

PERFORMANCE

Maximum speed 92mph; 0-100kph (62mph)17.6sec; standing km (quarter mile) 20.4sec; 20.5kg/kW (15.4lb/kW); average fuel consumption 26.2mpg (10.7l/100km) test fig.

After 26 years the Audi name was resurrected, although much of the car was not altogether new. The conservatively-styled body, similar to the DKW F-102, was a move up-market from the curvy two-stroke models.

Where the Audi differed was in its engine design. Front wheel drive was retained, but now there was a four cylinder, four-stroke engine providing the power. Designed by Daimler-Benz, it featured some very advanced engineering. Instead of the combustion chambers being in the cylinder head, they were in the piston crowns, with a very high-turbulence induction design allowing a high compression ratio of 11.2:1 to be used. The layout, with the engine hung out ahead of the front axle line, and with the four-speed all-synchromesh gearbox in unit with the final drive, was to become an Audi feature for many years. The move to a four stroke engine gave Audi a clean break from the two-stroke image created by DKW.

It quickly moved to re-occupy the ground left vacant by the middle-class low-volume, premium-priced cars of the pre-war Auto Union.

BODY
Saloon; 2/4 doors; 5 seats; weight 980kg (2156lb).

ENGINE
4 cylinders, in line; front; 80.0x84.4mm, 1696cc; compr 11.2:1; 54kW (72bhp) @ 5000rpm; 31.8kW/l (31.8bhp/l); 127Nm (13.0mkp) @ 2800rpm.

ENGINE STRUCTURE
Ohv; 2 valves per cylinder; 1 chain driven side camshaft; aluminium alloy cylinder head; cast iron block; 5 bearing crankshaft; Solex 38 PDSI carburettor; water cooled.

TRANSMISSION
Front wheel drive; 4 speed; spiral bevel final drive, 3.888.

CHASSIS DETAILS
Steel unitary construction; independent front suspension, wishbones, torsion bars; rear suspension, torsion beam axle, trailing arms, Panhard rod, torsion bars;

front anti-roll bar; telescopic dampers; disc front, drum rear brakes; single braking circuit; rack and pinion steering; 165/13 tyres, 4.5in rim width.

DIMENSIONS
Wheelbase 249.0cm (98.0in), front track 1340.0cm (52.8in), rear track 133cm (52.4in), ground clearance 16.0cm (6.3in), turning circle 10.9m (36.0ft), overall length 438.0cm (172.4in), overall width 163.0cm (64.2in), overall height 146.0cm (57.5in).

PERFORMANCE
Maximum speed 92mph (148kph); 29.0kph (18.0mph @ 1000rpm; 18.1kg/kW (13.6kg bhp); average fuel consumption 33.6mpg (8.4l/100km).

AUDI Super 90 1966

The Super 90 set new standards in both performance and equipment. The engine with the Heron high swirl piston combustion chamber was retained, with the larger capacity now giving 67kW. The very high compression ratio of the smaller capacity designs was reduced slightly, but was still far greater than that used by most competitors.

The basic front wheel drive design lacked the refinement of later models, while the firm ride was typical of German cars of the period. Despite the superior performance, the Super 90 stayed with the same disc front, drum rear braking system layout used in the other cars in the range.

The 90 and the later 75 exemplified the conservative side of Audi styling, changing car shapes subtly and slowly, each new feature evolving rather than appearing suddenly.

BODY
2/4 door saloon; 5 door estate; 5 seats; weight 1030kg (2266lb).

ENGINE
4 cylinders, in line; front; 81.5x84.4, 1760cc; compr 10.6:1; 67kW (90bhp) @ 5200rpm; 37.8kW/l (50.8bhp/l); 147Nm (15.0mkp) @ 3000rpm.

ENGINE STRUCTURE
Ohv; 2 valves per cylinder; 1 chain driven side camshaft; aluminium alloy cylinder head; cast iron block; 5 bearing crankshaft; Solex 32/32DIDTA carburettor; water cooled.

TRANSMISSION
Front wheel drive; 4 speed gearbox; spiral bevel final drive, 3.888.

CHASSIS DETAILS
Steel unitary construction; independent front suspension, wishbones, torsion bars; rear suspension, torsion beam axle, trailing arms, Panhard rod, torsion bars; telescopic dampers; disc front, drum rear; dual braking circuits; rack and pinion steering; 53l (11.7 Imp gal) (14 US gal) fuel tank; 165R13 tyres, 4.5in rim width.

DIMENSIONS
Wheelbase 249.0cm (98.0in), front track 133.0cm (52.4in), rear track 133.0cm (52.4in), ground clearance 19.0cm (7.5in), turning circle 10.9ft (36.0ft), overall length 438.0cm (172.4in), overall width 163.0cm (53.5in), overall height 145.0cm (57.1in).

PERFORMANCE
Maximum speed 101mph (163kph), 30kph (18.6mph) @ 1000rpm; acceleration 0-100kph (62mph) 12.5sec; 15.4kg/kW (11.4kg/bhp); average fuel consumption 31.7mpg (8.9l/100km).

NSU Type 110/1200 1967

NSU might have been tempted to use its new Wankel engine technology for the Type 110. But caution prevailed, and it was given a conventional piston engine. The air-cooled engine was an enlargement of the 1000, with iron cylinder barrels and aluminium alloy head, plus a single chain-driven overhead camshaft. As with the previous models, the Type 110 engine was located transversely above the rear axle line, driving to the end-on gearbox through step-down gearing.

The suspension was similar to other small NSUs, with wishbones at the front and swing axles located by semi-trailing wishbones at the rear, and the Type 110 kept a longer wheelbase version of the Corvair-influenced two door body, with a rather spartan interior. Despite the tail-heavy weight distribution and swing axle suspension, the handling was remarkably good.

This was to be the largest post-war piston-engined model to carry NSU badges. The larger K70, which was to fill the gap between the Type 110 and Ro80, was eventually to appear as a short-lived Volkswagen model.

BODY
Saloon; 2 doors; 5 seats; weight 710kg (1562lb).

ENGINE
4 cylinders, in line; rear; 75.0x66.6mm, 1177cc; compr 8.0:1; 41kW (55bhp) @ 5500rpm; 34.8kW/l (46.7bhp/l); 85.5Nm (8.6mkp) @ 3500rpm.

ENGINE STRUCTURE
Ohv; 2 valves per cylinder; 1 chain driven ohc; aluminium alloy cylinder head; cast iron block; 5 bearing crankshaft; Solex 34PCI carburettor; air cooled.

TRANSMISSION
Rear wheel drive; 4 speed; helical spur gear final drive, 3.786.

CHASSIS DETAILS
Steel unitary construction; independent front suspension, wishbones, coil springs; independent rear suspension, swing axles; semi-trailing wishbones, coil springs; telescopic dampers; drum brakes; single braking circuit; rack and pinion steering; 44.0l (9.8 Imp gal) (10.8 US gal) fuel tank; 155R13 tyres, 4.5in rim width.

DIMENSIONS
Wheelbase 244.0cm (96.1in); front track 125.0cm (49.2in), rear track 123.5cm (48.6in); ground clearance 16.0cm (6.3in), turning circle 9.9m (29.7ft) overall length 400.0cm (157.5in), overall width 150.0cm (59.1in), overall height 139.0cm (54.7in).

PERFORMANCE
Maximum speed 93mph (150kph), 32.3kph (20.1mph) @ 1000rpm; acceleration 0-100kph (62mph) 14.5sec; standing km 37.3sec; 17.3kg/kW (12.9kg/bhp); average fuel consumption 23.5mpg (12.0l/100km).

NSU Ro 80 1967

If the launch of the world's first production Wankel-engine cars by NSU in 1964 did not exactly make history, the Ro80 most certainly did. One reason was that it was a completely new car from stem to stern – and that included the far more advanced and refined twin rotor engine.

As before, there was some disagreement between NSU and officialdom over its capacity. NSU claimed that the swept volume was 995cc, or twice the individual rotor combustion chamber swept volume of 497.5cc. More realistically the official view that the Ro80's engine had an equivalent capacity of 1990cc, more in keeping with its 85kW output.

The new twin-rotor engine used two spark plugs per rotor casing, one behind the other. The 'trailing' plug firing milliseconds behind the leading one, ensuring better combustion and smoother running. Each half of the engine was fed by a separate twin-choke Solex carburettor.

In the 1964 Spider the single rotor engine had been at the back, driving the rear wheels. For the Ro80 the engine was at the front, located fore-and-aft, and

BODY
4 door saloon; 5 seats; 1213kg (2668lb).

ENGINE
Twin rotor Wankel; front; compr 9:1; 2x497.5cc, 1990cc nominal; 85kW (114bhp) @ 5500rpm; 42.7kW/l (57.3bhp/l);156.9Nm (16mkp) @ 4500rpm.

ENGINE STRUCTURE
Induction and exhaust via ports in rotor casing; cast iron rotor and casing; 4 rotor bearings; 2 Solex 18/32 twin choke carburettors; electronic thysistor capacitor discharge ignition; water cooled.

TRANSMISSION
Front wheel drive; 3 speed with servo clutch and torque converter; hypoid bevel final drive; 4.86.

CHASSIS DETAILS
Steel unitary construction; independent front suspension, struts, coil springs; independent

rear suspension, trailing arms, struts, coil springs; telescopic dampers; disc brakes; vacuum servo power assistance; rack and pinion steering; PAS; 81.8l (18.0 Imp gal) (21.6US gal) fuel tank; 175R14 tyres, 5.0 in rim width.

DIMENSIONS
Wheelbase 286.2cm (112.7in), front track 148.6cm (58.5in), rear track 143.5cm (56.5in), ground clearance 11.4cm (4.5in), turning circle 10.9m (36ft), overall length 482.6cm (190.0in).

PERFORMANCE
Maximum speed 107mph (172kph); 18.6mph (30kph) @ 1000rpm in top gear; acceleration to 62mph, 14.2sec; 11.2kg/bhp (29.7lb/bhp); average fuel consumption 28mpg (11.2l/100km).

now driving the front wheels. The transmission NSU developed was as unusual, at the time, as the Wankel engine. Rather than use a conventional four- or five-speed manual box, with a pedal operated clutch, the Ro80 had a three-speed manual box, with a Fichtel and Sachs servo operated clutch. This was disengaged as the gear lever knob was moved and engaged again as it was released. To smooth out drive and bridge the wide spaces between the gear ratios, a torque converter was fitted between engine and gearbox. This meant that in urban driving, for instance, the gearbox could be left in second, with the torque converter covering the likely speed range.

The prescient Ro80 body, with low, smooth front and high tail, was the result of wind tunnel design. The wheels were set at each corner of the car, and with long suspension travel and power

steering, the Ro80's handling was precise, with a supple ride. Justifiably, it was named Car of The Year in 1968.

As with the Spider's engine, rotor tip seal wear was again to become a major problem. Fuel consumption too proved to be far heavier than with rivals of similar capacity and performance, and the Ro80 had less success than it undoubtedly deserved.

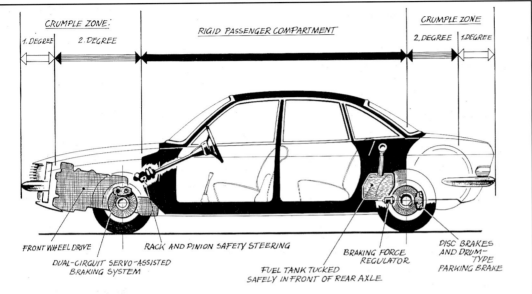

CRUMPLE ZONE:

1. DEGREE 2. DEGREE

RIGID PASSENGER COMPARTMENT

CRUMPLE ZONE

2. DEGREE 1. DEGREE

FRONT WHEEL DRIVE

DUAL-CIRCUIT SERVO-ASSISTED
BRAKING SYSTEM

RACK AND PINION SAFETY STEERING

FUEL TANK TUCKED
SAFELY IN FRONT OF REAR AXLE

BRAKING FORCE
REGULATOR

DISC BRAKES
AND DRUM-
TYPE
PARKING BRAKE

AUDI 75 1968

Building carefully on the success of the new 90 introduced in 1966, Audi started to expand its range. The two and four door saloon versions were joined by a five-door estate to meet the growing demands for more space inside. Changes to the high-swirl engine gave more power from the 1.7 litres, with the 75 title referring to the DIN power output in bhp.

Audis of the period were unusual in using torsion bar independent suspension front and rear. But with a high proportion of the car's weight being carried over the front wheels, they did suffer from understeer when being driven quickly on twisting roads. The estate car, with its neatly sloping tailgate and big windows, accounted for a remarkably high percentage of sales. The 75 range remained on sale until 1972.

BODY
2/4 door saloon, 5 door estate; 5 seats; weight 1025kg (2255lb).

ENGINE
4 cylinders, in line; front; 80.0x84.4mm, 1696cc; compr 11.2:1; 55kW (75bhp) @ 5000rpm; 32.4kW/l (44.2bhp/l); 130Nm (13.0mkp) @ 3000rpm.

ENGINE STRUCTURE
Ohv; 2 valves per cylinder; 1 chain driven side camshaft; aluminium alloy cylinder head; cast iron block; 5 bearing crankshaft; Solex 35 PDSIT/5 carburettor; water cooled.

TRANSMISSION
Front wheel drive; 4 speed gearbox; spiral bevel final drive, 3.888.

CHASSIS DETAILS
Steel unitary construction; independent front suspension, wishbones, torsion bars; rear suspension, torsion beam axle, trailing arms, Panhard rod, torsion bars; telescopic dampers; disc front, drum rear; single braking circuit; rack and pinion steering; 53.0l (11.7 Imp gal) (14.0 US gal) fuel tank; 165R13 tyres, 4.5in rim width.

DIMENSIONS
Wheelbase 249.0cm (98.0in), front track 133.0cm (52.4in), rear track 133.0cm (52.4in), ground clearance 19.0cm (7.5in), turning circle 10.9ft (36.0ft), overall length 438.0cm (172.4in), overall width 163.0cm (53.5in), overall height 145.0cm (57.1in).

PERFORMANCE
Maximum speed 94mph (152mph), 29.0km (18.0mph) @ 1000rpm; acceleration 0-100kph (62mph) 14.0sec; 18.6kg/kW (13.7kg/bhp); average fuel consumption 33.6mpg (8.4l/100km).

AUDI 60 1968

In a move to expand the new model's range, Audi added a small-engined version, the 60. The Daimler-Benz designed engine kept the same 80.0mm bore, but the stroke was reduced to 74.4mm to give a capacity of 1.5 litre, and an output of just 41kW.

The 60 was made as a two and four door saloon and three-door estate, but even with a lower final drive ratio performance hardly sparkled. It was a car designed very much for mainland European markets, where the annual road tax was based on engine capacity. Keeping the engine under 1.5 litre brought the 60 into a lower tax bracket. This was the last of the original Audis with the DKW F-102 inspired body design, and one of the few new Audis under 1.5 litres for nearly thirty years.

BODY
2/4 door saloon, 3 door estate; 5 seats; weight 970kg (2138lb).

ENGINE
4 cylinders, in line; front; 80.0x74.4mm, 1496cc; compr 9.0:1; 41kW (55bhp) @ 4750rpm; 27kW/l (36.8bhp/l); 113Nm (11.5mkp) @ 2500rpm.

ENGINE STRUCTURE
Ohv; 2 valves per cylinder; 1 chain driven side camshaft; aluminium cylinder head; cast iron block; 5 bearing crankshaft; Solex 35 PDSIT-5 carburettor; water cooled.

TRANSMISSION
Front wheel drive; 4 speed gearbox; spiral bevel final drive, 4.1111.

CHASSIS DETAILS
Steel unitary constuction; independent front suspension, wishbones, torsion bars; rear suspension, dead axle, trailing arms, Panhard rod, torsion bars; telescopic dampers; discs front, drums rear; single braking circuit; rack and pinion steering; 58.0l (12.8 Imp gal) (15.3 US gal) fuel tank; 155R13 tyres, 4.5 rim width.

DIMENSIONS
Wheelbase 249.0cm (98.0in), front track 134.0cm (52.8in), rear track 132.5cm (52.2in), ground clearance 19.0cm (7.5in), turning circle 10.9m (3.6.0ft), overall length 438.0cm (172.4in), overall width 163.0cm (64.1in), overall height 145.0cm (57.1in).

PERFORMANCE
Maximum speed 86mph (138mph), 26.0kph (16.1mph) @ 1000rpm; acceleration 0-100kph (62mph) 18.0sec; 23.7kg/kW (17.6kg/bhp); average fuel consumption 32.5mpg (8.7l/100km).

AUDI 100/100S/100LS 1968

The Audi 100 title adopted in 1968 remained a model name for 27 years. Ownership of the make passed from Daimler-Benz to Volkswagen, but the styling of the four door saloon suggested that Stuttgart had had a major part in its design.

The engine was the high-swirl ohv 1760cc four cylinder unit designed by Mercedes-Benz and previously used in the Super 90. It was later enlarged to 1871cc for the 100GL and Coupe S. The four-speed gearbox was also retained, as was the forward-mounted engine. At the front there was a modified version of the wishbone suspension, and at the rear the same type of dead axle, located by trailing arms and a Panhard rod, as was used in the 60, 75 and Super 90. The 100 set out to be a car with a wide appeal in a growing sector of the new executive market.

BODY
4 door saloon; 5 seats; weight 1050kg (2315lb).

ENGINE
4 cylinders, in line; front; 81.5x84.4mm, 1760cc; compr 9.1:1; 60kW (80bhp) @ 5000rpm; 34.0kW/l (45.5bhp/l); 135Nm (13.8mkp) @ 3000rpm.

ENGINE STRUCTURE
Ohv; 2 valves per cylinder; 1 chain driven side camshaft; aluminium alloy cylinder head; cast iron block; 5 bearing crankshaft; Solex 35PDSIT-5 carburettor; water cooled.

TRANSMISSION
Front wheel drive; 4 speed gearbox, spiral bevel final drive, 4.111.

CHASSIS DETAILS
Steel unitary construction; independent front suspension, wishbones, coils; rear suspension, dead axle, trailing arms, Panhard rod, torsion bars; anti-roll bars front and rear; telescopic dampers. disc front, drum rear; dual braking circuits; rack and pinion steering; 58.0l (12.8 Imp gal) (15.3 US gal) fuel tank; 165SR14in tyres, 4.5in rim width.

DIMENSIONS
Wheelbase 267.5cm (105.3in), front track 142.0cm (55.9in), rear track 142.5cm (56.1in), ground clearance19.5cm (7.7in), turning circle 11.2m (40.0ft), overall length 459.0cm (180.7in), overall width 173.0cm (68.1in), overall height 142cm (55.6in).

PERFORMANCE
Maximum speed 99mph (156kph), 28.3kph (17.6mph) @ 1000rpm; acceleration 0-100kph (62mph) 13.5sec; standing km 35.3sec; 17.5kg/kW (13.1kg/bhp); average fuel consumption 31.7mpg (8.9 l/100km).

NSU TTS 1968

It was easy to spot a TTS, especially from the rear, because the engine cover was usually propped open to assist cooling. With raised compression ratio and advanced camshaft, plus two twin-choke Solex carburettors, what was essentially a Prinz 1000 engine produced 52kW, creating a lot of heat as well as power.

    The factory offered a variety of competition extras, such as a 63kW engine, an assortment of tyre sizes, and two final drive ratios. To handle the extra performance, the TTS came with disc front brakes and wider rim wheels. Spring and damper rates too were uprated slightly, so the model had very neat and nimble handling, plus a 100mph top speed in standard form. The four headlamp system was exclusive to the TTS and its fore-runner the TT. Just over 2400 were made, with the majority used either for rallying or racing although production continued until mid-1971.

    In another 28 years the TT title would be invoked for yet another car in a sporting idiom from Audi.

BODY
Saloon; 2 doors; 4 seats; weight 700kg (1540lb).

ENGINE
4 cylinders, in line; rear; 69.0x66.6mm, 996cc; compr 10.5:1; 52kW (70bhp) @ 6150rpm; 52.2kW/l (70.3bhp/l); 84Nm (8.6mpk) @ 5500rpm.

ENGINE STRUCTURE
Ohv; 2 valves per cylinder; 1 chain driven ohc; aluminium cylinder head and block; 5 bearing crankshaft; twin Solex 40PHH carburettors, air cooled.

TRANSMISSION
Rear wheel drive; 4 speed gearbox; helical spur gear final drive, 4.231 or 4.538.

CHASSIS DETAILS
Steel unitary construction; independent front suspension, wishbones, coil springs; independent rear suspension, swing axles, semi-trailing wishbones; coil springs; telescopic dampers; disc front, drum rear brakes; single braking circuit; rack and pinion steering; 37.0l (8.1 Imp gal) (9.8 US gal) fuel tank; 135 SR13in or 145 SR12 tyres, 4.5in rim width.

DIMENSIONS
Wheelbase 224.8cm (88.5in), front track 149.9cm (59.0in), rear track 137.2cm (54.0in), ground clearance 10.1cm (7.5in), turning circle 8.0m (26.5ft), overall length 379.2cm (149.3in), overall width 149.6cm (58.9in), overall height 136.4cm (53.7in).

PERFORMANCE
Maximum speed 99mph mph (160kph), 24.8 kph (15.4mph) @ 1000rpm; acceleration 0-100kph (62mph) 12.3sec; 13.5 kg/kW (10kg/bhp); average fuel consumption 31mpg (9.1l/100km) test fig.

AUDI 100 Coupe S 1969

Audi's new handsome Coupe was a radical break from anything previously seen. The fastback design, which had a conventional boot rather than a more practical hatchback tailgate, was reinforced by the five 'shark gill' vents on the rear quarters. The Coupe's body was identical to the saloon's from the A-pillar forward, but the wheelbase was 11.5cm shorter, giving more agile handling – and rather less space for rear seat passengers. The four headlamp grille layout was the same as that on the top-of-the-range 100 saloons.

It was only made with the 1.9 engine. Early models had two twin-choke carburettors and developed 84kW (115bhp). From 1971 a single carburettor was fitted, and power fell slightly to 82kW (112bhp). Production was limited, so that the few Coupes which have survived have become collectable.

BODY
Coupe; 2 doors; 4 seats; weight 1045kg (2299lb).

ENGINE
4 cylinders, in line; front; 84.0x84.4mm, 1871cc; compr 10.2:1; 84kW (115bhp) @ 5500rpm; 44.9kW/l (61.5bhp/l); 159Nm (16.2mkp) @ 4000rpm.

ENGINE STRUCTURE
Ohv; 2 valves per cylinder; 1 chain driven side camshaft; aluminium cylinder head; cast iron block; 5 bearing crankshaft; Solex 32/32 TDID carburettor; water cooled.

TRANSMISSION
Front wheel drive; 4 speed gearbox; spiral bevel final drive, 3.70.

CHASSIS DETAILS
Steel unitary construction; independent front suspension, wishbones, coil springs; rear suspension, dead axle, trailing arms, Panhard rod, torsion bars; anti-roll bars front and rear; telescopic dampers; inboard ventilated discs front, drums rear; dual braking circuits; vacuum servo power assistance; rack and pinion steering; 58.0l (12.8 Imp gal) (15.4 US gal) fuel tank; 185/70HT14 tyres, 5.0 rim width.

DIMENSIONS
Wheelbase 256.0cm (100.8in), front track 144.0cm (56.7in), rear track 144.0cm (56.7in), turning circle 10.9m (36.0ft), overall length 440.0cm (173.2in), overall width 175.0cm (68.9in), overall height 133.0cm (52.4in).

PERFORMANCE
Maximum 115speed mph (185kph), 33.0kph (20.4mph) @ 1000rpm; acceleration 0-100kph (62mph) 10.0sec; 12.4kg/kW (9.1kg/bhp); average fuel consumption 26.9mpg (10.5l/100km).

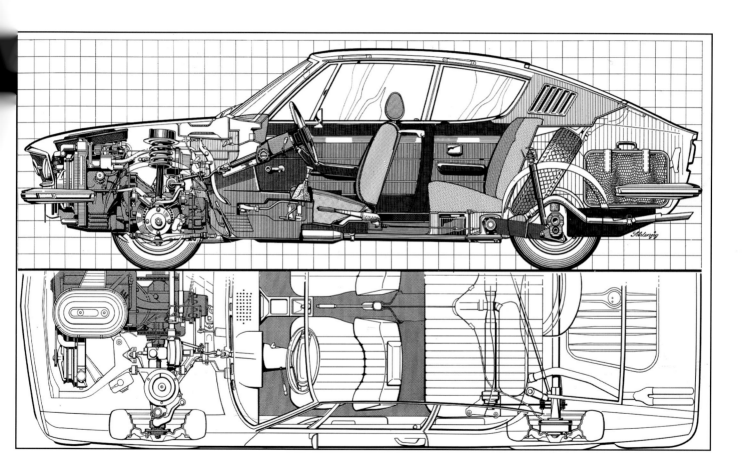

NSU VW K70 1969

The K70 was originally designed by NSU as a model to fit in between the revolutionary Wankel-engined Ro80 and the smaller Prinz/1200 range. It used some of the Ro80's underpan, centre-section and suspension elements, and in place of the Wankel engine it had a four cylinder piston engine that was an enlarged, water-cooled derivative of the air-cooled 1200.

When Volkswagen acquired NSU, the project was adapted, creating VW's first front wheel drive, water-cooled car. More importantly, the K70 was an alternative to the air-cooled, rear-engined 411/412 range. Mechanically, the K70 was pure NSU, and early production cars still had 'NSU' on the four pressed covers over the valve rockers. With new front and rear styling, the K70 was given a Volkswagen identity, although none of its components were ever used on any other VW model. The independent suspension, with struts front and rear, was similar to that on the Ro80, but the K70 had a conventional four-speed gearbox, with no automatic option. Production lasted just five years, until the launch of the first Passat. In 1974 there was an LS model with 1.8 100bhp engine.

BODY
4 door saloon; 5 seats; weight 1072kg (2360lb).

ENGINE
4 cylinders in line; front; 82.0x76.0mm, 1605cc; compr 9.5:1; 67kW (90bhp) @ 5200rpm; 41.7kW/l (56.1bhp/l); 134Nm (13.7mkp)@ 4000rpm.

ENGINE STRUCTURE
Ohv; 2 valves per cylinder; 1 chain driven ohc; aluminium alloy cylinder head; cast iron block; 5 bearing crankshaft; Solex 40DDHT twin choke carburettor; water cooled.

TRANSMISSION
Front wheel drive; 4 speed gearbox; hypoid bevel final drive, 4.375.

CHASSIS
Steel unitary construction; independent front suspension, struts, coil springs; independent rear suspension, semi-trailing arms, coil springs; anti-roll bars front and rear; inboard disc front, drum rear brakes; dual braking circuits; vacuum power assistance; rack and pinion steering; 54.0l (11.9 Imp gal) (14.3 US gal) fuel tank; 165SR14 tyres, 4.5in rim width.

DIMENSIONS
Wheelbase 264.2cm (104.0in), front track 127.0cm (50.0in), rear track 142.2cm (56.0in), ground clearance 12.7cm (5.0in), turning circle 10.0m (33ft), overall length 462.3cm (182.0in), overall width 167.6cm (66.0in), overall height 147.3cm (58.0in).

PERFORMANCE
Maximum speed 98mph (158kph); acceleration 0-100kph (62mph) 13.6sec; standing km 35.9sec (18.8sec); 16.0kg/kW (11.9kg/bhp); average fuel consumption 23.0mpg (12.3l/100km).

AUDI 100 2-door 1971

At this period in the late 1960s, several European manufacturers, including Jaguar and Audi, produced two-door versions of their conventional four-door saloons, aimed at drivers more concerned with style than with room for a whole family.

The two-door design, with fewer vertical shut lines along the sides helped make a car look longer and lower. New dies were needed for the door and side panel pressings, as well as different glazing for door and quarter windows. This added to production costs and complications, and it was a short-lived fashion which never gained any real foothold in the UK.

Audis were starting to earn the plaudits of the press. "Few cars can have improved so much from what appeared to be just a body change" enthused The Motor in 1971. The 100GL two door was reckoned better value at £1899 than the fastback Coupe which cost £500 more. Rear seat accommodation was superior and rearwards visibility better.

BODY
2 door saloon; 5 seats; weight 1100kg (2425lb).

ENGINE
4 cylinders, in line; front; 84.0x84.4mm, 1871cc; compr 10:1; 83.5kW (112bhp) @ 5600rpm; 46.8kW/l (59.8bhp/l); 160Nm (16.3mkp) @ 3500rpm.

ENGINE STRUCTURE
Ohv; 2 valves per cylinder; 1 chain driven side camshaft; aluminium alloy cylinder head; cast iron block; 5 bearing crankshaft; Solex 32/35TDID carburettor; water cooled.

TRANSMISSION
Front wheel drive; 4 speed gearbox, spiral bevel final drive, 4.111.

CHASSIS DETAILS
Steel unitary construction; independent front suspension, wishbones, coils; rear suspension, dead axle, trailing arms, Panhard rod, coils; anti-roll bars front and rear; telescopic dampers. disc front, drum rear; dual braking circuits; rack and pinion steering; 58.0l (12.8 Imp gal) (15.3 US gal) fuel tank; 165SR14 tyres, 4.5in rim width.

DIMENSIONS
Wheelbase 267.5cm (105.3in), front track 142.0cm (55.9in), rear track 142.5cm (56.1in), ground clearance19.5cm (7.7in), turning circle 11.2m (40.0ft), overall length 459.0cm (180.7in), overall width 173.0cm (68.1in), overall height 142cm (55.6in).

PERFORMANCE
Maximum speed 106mph (170kph), 28.3kph (17.6mph) @ 1000rpm; acceleration 0-100kph (62mph) 11.9; 13.9kg/kW (10.5kg/bhp); average fuel consumption 30.5mpg (8.6 l/100km).

AUDI 100 GL 112hp 1971

Audi had been carefully building its 100 range, keeping the title GL for the most powerful. Engine capacity remained at 1871cc, but with raised compression ratio and a twin-choke Solex carburettor, it was steadily improved and refined with a small increase in torque.

As with the rest of the range, the GL remained with a four-speed gearbox, with a three-speed automatic among the listed extras. It also kept the disc front, drum rear brake arrangement, backed by a vacuum servo. Power steering however was not available. Wider section tyres helped the handling although, like the rest of the 100 range, it

tended towards heavy understeer when pushed too hard through corners. As the top model in the 100 range, the GL featured the four headlamp grille.

BODY
2/4 door saloon; 5 seats; weight 1100kg (2420lb).

ENGINE
4 cylinders, in line; front; 84.0x84.4mm, 1871cc; compr 10.0:1; 84kW (112bhp) @ 5600rpm; 44.9kW/l (60.0bhp/l); 160Nm (16.3mkp) @ 3500rpm.

ENGINE STRUCTURE
Ohv; 2 valves per cylinder; 1 chain driven side camshaft; aluminium cylinder head; cast iron block; 5 bearing crankshaft; Solex 32/35TDID carburettor.

TRANSMISSION
Front wheel drive; 4 speed gearbox; hypoid bevel final drive, 3.70; 3 speed automatic option.

CHASSIS DETAILS
Steel unitary construction; independent front suspension, wishbones, coil springs; rear suspension, dead axle, trailing arms, Panhard rod, coil springs; anti-roll bars front and rear;

telescopic dampers; disc front, drums rear; dual circuits; vacuum servo power assistance; rack and pinion steering; 58.0l (12.8 Imp gal) (15.3 US gal) fuel tank; 175/70SR14 tyres, 5.0in rim width.

DIMENSIONS
Wheelbase 267.5cm (105.3in), front track 142.0cm (55.9in), rear track 142.5cm (56.1in), ground clearance19.5cm (7.7in), turning circle 11.2m (40.0ft), overall length 459.0cm (180.7in), overall width 173.0cm (68.1in), overall height 142cm (55.6in).

PERFORMANCE
Maximum speed 111mph (179kph), 31.4kph (19.5mph)@ 1000rpm; acceleration 0-100kph (62mph) 10.8sec; 13.1kg/kW (9.8kg/bhp); average fuel consumption 31.7mpg (8.9 l/100km).

AUDI 80, 80L 55HP; 80 S, 80 LS 60HP; 80 GL 85hp 1972

The original DKW-based Audi continued alongside the new 100, but sales never prospered. The new 80, however, was totally fresh and had nothing in common with any previous Audi. In fact the 80, with a new Audi-designed overhead camshaft engine, was to become the basis for Volkswagen's yet-to-be-announced Passat. MacPherson strut front suspension was used in place of the more complex and heavier wishbones. A major innovation was the negative offset steering geometry which gave a self-stabilising effect in the event of a tyre blow-out. Like the 100, the 80 also used a dead rear axle layout, located by trailing arms, with a Panhard rod. Audi kept what by now had become its traditional engine location, cantilevered out ahead of the front axle line and tilted 20 degrees to the right, with the final drive in unit with the four-speed gearbox. Within the parent company's marketing plans, the 80 was to remain as a saloon until well into the 1990s.

The Audi won its first annual Car of the Year title for 1973 with 114 points, against the Renault 5 with 109 points and the Alfa Romeo Alfetta with 95 points from the international jury.

BODY
2/4 door saloon; 5 seats; weight 835kg (1670lb).

ENGINE
4 cylinders, in line, front; 75.0x73.4mm, 1297cc; compr 8.5:1; 41kW (55bhp) @ 5500rpm; 31.6kW/l (42.4bhp/l); 94Nm (9.6mkp) @ 2500rpm.

ENGINE STRUCTURE
Ohv; 2 valves per cylinder; 1 belt driven ohc; aluminium cylinder head; cast iron block; 5 bearing crankshaft; Solex 30/35 PDSI (T)

TRANSMISSION
Front wheel drive; 4 speed gearbox; hypoid bevel final drive, 4.555.

CHASSIS DETAILS
Steel unitary construction; independent front suspension, struts, coil springs; rear suspension, dead axle, trailing arms, Panhard rod, coil springs; anti-roll bars front and rear; telescopic dampers; disc front, drum rear, dual braking circuits; vacuum servo power assistance; rack and pinion steering; 46.0l (10.1 Imp gal) (12.1 US gal) fuel tank; 155R13 tyres, 4.5in rim width.

DIMENSIONS
Wheelbase 247.0cm (97.2in), front track 134.0cm (52.8in), rear track 133.5cm (53.1in), ground clearance 18.0cm (7.1in), turning circle 10.3m (31.2ft), overall length 417.5cm (164.4in), overall width 160.0cm (63.0in), overall height 137.0cm (53.9in).

PERFORMANCE
90mph (145kph); 24.0km (14.9mph) @ 1000rpm; acceleration 0-100kph (62mph) 16.9sec; 20.4kg/kW (15.5kg.bhp); average fuel consumption 24.9mpg (8.8l/100km).

Other engines 1.3 litre 45kW, 1.5 litre 63kW.

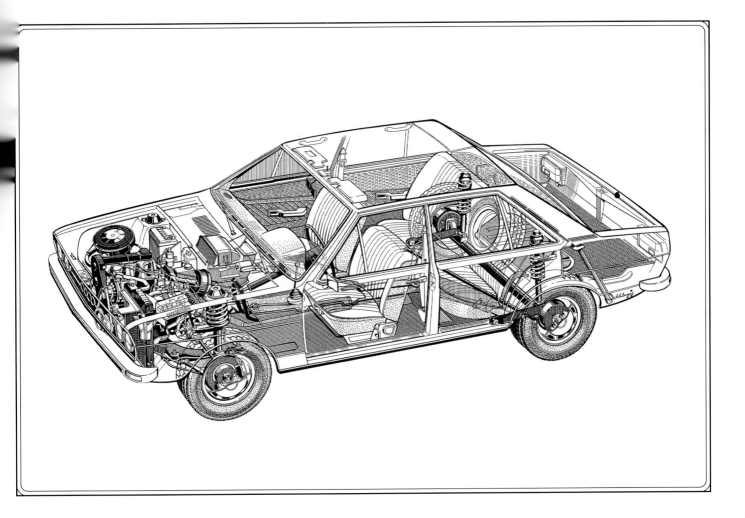

AUDI 80 GT 1973; 80 GTE 1976

As demand for high-performance versions of standard cars grew, Audi waited only a year before bringing out a GT version of the 80. While the standard cars had either 1.3 or 1.5 litre engines, the GT had a new 1.6-litre version of the overhead camshaft unit. Fuel injection was still in the future, so the 75kW GT continued with a twin-choke Solex carburettor. To complement the additional power, the GT's final drive ratio was raised slightly to give more relaxed high-speed cruising, while wider-section tyres on 5.0in rims were standard. A vacuum servo was fitted as standard to reduce the pedal pressure for the disc front, drum rear brakes.

Unlike the smaller-engined 80s, the GT was made only in two-door form. The compact dimensions meant that rear seat passenger space was restricted, but boot space was quite generous.

In 1976 the GT's power output was raised to 82kW (110bhp) and the carburettor was replaced by Bosch fuel injection. It was then known as 80 GTE. The same engine was later fitted to the Golf GTI.

80 GT:
BODY
2 door; 5 seats; weight 855kg (1881lb).

ENGINE
4 cylinders, in line; front; 79.5x80.0mm, 1588cc; compr 9.7:1; 75kW (100bhp) @ 6000rpm; 47.2kW/l (63.0bhp/l); 134Nm (13.6mkp) @ 4000rpm.

ENGINE STRUCTURE
Ohv; 2 valves per cylinder; 1 belt driven ohc; aluminium alloy cylinder head; cast iron block; 5 bearing crankshaft; Solex 35/40 DIDTA carburettor; water cooled.

TRANSMISSION
Front wheel drive; 4 speed gearbox; hypoid bevel final drive; 4.111.

CHASSIS DETAILS
Steel unitary construction; independent front suspension, struts, coil springs; rear suspension, dead axle, trailing arms, coil springs; anti-roll bars front and rear; telescopic dampers; disc front, drum rear, dual braking circuits; vacuum servo power assistance; rack and pinion steering; 46.0l (10.1 Imp gal) (12.1 US gal) fuel tank; 175/70SR13 tyres, 5.0in rim width.

DIMENSIONS
Wheelbase 247.0cm (97.2in), front track 134.0cm (52.8in), rear track 133.5cm (53.1in), ground clearance 18.0cm (7.1in), turning circle 10.3m (31.2ft), overall length 420cm (165.4in), overall width 160.0cm (63.0in), overall height 136.0 (53.5in).

PERFORMANCE
Maximum speed 109mph (175mph); 28.2kph (17.5mph) @ 1000rpm; acceleration 0-100kph (62mph) 10.2sec; 11.4kg/kW (8.6kg/bhp); average fuel consumption 31.7mpg (8.9l/100km).

If the 80's platform and engines were the basis of the first Volkswagen Passat, the 50 introduced in September 1974 strongly resembled the VW Polo revealed at Geneva in March 1975. Interestingly, this was the only time Volkswagen adopted this strategy, and the Audi 50 was dropped after a relatively short run. The design, however, was to become a classic among the growing range of superminis.

For the 50 only the 1.1 litre engine was available at first, although there was a choice of power output, between 37 and 45kW. Both it and Polo had a wider range of engines, up to 1.3 litres. MacPherson struts and coil springs were used at the front, but it differed from the 100 and 80 at the rear: the torsion beam was moved forward, the trailing arms made rigid, and the Panhard rod deleted. Rather than create confusion among its carefully nurtured Audi customers, the importer sensibly decided against selling the 50 in the UK in competition with its new Polo.

BODY
Hatchback; 3 doors; 4 seats; 685kg (1510lb)weight.

ENGINE
4 cylinders, in line; front; 69.5x72.0mm, 1093cc; compr 8.0:1; 37kW (50bhp) @ 5800rpm; 33.9kW/l (45.7bhp/l); 77Nm (7.8mkp) @ 3500rpm.

ENGINE STRUCTURE
Ohv; 2 valves per cylinder; 1 belt driven ohc; aluminium alloy cylinder head; cast iron block; 5 bearing crankshaft; Solex 31 PICT.5 carburettor; water cooled.

TRANSMISSION
Front wheel drive; 4 speed gearbox; helical spur gear final drive, 4.267.

CHASSIS DETAILS
Steel unitary construction; independent front suspension, struts, coil springs; rear suspension, torsion beam and trailing arms; telescopic dampers; disc front, drum rear brakes; dual braking circuits; rack and pinion steering; 36.0l (7.9 Imp gal) (9.5 US gal) fuel tank; 135SR13 tyres, 4.5in rim width.

DIMENSIONS
Wheelbase 233.5cm (91.9in), front track 130.0cm (51.1in), rear track 131.0cm (51.6in), turning circle 9.6m (29.0ft), overall length 350.0cm (137.8in), overall width 156.0cm (61.4in), overall height 134.5cm (52.9in).

PERFORMANCE
Maximum speed 88mph (142kph); 24.3.kph (15.1mph) @ 1000rpm; acceleration 0-100kph (62mph) 15.4sec; 18.5kg/kW (13.7kg/bhp); average fuel consumption 35.8mpg (7.3l/100km).

Features of Audi 50:
Toothed belt drive
for ohc *(left)*
and rear suspension struts
with trailing arms *(right).*

AUDI 100 1.6, 1.8 1974

Audi gave the 100 a new look in 1974, although the platform remained essentially as before. It gained a new 1.6 engine in 1974 with refinements such as optional power steering, servo brakes and diagonally linked dual braking circuits, and the 80's self-stabilising negative offset steering.

The 1.6 litre engine was the overhead cam 63kW (85bhp) unit from the 80 GL. The four-speed gearbox, with the 4.111 final drive, was unchanged. Suspension remained basically unaltered too, although anti-roll bars became standard front and rear. Even with the smaller 1.6 litre engine, the 100 could accelerate to 100kph in 13.5sec, and reach close to 100mph.

Yet the significant feature of Audis was the impression they created. In 1974 The Motor said, "..the feel of the car inspires confidence... the Audi range has matured steadily."

BODY
2/4 door; 5 seats; weight 1050kg (2310lb).

ENGINE
4 cylinders, in line; front; 79.5x80.0mm, 1588cc; compr 8.2:1; 63kW (85bhp) @ 5800rpm; 39.7kW/l (53.5bhp/l); 122Nm (12.4mkp) @ 3500rpm.

ENGINE STRUCTURE
Ohv; 2 valves per cylinder; 1 belt driven ohc; aluminium alloy cylinder head; cast iron block; 5 bearing crankshaft; Solex 32/35 DIDTA carburettor; water cooled.

TRANSMISSION
Front wheel drive; 4 speed gearbox; spiral bevel final drive, 4.111.

CHASSIS DETAILS
Steel unitary construction; independent front suspension, struts, coil springs; rear suspension, dead axle, trailing arms; Panhard rod, coil springs. Anti-roll bars front and rear; ventilated discs front, drum rear; dual braking circuits; vacuum servo power assistance; rack and pinion steering, optional PAS; 58.0l (12.8 Imp gal) (15.3 US gal) fuel tank; 155SR14 tyres, 5.0in rim width.

DIMENSIONS
Wheelbase 267.5cm (105.3in), front track 145.0cm (57.1in), rear track 142.5cm (5.61cm), ground clearance 19.5cm (7.7in), turning circle 11.2m (40.0ft), overall length 459.0cm (180.7in), overall width 173.0cm (68.1in), overall height 142.0cm (55.9in).

PERFORMANCE
for 1588cc 85bhp
Maximum speed 99mph (160kph); 27.7kph (17.0mph) @ 1000rpm; acceleration 0-100kph (62mph) 13.5sec; 16.7kg/kW (12.4kg/bhp); average fuel consumption 31.7mpg (8.9l/2100km).

PORSCHE 924 1975

For a company which hung its flat four or six air-cooled engines behind the rear axle, the idea of putting the engine at the front was dramatic enough. To make it a water-cooled, in-line unit was a radical reversal of policy for Porsche with the 924 which was made in the Audi works at Neckarsulm.

The 924 started life as an engineering design commissioned by Volkswagen as a new coupe. Porsche Design was to carry out the work, using as many VW or Audi components already in production as it could. The 2.0 single overhead camshaft engine started as a project to power the VW LT van and the 1977 Audi 100. With Porsche modifications, including Bosch K-Jetronic fuel injection, power output was increased to 92kW. The four speed gearbox was in unit with the rear axle: later a five-speed gearbox became standard, while a few 924s were sold with a three-speed automatic. Front suspension used VW Beetle 1302 MacPherson struts and at the rear there were semi-trailing arms and transverse torsion bars.

Despite its performance potential, the new car used a rather mundane mix of disc brakes at the front

BODY
2 door coupe; 2+2 seats; weight 1130kg (2486lb).

ENGINE
4 cylinders, in line; front; 86.5x84.4mm, 1984cc; 92kW/ 125bhp @ 5800rpm; 46.4kW/l (63.0bhp/l); 165Nm (16.8mkp) @ 3500rpm.

ENGINE STRUCTURE
Ohv; 2 valves per cylinder; 1 belt driven ohc; aluminium alloy head; cast iron block; 5 bearing crankshaft; Bosch K-Jetronic injection; water cooled.

TRANSMISSION
2 wheel drive; 4 speed gearbox; hypoid bevel final drive, 3.889. 3 speed automatic option.

CHASSIS DETAILS
Steel unitary construction; independent front suspension, struts, coil springs; independent rear suspension, semi-trailing arms, transverse torsion bars; telescopic dampers, disc front,

drum rear brakes; dual braking circuits; vacuum servo power assistance; no ABS; rack and pinion steering; 66.0l (14.5 Imp gal) (17.4 US gal) fuel tank; 185/70HR14 tyres, 6.0in rims.

DIMENSIONS
Wheelbase 240.0cm (94.5in), front track 142.0c, (55.9in), rear track 137.0cm (53.9in), grount clearance 12.5cm (4.9in), turning circle 12.5m (33.3ft), overall length 421.0cm (165.7in), overall width 168.5cm (66.3in), overall height 127.0cm (50.0in).

PERFORMANCE
Maximum speed126mph (204kph); 21.4mph (34.4kph) @ 1000rpm; acceleration 0-100kph (62mph) 9.6sec; 12.3kg/kW (9.0kg/bhp); average fuel consumption. 30.8mpg (8.7l/100km) Euromix.

Left: Crisply styled 924 featured large rear window which opened upwards, giving access to luggage. Later 924 had wide wheelarches and spoiler at base of back window which sullied clean lines.

Right: Engine was inclined at 40 degrees: 125bhp gave 125mph. The 924 reached 60mph in 10 sec and could return 30mpg. Pop-up headlights were sign of the times

and drums at the rear. The same could be said of the tyres, which were rather ordinary 185/70SR14, although wider section, 60-profile covers were later offered as an option. The body design was notable for Porsche's careful attention to aerodynamics and the late decision to make the body hot-dip galvanised which gave the model a six-year anti-corrosion warranty from the start.

It was also late in the new model's development that Volkswagen decided that the car did not meet its marketing plans. So what had started life as a successor to the VW-Porsche 914 became a fully fledged Porsche model in its own right.

Over 122,000 were made between 1976 and 1985, 300,000 including its derivative 924 Turbo and 944 variants, production of which stopped only in the 1990s. Their quality was high and the Audi manufacturers gained an industry lead in the production techniques of rust-resistant galvanized steel bodies.

The 924 was one of a number of Audi-Porsche co-operative ventures. The connection between the makes was affirmed in America by the 917 Can-Am cars entered as Porsche-Audis. Mark Donohue set a world record speed for a closed circuit at Talladega in a Porsche + Audi 917-30.

AUDI 100 1976

The 1968 100 confirmed Audi as a serious competitor to Mercedes-Benz and the top models of BMW, Opel, and Ford. It also set Audi AG on a course of its own rather than as a close clone of its owner Volkswagen. The Audi 100 had eclipsed in-house rivals like the VW411 and NSU-designed K70, so after seven years its second-generation was eagerly awaited. It was all the more remarkable as the first production car with a five cylinder engine.

The logic was plain enough. Audi wanted an engine smoother than a four cylinder without taking up the space of a six. The evolution of the 100 coincided with the arrival of the brilliant Dr Ferdinand Piëch following a purge of Porsche scions from the family firm. Grandson of the founder and fresh from designing radical racing cars such as the Porsche 917, Piëch advocated the five-cylinder following involvement with engineering work on a Mercedes-Benz five cylinder diesel which also had crankshaft throws at 144 degree intervals. The new Audi was introduced in Germany with a choice of 1.6 litre and 2.0 litre four cylinder engines canted to the right at 20 degrees.

BODY
4 door saloon; 5 seats; weight 1170kg (2578lb).

ENGINE
5 cylinders, in line; front; longitudinal; inclined to right; 79.5x86.4mm, 2144cc; compr 9.3:1; 100kW (136bhp) @ 5700rpm; 46.6kW/l (63.4bhp/l); 181Nm (18.5mkp) @ 4200rpm.

ENGINE STRUCTURE
Ohv; 2 valves per cylinder; 1 belt driven ohc; aluminium cylinder head; cast iron block; 6 bearing crankshaft; Bosch K-Jetronic fuel injection; water cooled.

TRANSMISSION
Front wheel drive; 4 speed gearbox, 3 speed automatic option; hypoid bevel final drive, 3.78:1.

CHASSIS DETAILS
Steel unitary construction; independent front suspension, McPherson struts, coil springs, telescopic dampers; rear dead axle, trailing arms and Panhard rod, coil springs; telescopic dampers with integral anti-roll bar at rear; brakes disc front, drum rear, vacuum servo; rack and pinion steering, PAS optional; 60l (13.2 Imp gal) (15.8 US gal) fuel tank; 185/70HR14 tyres, steel, 5.5x14 or alloy 6x14 wheels.

DIMENSIONS
Wheelbase 267.5cm (105.3in), front track 147.0 cm (57.9in), rear track 144.5cm (56.9in), ground clearance 13.0cm (5.1in), turning circle 11.3m (37.3ft), overall length 459.0cm (180.7in), overall width 177.0cm (69.7in), overall height 139,0cm (54.7in).

PERFORMANCE
Max speed 118mph (190kph); 18.1mph (28.9kph); acceleration 0-60mph (96kph) 9.5sec; 11.7kg/kW (8.6bhp/kg); average fuel consumption 25.6mpg (10.99l/100km).

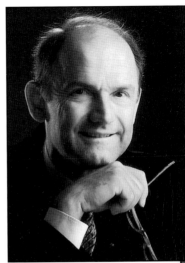

Above: Technical
genius behind Audi.
Ferdinand Porsche's
grandson, Ferdinand
Piëch.

AUDI 100 Avant 1977

An increasing number of hatchbacks was starting to appear in the medium-sized family car sector, so Audi adapted the 100 saloon, and gave the new model the Avant title. No changes were needed for the floorpan, drivetrain or suspension, and the Avant had the same overall dimensions as the saloon.

The main change was at the back, where a top-hinged, steeply sloping tailgate opened down to the top of the rear lamp clusters. This allowed many of the lower body pressings to be shared with the saloon. To prevent the back looking plain, Audi stylists put a single, shallow angle between the rear window and the lower part of the tailgate, flanking it with shallow strakes.

With the rear seats in use, the Avant had rather less boot space than the saloon. However, when the rear seats were folded down, the available space could be virtually doubled, giving Audi its first load carrier since the 75 Variant of the late 1960s.

The Avant started out with the same four-cylinder engine range as the 100 including the new five-cylinder engines and later the diesel as well.

BODY
5-door hatchback; 4 seats; weight 1110kg (2402lb).

ENGINE
4 cylinders, in line; front; 79.5x80.0mm, 1588cc; compr 8.2:1; 62.5kW (85bhp) @ 5600rpm; 39.4kW/l (53.5bhp/l); 121Nm (12.4mkp) @ 3200rpm.

ENGINE STRUCTURE
ohv; 2 valves per cylinder; 1 belt driven overhead camshaft; aluminium alloy cylinder head; cast iron block; 5 bearing crankshaft; Solex 2B2 carburettor; water cooled.

TRANSMISSION
Front wheel drive; 5-speed gearbox; hypoid bevel final drive, 4.444; 4 speed manual, 3 speed automatic options.

CHASSIS DETAILS
Steel unitary construction; independent front suspension, struts, coil springs; rear dead axle, trailing arms, Panhard rod, coil springs; anti-roll bars front and rear; telescopic dampers; disc front, drum rear brakes; dual braking circuits, vacuum servo assistance; rack and pinion steering; 60.0l (13.2 Imp gal) (15.8 US gal) fuel tank; 165SR14 tyres, 5.5in rim width.

DIMENSIONS
Wheelbase 267.5cm (105.3in), front track 147.0cm (57.9in), rear track 144.5cm (45.1in), ground clearance 13.0cm (5.1in), turning circle 11.3m (37.3ft), overall length 459.0cm (180.1in), overall width 177.0cm (70.0in), overall height 139.0cm (54.7in).

PERFORMANCE
Maximum speed 99mph (160kph); 17.1mph (27.6kph) @ 1000rpm; acceleration 0-100kph (62mph) 13.4sec; average fuel consumption 31.9mpg (8.9l/ 100km) Euromix.

AUDI VW Iltis 1977

Few people outside the Iltis project team had the slightest idea that an entire new dynasty of cars would stem from it. The West German defence ministry commissioned Audi to design a new 'go anywhere' lightweight four wheel drive vehicle to replace the ageing DKW Munga. Basing the design on the 1.7 engine used in the Audi 80/VW Passat, a four wheel drive system was developed, taking the drive to the rear wheels from the hollow output shaft of the five-speed gearbox. The independent suspension gave ample wheel travel, while the uncompromisingly basic bodywork was deemed soldierproof.

Although Iltis wore VW badges, it was actually built at Audi's Ingolstadt plant. Audi had no plans to produce four wheel drive mainstream models, but an unofficial team developed a prototype, based on the Audi 80, using an Iltis driveline with a small centre differential added between the gearbox and rear differential. The result impressed the management team and the go-ahead was given for the project to become official. The first car to emerge with the new four wheel drive system was the turbocharged Quattro in 1980.

BODY
Soft-top off-roader; 4 seats; no doors; weight 1300kg (2860lb).

ENGINE
4 cylinders, in line; front; 79.5x86.4mm, 1716cc; compr 8.2:1; 55kW (75bhp) @ 5500rpm; 32.1kW/l (43.7bhp/l); 135Nm (13.8mkp) @ 2800rpm.

ENGINE STRUCTURE
Ohv; 2 valves per cylinder; 1 belt driven ohc; aluminium cylinder head; cast iron block; 5 bearing crankshaft; Solex 1B1.

TRANSMISSION
4 wheel drive; 5 speed gearbox; hypoid bevel final drives, 5.268; diff locks front and rear.

CHASSIS DETAILS
Steel unitary construction; independent suspension front and rear, wishbones, transverse leaf springs; telescopic dampers; drum brakes; dual braking circuits; vacuum servo power assistance; rack and pinion steering; 85.0l (18.7imp gal) (22.4 US gal) fuel tank; 6.50R16 tyres, 5.5in rim width.

DIMENSIONS
Wheelbase 201.5cm (79.3in), front track 123.0cm (48.4in), rear track 126 cm (49.6in), ground clearance 22.5cm (8.9in), turning circle overall n/a, length overall 388.5cm (153.0in), overall width 152.0cm (59.8in), overall height 183.5cm (72.0in).

PERFORMANCE
Maximum speed 81mph (130kph); 14.9mph (24kph) @ 1000rpm; acceleration 0-100kph 21.0sec; 23.6kg/kW (17.3kg/ bhp); fuel consumption 21.1mpg (13.4l/100km) Euromix.

Right: Iltis in the field. Four wheel drive traction for the military effectively miniaturised for the first time was engineering triumph.

AUDI 100 diesel 1978

Introduced at the Paris motor show in 1978, the new five cylinder diesel of the Audi 100 announced in the wake of the oil crises of the 1970s aimed to exploit the new vogue for economy. VW and Audi had a modular range of diesel engines with the same cylinder bore of 76.5mm; a four cylinder for the Golf (80mm stroke giving 1471cc), a five cylinder for the Audi (86.4mm stroke giving 1986cc), and the same for a six cylinder which made its debut inconspicuously in the VW LT van in the summer of 1978. It was also adopted by Volvo for the 244GL D6 which gave the Swedish firm the distinction of introducing the world's first six cylinder diesel saloon. The very existence of a six cylinder engine in the group led to much speculation that there were plans for a large luxury saloon in 1980 which would revive the Horch name.

Audi was more interested in being the world's first maker of a five cylinder diesel, which resembled the motor sold to Volvo in having a single overhead camshaft, aluminium cylinder head, and distributor pump drive at the back of the camshaft, but with one cylinder less and 144 degree crank throws.

BODY
4-door saloon, 5-door hatchback; 5 seats; weight 1170kg (2574lb).

ENGINE
5 cylinders, in line; front; 76.5x86.4mm, 1986cc; compr 23.0:1; 51kW (70bhp)@ 4800rpm; 25.7kW/l (35.2bhp/l); 123Nm (12.3mkp) @ 3000rpm.

ENGINE STRUCTURE
Ohv; 2 valves per cylinder; 1 belt driven overhead camshaft; aluminium alloy cylinder head; cast iron block; 6 bearing crankshaft; diesel indirect injection; water cooled.

TRANSMISSION
Front wheel drive; 5 speed gearbox; hypoid bevel final drive, 5.221.

CHASSIS DETAILS
Steel unitary construction; independent suspension, struts, coil springs; rear dead axle, trailing arms, Panhard rod, coil springs; anti-roll bars front and rear; telescopic dampers; disc front, drum rear brakes; dual braking circuits; vacuum servo power assistance; rack and pinion steering; 60.0l (13.2 Imp Gal) (15.8 US gal) fuel tank; 175SR14 tyres, 5.5in rims.

DIMENSIONS
Wheelbase 267.5cm (105.3in). front track 147.0cm (57.9in), rear track 144.5cm (56.9in), ground clearance 13.0cm (5.1in), turning circle 11.3m (37.3ft), overall length 459.0cm (180.7in), overall width 177.0cm (69.7in), overall height 139.0cm (54.7in).

PERFORMANCE
Maximum speed 93mph (149.3kph); acceleration 0-100kph (62mph) 17.5sec; 22.9kg/kW (16.7kg/bhp); average fuel consumption 42mpg (6.7l/100km).

AUDI 80 1978

The new 80 used a lengthened version of the original 80's floorpan. Audi tried hard to distance it from the revised Volkswagen Passat, but it had some common dimensions and body components.

As before there were two and four door saloon versions, but Audi decided against adding an estate. The base engine was a 40.5kW 1.3 litre ohc unit, while there were no fewer than three renderings of the 1.6-litre. The 55kW and 62.5kW versions ran with a single Solex carburettor, the 81kW version, used in the GLE had Bosch K-Jetronic petrol injection, and there was also a 1.6-litre, 40kW diesel. Initially all models had a four-speed gearbox, with a three-speed automatic optional on the carburettor-engined models. From 1981 the 62.5kW (85bhp) GLS and 81kW (108.6bhp) GLE had five-speed manual transmissions, fifth being an extra-high 'economy' ratio.

Suspension was typical of Audi, with struts at the front and the dead axle, located by trailing arms and Panhard rod at the rear. The 80's platform later formed the basis of the Coupe and quattro introduced on 1 September 1980 with the five-cylinder engine.

80:
BODY
4 door saloon; 5 seats; weight 950kg (2090lb).
ENGINE
4 cylinders, in line; front; 79.5x80.0mm, 1588cc; compr 8.2:1; 62.5kW (85bhp) @ 5600rpm; 39.4kW/l (53.5bhp/l); 124Nm (12.7mkp) @ 3200rpm.
ENGINE STRUCTURE
Ohv; 2 valves per cylinder; 1 belt driven overhead camshaft; aluminium alloy cylinder head; cast iron block; 5 bearing crankshaft; Solex carburettor; water cooled.
TRANSMISSION
Front wheel drive; 5 speed gearbox; hypoid bevel final drive, 4.111; 4-speed manual, 3 speed automatic options.
CHASSIS DETAILS
Steel unitary construction; independent front suspension, struts, coil springs; rear dead axle, trailing arms, Panhard rod, coil springs; anti-roll bars front and rear; telescopic shock absorbers; disc front, drum rear; vacuum servo power assistance; rack and pinion steering; 68.0l (15.0 Imp gal) (17.9 US gal) fuel tank; 175/70SR13 tyres, 5.0in rim width.
DIMENSIONS
Wheelbase 254.0cm (100.0in), front track 140.0cm (55.1in), rear track 142.0 (55.9in); ground clearance 18.0cm (7.1in); turning circle 10.4m (34.3ft), overall length 428.5cm (168.7in), overall width 168.0cm (66.1in); overall height 136.5cm (53.7in).
PERFORMANCE
Maximum speed 104mph (165kph); 17.7mph (29.5kph); acceleration 0-100kph (62mph) 12.1sec; 14.9kg/kW (10.9kg/bhp); average fuel consumption 35.9mpg (7.9l/100km).

AUDI 200 2.2 litre 5 cylinder; 2.2 Turbo 1979

The Audi 200 was essentially a 100 body shell with a better standard of equipment and distinctive appearance. Aluminium wheels, a side rubbing strip and heavier bumpers made it look quite different. The 200 was always sold with the fuel injected five cylinder engine and five-speed gearbox, the 200 5E with the 100's 100kW 2.2 litre engine, and the 200 5T with Audi's first turbocharger. This was a very quick luxury saloon by any standards. The three-speed automatic gave an acceleration time to 100kmh of 9.4sec. The car's principal demerit was its lack of refinement against Jaguar, BMW and Mercedes-Benz opposition. Performance was swift though the 5T could be unruly in the wet.

BODY

2 door saloon; 5 seats; weight 1260kg (2772lb).

ENGINE

5 cylinders, in line; front; 79.5x86.4mm, 2144cc; compr 7.0:1; 125kW (170bhp) @ 5300rpm; 58.3kW/l (79.3bhp/l); 265Nm (27.0mkp) @ 3300rpm.

ENGINE STRUCTURE

Ohv; 2 valves per cylinder; 1 belt driven ohc; aluminium cylinder head; cast iron block; 6 bearing crankshaft; Bosch K-Jetronic injection; KKK turbocharger; water cooled.

TRANSMISSION

Front wheel drive; 5-speed, 3-speed automatic option; hypoid bevel final drive, 3.889.

CHASSIS DETAILS

Steel unitary construction; independent front suspension, struts, coils springs. Rear dead axle, trailing arms, Panhard rod, coil springs; anti-roll bars front and rear; telescopic dampers; disc brakes, ventilated at front; dual diagonally split braking circuits; hydraulic servo power assistance; rack and pinion steering, PAS; 75l (16.5 Imp gal) (19.8 US gal) fuel tank; 205/60HR15 tyres, 6.0in rim width.

DIMENSIONS

Wheelbase 267.5cm (105.3in), front track 147.5cm (58.1in), rear track 145.5cm (57.3in). ground clearance 13.0cm (5.1in), turning circle 11.3m (37.3ft), overall length 469.5cm (184.8in), overall width 177.0 (69.7in), overall height 139.0cm (54.7in).

PERFORMANCE
for 5T only

Max 126mph (202kph); 21.6mph (34.9kph) @ 1000rpm; 0-100kph (62mph) 8.6sec; 10.1kg/kW (7.4 kg/bhp); average consumption 25.2mpg (11.2l/100km) Euromix.

AUDI Quattro 1980

The four wheel drive system used for the Audi Quattro was designed by Audi for a new military vehicle, the Volkswagen Iltis (q.v.), using the in-line 1.6-litre engine and gearbox unit found in the Volkswagen Passat and Audi 80. It was a relatively simple engineering task to take a drive to the rear wheels from the output shaft at the back of the gearbox. This same system, with modifications, was to form the basis of the Audi quattro.

The new coupe, based on the 80 floorpan and running gear, served as the foundation of Audi's new high performance model. The two-door design gave reasonable space for four adults and luggage, with the fastback design having great sporting appeal. A new floorpan was needed, mainly to accommodate the fully independent rear suspension, differential and drive shafts. In place of the Coupe's dead axle layout, the quattro had lower wishbones and struts.

The five-cylinder 2.1 litre engine was a development of that used in the 200, with a KKK turbocharger and Bosch K-Jetronic injection giving an output of 147kW at 6500rpm and a correspondingly healthy torque output. To get the engine and all its

BODY
2door coupe; 4 seats; weight 1300kg (2860lb).

ENGINE
5 cylinders, in line; front; 79.5x86.4mm; 2144cc; compr 8.0:1; 147kW (200bhp) @ 6500rpm; 68.7kW/l (93.3bhp/l); 285Nm (29mkp)@ 2250rpm.

ENGINE STRUCTURE
Ohv; 2 valves per cylinder; one belt-driven ohc; aluminium alloy cylinder head, cast iron cylinder block; 6 bearing crankshaft; Bosch K-Jetronic carburettor, KKK turbocharger with intercooler; water cooled.

TRANSMISSION
4 wheel drive; 5 speed gearbox; bevel final drive; 3.889; lockable centre and rear diffs.

CHASSIS DETAILS
Unitary construction; independent front suspension, struts, coil springs; independent rear suspension, struts, lower wishbones, coil springs; front and rear anti-roll bar; telescopic dampers; disc brakes, ventilated at front; dual braking circuits; hydraulic servo power assistance; rack and pinion PAS; 90l (19.8 Imp gal) (23.8 US gal) fuel tank; tyres 205/60VR15, rim width 6in.

DIMENSIONS
Wheelbase 252cm (99.4in), front track 142cm (55.9in), rear track 145cm (57.1in), ground clearance 12cm (4.7in), turning circle 11.3m (37.1ft), overall length 440cm (173.4in), overall width 172cm (67.8in), overall height 134cm (52.9in).

PERFORMANCE
Maximum speed 137mph (222kmh); 23.3mph (37.5kph) @ 1000rpm; 0-100kph (62mph) 7.1sec; 8.8kg/kW (6.5kg/bhp); average fuel consumption 26.0mpg (10.7l/100km) Euromix.

IN-NH 35

ancillaries under the bonnet, it had to be canted 20deg to the right, with the radiator alongside rather than ahead of the engine.

The main alteration to the permanent four wheel drive system was a small differential between the gearbox and the drive shaft to the rear axle, to prevent transmission 'wind up'. The Quattro had a fixed 50:50 front to rear torque distribution, with lockable centre and rear differentials to help traction in icy or slippery conditions.

To handle the extra power and performance, the Quattro had power steering and disc brakes all round, those at the front ventilated, but there was no ABS.

Wide cast alloy wheels, with 205/60VR15in tyres completed the package.

Audi kept the Quattro almost understated in its appearance. The four Auto Union interlinked rings appeared at the base of the doors, while 'quattro' appeared at the bottom of the rear side windows. The first cars were made in left hand drive only. With the vastly increased torque and traction, drivers had to learn new techniques to get the best from the Quattro. Turbo lag, the time taken for the turbocharger to respond meant a pause between opening the throttle and power arriving at the driving wheels, so rally drivers used the left-foot braking technique to maintain turbo boost while braking and cornering.

AUDI Coupe 1980

Once the 80 was firmly established, Audi was able to use its floorpan as the foundation for a new coupe. The steeply sloping back gave it the appearance of a hatchback, but the window was fixed, and there was a conventional boot behind the rear seats. The sensible use of space inside meant that there was ample room in the rear seat for adults.

Although the 1.6 litre/55kW model used the same four cylinder engine as the 80 saloon, the 1.9-litre/84.5kW five cylinder engine, with a single twin-choke Solex carburettor was a new departure for Audi and pointed the way for the new 90 range. The standard transmission was a five-speed manual gearbox, with a three-speed automatic available at extra cost.

The coupe's suspension was taken directly from the 80 saloon, with the semi-rigid dead rear axle located by trailing arms and Panhard rod, while at the front there were struts and coil springs. Braking was by discs at the front and drums at the rear, with a vacuum servo. The steering did not have the benefit of power assistance.

BODY
Coupe; 2 door; 5 seats; weight 1020kg (2244lb).

ENGINE
5 cylinders in line, front, in line; 79.5x77.4mm; 1921cc; compr 10.0:1; 84.5kW/115bhp @ 5900rpm; 44kW/l, 59.9bhp/l; 154Nm/15.7mkp @ 3700rpm.

ENGINE STRUCTURE
Ohv; 2 valves per cylinder; ohc; one belt-driven camshaft; aluminium alloy cylinder head material; cast iron cylinder block; 6 bearing crankshaft; Solex 2B2 carburettor; water cooled.

TRANSMISSION
Front wheel drive; 5 speed gearbox; hypoid bevel final drive; final drive ratio 4.9; optional 3 speed automatic.

CHASSIS DETAILS
Unitary construction; front independent suspension, struts, coil springs; rear suspension dead axle, trailing arms, Panhard rod, coil springs; telescopic dampers; front brakes disc, rear brakes drum; dual braking circuits; vacuum servo power assistance; rack and pinion steering; 68l (15 Imp gal) (18.0 US gal) fuel tank; tyres 175/70HR13, rim width 5.5in.

DIMENSIONS
Wheelbase 254cm (100in); front track 149cm (58.7in); rear track 142cm (55.9in); ground clearance 18cm (7.1in); turning circle 10.4m (34.1ft); overall length 435cm; overall width 168cm (66.1in); overall height 135cm (53.1in).

PERFORMANCE
Maximum speed 114mph (183kph); 25.2mph (40.4kph) @ 1000rpm in top gear ; acceleration 0-100kph (62mph)10.3sec; 12.7kg/kW (8.9kg/bhp); average fuel consumption 30.5mpg (9.3l/ 100km) Euromix.

AUDI BMFT concept car 1981

West Germany's Federal Ministry for Research and Technology commissioned the country's major motor manufacturers to reveal their ideas for a car of the future. Audi's concept car at the Frankfurt Show in the autumn of 1981, was, as far as the external lines went, the new 100, not due to be launched for a further 12 months. Its designers' claims for a drag coefficient of 0.30 seemed extravagant. The flush windows and smooth underside were some way from perfection. Audi took the opportunity to explore the use of other materials. The passenger cabin had a glass fibre and aluminium 'sandwich' for the roof, carried in a steel frame; the floor was another sandwich, this time with polyurethane foam between plastic sheets. The bonnet was fabricated from two aluminium pressings, with plastic foam in the voids to act as an energy absorber in an accident. Safety in the cabin was provided by air bags and knee bolsters, while a child seat folded away in the rear centre armrest. Power was supplied by a light-pressure turbocharged 1.6 engine, giving 81kW. The turbocharger was designed to give its maximum boost at between 1000 and 2000rpm.

BODY
4 door saloon, 4 seats; weight 1200kg (2640lb).

ENGINE
4 cylinders, in line; front 81.0x 77.4mm, 1595cc; 81.0 kW (110bhp); 50.8kW/l (70.0bhp/l).

ENGINE STRUCTURE
Ohv; 2 valves per cylinder; belt-driven camshaft; aluminium alloy cylinder head; cast iron block; 5 bearing crankshaft; Bosch fuel injection; turbocharger; water cooled.

TRANSMISSION
Front wheel drive; 5 speed gearbox; hypoid bevel final drive.

CHASSIS DETAILS
Composite glass fibre, aluminium and polyurethane foam, with steel frame. Independent front suspension, struts, coil springs; semi-independent rear suspension, coil springs; telescopic dampers; disc front, drum rear brakes; dual hydraulic circuit; vacuum servo power assistance; rack and pinion, PAS; 80.0l (17.6 Imp gal) (21.5 US gal) fuel tank.

DIMENSIONS
Wheelbase 272.6cm (107.3in), overall length 476.4cm (187.6 in), overall width 178.7cm (70.4in), overall height 140.8cm (55.4in).

PERFORMANCE
Maximum speed 113mph (180kph); acceleration 0-100km/h (62mph) 12.0sec; 14.8kg/kW (10.9kg/bhp); average fuel consumption 39.2mpg (7.2l/100km)Euromix.

Right: Audi's research into low energy requirements in manufacturing began in the 1970s. The BMFT Concept car's engine was encased in an insulated capsule with ducted airflow.

AUDI 100 0.30 Cd 1982

Until 1982, drag coefficient – Cd – was only of significance to engineers. Audi then set new standards, because 0.30Cd had seemed impractical for a production car.. The windscreen was blended into the pillars and roof, while around the radiator grille and bonnet opening, seals ensured that air flow was carefully managed, rather than being allowed to find its own way. The 100 ran with very high top gearing, 43.9kph/27.3mph per 1000rpm for long-legged and quiet motorway cruising. Rain guttering was trimmed away and the result was a cleanly-styled car which influenced many others of the 1980s and 1990s.

As well as five cylinder 2.0/74kW and 2.2/100kW engines, there were a pair of 2.0 petrol and diesels, the latter giving 64kW in turbo form. Wind tunnel tests reduced air drag with the aims of improving fuel consumption and reducing wind noise. The demand for lower fuel consumption had increased following the fuel crises of the 1970s. Audi had managed to make a 2.0 litre engine provide the performance of a 3.0 litre by improving aerodynamics and reducing weight.

BODY
Saloon; 4 door; 5 seats; weight 1145kg (2525lb).

ENGINE
5 cylinders, in line; front; 79.5x77.4; 1921cc; compr 10.0:1; 74kW (100bhp) @ 5600rpm; 38.5kW/l (52.1bhp/l); 150Nm (15.3mkp) @ 3200rpm.

ENGINE STRUCTURE
Ohv; 2 valves per cylinder; ohc; one belt-driven camshaft in cylinder head; aluminium alloy cylinder head; cast iron cylinder block; 6 bearing crankshaft; Solex twin choke 2B2 carburettor, water cooled.

TRANSMISSION
Front wheel drive; 5 speed gearbox; hypoid bevel final drive; 5.222; 3 speed automatic option

CHASSIS DETAILS
Unitary construction; independent front suspension, struts, coil springs; rigid axle rear suspension, trailing arms, Panhard rod, coil springs; front and rear anti-roll bar; telescopic dampers; front brakes disc, rear brakes drum; dual braking circuits, hydraulic servo power assistance; rack and pinion steering; 80l (17.6 Imp gal) (21.1 US gal) fuel tank; tyre size 185/70SR14, rim width 5.5in.

DIMENSIONS
Wheelbase 269cm (105.9in), front track 147cm (57.9in), rear track 144cm (56.7in), ground clearance 12cm (4.8in), turning circle 11.6m (38.1ft), overall length 468.5cm, overall width 177cm, overall height 139cm.

PERFORMANCE
Maximum speed 111.5mph (179kph); 43.9kph (27.3mph)@ 1000rpm; acceleration 0-100kph (62mph) 12.1sec; 7.6kg/kW, 11.5kg/bhp; average cons 31.5mpg (9l/100km) Euromix.

AUDI 80 quattro 1983

Although Audi's permanent four wheel drive system was first used on the high-performance Quattro, it quickly became in demand by those living in mountain areas where snow and ice made two wheel drive motoring difficult. The 1978 Audi 80 was a longer and wider version of the 1972 car, and in 1981 it was relaunched as a new model with an enhanced power train. The first 4wd car was Quattro, the transmission alone quattro.

The two or four-door 80 quattro was only available with four wheel drive, and used the five cylinder engine developed for the 100. The 2.0-litre developed 85kW, with a more sporting model using the 100kW 2.2 engine. The drive system was the same as on the Quattro, with a small differential set between the output shaft of the gearbox and the propeller shaft to the rear diff. Both the centre and rear axle differentials could be locked to give added traction. In place of the normal 80's dead axle rear suspension, the quattro version used full-independent struts and lower wishbones. To handle the extra performance and weight, the 80 quattro had PAS and disc brakes front and rear.

BODY
4 door; 5 seats; weight 1190kg (2618lb).

ENGINE
5 cylinders, in line; front; 79.5x86.4mm, 2144cc; compr 9.3:1; 100kW (136bhp) @ 5900rpm; 46.6kW/l (63.4bhp/l); 176Nm (18.0mkp) @ 4500rpm.

ENGINE STRUCTURE
Ohv; 2 valves per cylinder; belt driven ohc; aluminium cylinder head; cast iron block; 6 bearing crankshaft; Bosch K-Jetronic injection; water cooled.

TRANSMISSION
4-wheel drive; 5-speed gearbox; lockable centre and rear diffs; hypoid bevel final drives, 4.111.

CHASSIS DETAILS
Steel unitary construction; independent front suspension, struts, coil springs; independent rear suspension, struts, lower wishbones, coil springs; anti-roll bars front and rear; dual braking circuits; vacuum servo power assistance; rack and pinion steering, PAS; 70l (15.4 Imp gal) (18.5 US gal) fuel tank; 175/70HR14 tyres, 5.5in rim width.

DIMENSIONS
Wheelbase 252.0cm (99.2in), front track 140.0cm (55.1in). rear track 141.0cm (55.5in), ground clearance 11.0cm (4.3in), turning circle 10.5m (34.7ft), overall length 438.0cm (172.4in), overall width 168.0cm (66.1in), overall height 138.0cm (54.3in).

PERFORMANCE
Maximum speed 120mph (192.6kph); 20.2mph (32.2kph) @ 1000rpm; acceleration 0-100kph (62mph) 9.4sec; 11.9kg/kW (8.8kg/bhp); average fuel consumption 31.7mpg (8.9l/100km) Euromix.

Right: **Square crisp body lines for the enlarged 80.**

AUDI 100 Avant 1983

The name Avant had been used before by Audi, to denote a five-door hatchback version of the 100. The new Avant managed to bridge the gap between the hatchback design and a classic estate car, with its close to vertical tailgate.

    The new design had a steeply sloping tailgate, with an ingenious larger upper and narrow lower window, the latter below the 'break' in the slope, giving better rearward vision low down behind the car. Unlike a conventional estate car, the Avant had a lip to the load platform. The Avant introduced rear seats with a split-fold facility to expand the load carrying abilities. From the back of the rear doors the roof panel was extended rearwards, with larger quarter windows.

    Despite looking bigger, the Avant shared the same overall dimensions as the saloon. The model was launched with four engine options in addition to the 2.3 E/100kW. The four cylinder 1.8 came in 55 and 66kW versions, while five cylinder 2.0 diesels gave 51 and, with turbocharging, 64kW.

    The 100 saloon was relaunched in September 1987 and the Avant in March 1983.

BODY
Estate; 5 door; 5 seats; weight 1260kg (2778lb).

ENGINE
5 cylinders; front; 79.5x86.4mm; 2144cc; compr 9.3:1; 100kW (136bhp) @ 5700rpm; 46.7kW/l (62.4bhp/l); 180Nm (18.4mkp) @ 4800rpm.

ENGINE STRUCTURE
Ohv; 2 valves per cylinder; ohc; 1 belt-driven camshaft in cylinder head; aluminium alloy cylinder head; cast iron cylinder block; 6 bearing crankshaft; Bosch K-Jetronic injection, water cooled.

TRANSMISSION
Front wheel drive; 5 speed, 3 speed automatic option; hypoid bevel final drive; 3.889.

CHASSIS DETAILS
Unitary construction; front independent suspension, struts, coil springs; rear rigid axle suspension, trailing arms, Panhard rod, coil springs; anti-roll bar front and rear; telescopic dampers; front brakes disc, ventilated; dual braking circuits; hydraulic servo power assistance; optional ABS; rack and pinion steering, PAS; 80l (17.6 Imp gal) (21.1 US gal); 185/70HR14 tyres, rim width 5.5in.

DIMENSIONS
Wheelbase 269cm (105.8in), front track 147cm (57.8in), rear track 147cm (57.8in), ground clearance 12cm (4.7in), turning circle 11.6m (31ft), overall length 479cm (188.7in), overall width 181cm (71.2in), overall height 142cm (56in).

PERFORMANCE
Maximum speed 122mph (196kph); 45.0kph (28.0mph) @ 1000rpm; acceleration 0-100kph (62mph) 11.3sec; 12.6kg/kW, 9.3kg/bhp; average fuel consumption 33.6mpg (8.4l/100km) Euromix.

AUDI 200 Turbo 1983

Even though the 200 shared the same fully galvanised body shell as the aerodynamic 100, Audi was looking for a rather different image. The 200 aimed to be the top-of-the-range, performance model. For the turbo version the 2.2 litre five-cylinder 134kW engine was used, with a KKK turbocharger and intercooler operating with Bosch K-Jetronic injection system. Initially drive was through the front wheels only, with the four wheel drive quattro system added in 1985. The five-speed gearbox was standard and a three-speed automatic available. As with the 100, the 200 used a rigid rear axle layout, carried on trailing arms and located by a Panhard rod. The usual Audi strut suspension arrangement was used at the front. The wide 205-section tyres detracted from the slimmer-wheeled 100's 0.30Cd drag factor, but the 200 was nevertheless a very fast and well equipped car, with a top speed of 230kph/143mph.

An Avant version, with four wheel drive, was added to the range in 1985. Despite its performance and equipment levels, the high price put the 200 out the running for many would-be buyers, and the model was discontinued in summer 1989.

BODY
Saloon; 4 doors; 5 doors; weight 1290kg (2844lb).

ENGINE
5 cylinders, in line; front; 79.5x86.4mm; 2144cc; compr 8.8:1; 134kW (182bhp) @ 5700rpm; 62.5kW/l (84.9bhp/l); 252Nm (26mkp) @ 3600rpm.

ENGINE STRUCTURE
Ohv; 2 valves per cylinder; ohc; one belt-driven camshaft; aluminium alloy cylinder head; cast iron cylinder block; 6 bearing crankshaft; Bosck K-Jetronic injection; KKK turbocharger with intercooler; water cooled.

TRANSMISSION
Front wheel drive; 5 speed gearbox; hypoid bevel final drive; 3.889; optional 3 speed automatic.

CHASSIS DETAILS
Unitary construction; independent front suspension, struts, coil springs, rear suspension dead axle, trailing arms, Panhard rod, coil springs; anti-roll bars front and rear; telescopic dampers; disc brakes, ventilated at front; dual braking circuits; hydraulic servo power assistance; ABS; PAS; rack and pinion steering; 80l (17.6 Imp gal) (21.1 US gal) fuel tank; tyres 205/60VR15, rim 6in.

DIMENSIONS
Wheelbase 269cm (105.8in), front track 147cm (57.7in), rear 147cm (57.7in), ground clearance 10cm (3.9in), turning circle 11.6cm (38in), length 481cm (189.3in), width 181cm (71.2in), height 142cm (56in).

PERFORMANCE
Maximum speed 143mph (230kph); 23.3mph (37.5kph) @ 1000rpm; acceleration 0-100kp (62mph) 8.7sec; 9.6kg/kW (7.1kg/ bhp); average fuel consumption 31.7mpg (8.9l/100km) Euromix.

Audi achieved almost instant success in international rallies with the first iron-block Quattro, but the original Coupe body was heavy, and put it at a disadvantage. As soon as the regulations allowed, a new Quattro, the Sport, was introduced with a 20-valve, alloy block turbocharged engine which not only reduced weight but provided 225kW against the original quattro's 147kW. The new engine also saw Audi using a cross-flow twin overhead camshaft cylinder head for the first time. The wheelbase was shorter by 32cm, the saving achieved behind the front seats and in front of the rear wheels. Legroom in the back was foreshortened to the extent that the seat cushion touched the back of the front seats. The roof, wings and front apron were made from Kevlar to save weight. The production Sport had trim, glass windows and full instrumentation, and the wheel arches front and rear were flared. The Sport marked the first occasion Audi felt the quattro four wheel drive system to be compatible with ABS braking. 214 were built; 164 were sold to customers, and 20 were used as competition cars by the Motorsport Department. The remainder were experimental and retained by the factory.

Sport quattro:

BODY
Coupe; 2 doors; 4 seats; weight 1300kg (2866lb).

ENGINE
5 cyl, in line; front; 79.3x86.4mm; 2133cc; compr 8.0:1; 225kW (306bhp) @ 6700rpm; 105.5kW/l (143.5bhp/l); 350Nm (35.7mkp) @ 3700rpm.

ENGINE STRUCTURE
Ohv; 4 valves per cylinder; ohc;two belt driven camshafts in cylinder head; aluminium alloy cylinder head and block, wet liners; 6 bearing crankshaft; Bosch HI-Jetronic, KKK turbocharger with intercooler, water cooled.

TRANSMISSION
4 wheel drive; 5 speed gearbox; hypoid bevel final drive; 3.875; lockable centre and rear diffs.

CHASSIS DETAILS
Unitary construction; independent front suspension, struts, coil springs; independent rear suspension, lower wishbones, struts, coil springs; anti-roll bar front and rear; telescopic dampers; disc brakes, ventilated at front; dual braking circuits; hydraulic servo power assistance; ABS standard; rack and pinion, PAS; 90l (19.8 Imp gal) (23.7 US gal) fuel tank; tyres 235/45VR15, 9in rim s.

DIMENSIONS
Wheelbase 220cm (86.8in), front track 152cm (59.7in), rear track 149cm (58.7in), ground clearance 11cm (4.3in), turning circle 11.2m (37ft), length 416cm (163.9in), width 180cm (71in), height 134cm (52.9in).

PERFORMANCE
Max. speed 155mph (250kph); 23.1mph (37.2kmh) @ 1000rpm; acceleration 0-100kph (62mph) 6.4sec; 5.8kg/kW (4.2kg/bhp); average fuel consumption 24mpg (11.8l/100km) estimated fig.

Above: In 1982 Audi won the World Rally Championship for Manufacturers and Michele Mouton was runner-up in the Drivers World Championship. Hannu Mikkola took the Drivers title in 1983 and, in 1984, Audi scored the double winning both the Drivers Championship with Stig Blomqvist, and the Manufacturers Championship.

Above: Major technical changes to the roadgoing quattro in 1988 included the Torsen centre differential, giving variable front/rear torque split, and the 2226cc engine with water-cooled turbo, hydraulic tappets and higher compression, giving increased low-speed torque.

AUDI 80 1984

When the 80 was re-launched in 1978 it broke away more thoroughly from the Volkswagen Passat influence, remaining steadfastly faithful to its fore-and-aft engine layout. The engine was hung out ahead of the front axle line, with the gearbox in unit with the final drive.
In 1983 the CD, a version of the 80, appeared with a five cylinder 2.0l engine, plus a short-lived 2.1-litre, quattro version. This confusion was resolved in 1984 when the five cylinder 90 range was launched, leaving the 80 models with four cylinder engines.

Although the 80 and 90 shared the same four-door bodyshell and suspension layout, the standard of equipment on the five-cylinder version was generally higher. The 80 was also available with 1.3 44 kW (59bhp) and 1.6 55kW (73.8bhp) petrol engines, and a 1.6 diesel developing 40kW (53.6bhp) or, in turbocharged form, 51kW (68.4bhp).

Known in the United States as the Audi 4000, the square-rigged 80 body had only two years left to run.

BODY
4 door saloon; 5 seats; weight 950kg (2090lb).

ENGINE
4 cylinders, in line; front; 81.0x86.4mm, 1781cc; compr 10.0:1; 66kW (90bhp) @ 5200rpm; 37.1kW/l (50.5bhhp/l); 145Nm (14.8mkp) @ 3300rpm.

ENGINE STRUCTURE
Ohv; 2 valves per cylinder; 1 belt driven ohc; aluminium cylinder head; cast iron block; 5 bearing crankshaft; Solex carburettor.

TRANSMISSION
Front wheel drive; 4 speed gearbox, 5 speed extra; spiral bevel final drive, 4.111.

CHASSIS DETAILS
Steel unitary construction; independent front suspension, struts, coil springs; rear suspension, dead axle, trailing arms, Panhard rod, coil springs; front anti roll bar; telescopic dampers; disc front, drum rear

brakes, dual braking circuits; vacuum servo assistance; 68.0l (15.0 Imp gal) (17.9 US gal) fuel tank; 175/50ST13 tyres, 5.0in rim width.

DIMENSIONS
Wheelbase 254.0cm (100.0in), front track 140.0cm (55.1in), rear track 142.0cm (55.9in), ground clearance 10.7cm (4.2in), turning circle 10.4m (43.1ft), overall length 428.0cm (172.6in), overall width 168.0cm (66.2in), overall height 136.0cm (53.4in).

PERFORMANCE
(for 1781cc petrol)
Maximum speed 104mph (168kph), 30.7kph (19.1mph) @ 1000rpm; acceleration 0-100kph (62mph) 11.8sec; 14.4kg/kW (10.6kg/bhp); average fuel consumption 34.4mpg (8.2l/100km) Euromix.

AUDI 80 0.29 Cd galvanised body 1986

By the time the new 80 was launched in September 1986, drag coefficient figures were being freely quoted throughout the industry. So after the new 100's figure of 0.30Cd, the 80's even lower figure of 0.29Cd made it just about the most aerodynamic model in its class. Also new was the use of galvanised steel for the whole body structure, allowing Audi to give its new model a 10 year anti-corrosion warranty.

Safety was given prominence, with the 80 being the first Audi to have the Procon-ten passive safety feature. By using a cable and pulley system, if the engine was driven backwards in a head-on impact, the steering column would be pulled forward, away from the driver, minimising injury risk. Wide doors made access easy, but the boot was rather small. Models on the UK market had the 4+E five speed gearbox, with the high fifth gear giving relaxed cruising. The base 1.6 and 1.8S models had a carburettor, while the 1.8E had Bosch fuel injection.

A new feature for the 80 quattro was the use of a torque-sensing Torsen centre differential in place of the fixed-split unit used in previous models.

BODY
4 door saloon; 5 seats; weight 1020kg (2040lb).

ENGINE
4 cylinders, in line; front; 81.0x86.4mm, 1781cc; compr 9.0:21; 66kW (90bhp) @ 5400rpm; 37.1kW/l (50.5bhp/l); 140Nm (14.4mkp) @ 3350rpm.

ENGINE STRUCTURE
Ohv; 2 valves per cylinder; 1 belt driven ohc; aluminium cylinder head; cast iron block; 5 bearing crankshaft; Keihin carburettor; water cooled.

TRANSMISSION
Front wheel drive; 5 speed gearbox; hypoid bevel final drive, 4.111; 4 speed manual, 3 speed automatic options.

CHASSIS DETAILS
Steel unitary construction; independent front suspension, struts, coil springs; rear suspension, torsion beam, trailing arms, Panhard rod, coil springs; anti-roll bars front and rear; telescopic dampers; disc brakes front, drums brakes rear; dual braking circuits; vacuum servo power assistance; rack and pinion steering; 68.0l (15.0 Imp gal) (18.0 US gal) fuel tank; 175/70HR14 tyres, 5.5in rim width.

DIMENSIONS
Wheelbase 254.5cm (100.0in), front track 141.0cm (55.5in), rear track 143.0cm (56.3in), ground clearance 13.0cm (5.1in), turning circle 10.3m (34.0ft), overall length 439.5cm (173.0in), overall width 169.5cm 66.7in), overall height 139.5cm 54.9in).

PERFORMANCE
Maximum speed 113mph (182kph); 39.5kph (24.5mph) @ 1000rpm; 0-100kph (62mph) 12.2sec; 15.5kg/kW (11.3kg/bhp); average fuel consumption 36.1mpg (7.8l/100km).

AUDI 90, 90 quattro 1987

Rather than use engine capacity figures to distinguish between models, Audi redesignated the new five cylinder engine versions of the 80 as the 90. The longer engine was a tight squeeze in the space available, so the radiator was placed on one side. The 90 range was limited to the 2.0 and 2.3 litre 85/100kW engines, with the latter available in front and four-wheel drive.

With the quattro system, the 90, like the 80, used a lower wishbone rear suspension layout in place of the front-drive models' torsion beam system. With four wheel drive a lower final drive ratio was used to compensate for the 110kg weight penalty. The 90 models also had disc brakes all round, with antilock available as an extra except on the quattro, where it was standard. Power steering was standard on all 90 models.

As with the 80, the 90 used the same galvanised steel bodyshell and the Procon-ten system, pictured opposite.

BODY
4 door, 5 seats; weight 1110kg (2442lb).

ENGINE
5 cylinder, in line; front; 81.0x77.4mm, 1994cc; compr 10.0:1; 85kW (115bhp) @ 5400rpm; 42.6kW/l (57.7bhp/l); 172Nm (17.5mkp) @ 4000rpm.

ENGINE STRUCTURE
Ohv; 2 valves per cylinder; 1 belt driven ohc; aluminium cylinder head, cast iron block; 6 bearing crankshaft; Bosch KE-Jetronic injection.

TRANSMISSION
Front wheel drive; 5 speed gearbox; hypoid bevel final drive, 3.70; 3 speed automatic option.

CHASSIS DETAILS
Steel unitary construction; independent front suspension, struts, coil springs; rear torsion beam, trailing arms, Panhard rod, coil springs; anti-roll bar front and rear; telescopic dampers; disc brakes front and rear; dual braking circuits; vacuum servo power assistance; rack and pinion steering; 68.0l (15.0 Imp gal) (18.0 US gal) fuel tank; 195/60HR14 tyres, rim width 5.5in.

DIMENSIONS
Wheelbase 254.5cm (100.0in), front track 141.0cm (55.5in), rear track 143.0cm (56.3in), ground clearance 13.0cm (5.1in), turning circle 10.3m (34.0ft), overall length 439.5cm (173.0in), overall width 169.5cm (66.7in), overall height 139.5cm (54.9in).

PERFORMANCE
Maximum speed 122.8mph (196kph); 21.4mph (34.5kph) @ 1000rpm; 0-100kph 9.8sec; 13.1kg/kW (9.7 kg/bhp); average fuel consumption 33.5mph (8.4l/100km) Euromix.

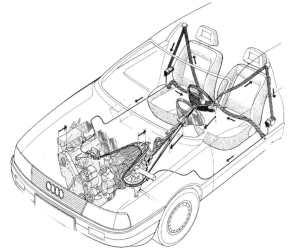

AUDI 200 quattro TransAm racer 1987

The 200 quattro made its first works appearance in the 1987 Monte Carlo Rally, but the 200 quattro which appeared at Long Beach in April, for the US TransAm series was very different. The basic engine remained much as in the road car, with, among other things, revised Bosch fuel injection and engine management system, plus more extreme camshaft profiling.

Output was more than doubled from the standard cat-equipped car's 171kW to 375kW. Drive to front and rear wheels was through a new six-speed gearbox, with a twin-plate clutch to handle the massive torque. Flared wheel arches covered the 13.5in wide rims, with the car running on ultra low profile 25.5 x 13.5 x 16 tyres. The car's eight wins in the series gave Audi an easy victory for the constructors' title.

BODY
2 door, 1 seat saloon; weight 1115kg (2453lb).

ENGINE
5 cylinders, in line; front; 79.5x 85.0mm, 2110cc; 375kW (510bhp) @ 7500rpm; 177.7kW/l (241.7 bhp/l); 500Nm (50.9mkp) @ 6000rpm.

ENGINE STRUCTURE
Ohv; 2 valves per cylinder; 2 overhead belt-driven camshafts; aluminium alloy cylinder head, cast iron block; 6 bearing crankshaft; Bosch fuel injection; turbocharger, intercooler; water cooled.

TRANSMISSION
4 wheel drive; 6 speed gearbox; hypoid bevel final drives.

CHASSIS DETAILS
Steel unitary construction; front suspension, struts, coil springs; independent rear suspension, double wishbones, coil springs; telescopic dampers; ventilated disc brakes, dual hydraulic circuit; rack and pinion steering, PAS; 25.5x16 tyres; 13.5in rims wet, 12.0in rims dry.

DIMENSIONS
Wheelbase 268.8cm (105.8in), front track 162.0cm (63.8in), rear track 162.0cm (63.8in), overall length 489.7cm (192.8in), width 203.3cm (80in), height 134.0cm (52.8in).

PERFORMANCE
Top speed, depending on gearing, approx 200mph (320kph); 3.0kg/kW (2.2kg/bhp).

Audi effectively re-wrote the specifications of a TransAm racer by not building a normal tube-frame chassis. Four wheel drive made the best use of large amounts of horsepower.

AUDI V8 3.6 1988

The introduction of the V8 moved Audi into the luxury sector of the market, dominated hitherto by BMW, Jaguar and Mercedes-Benz. Its introduction in September 1988 showed how determined Audi was to penetrate this exclusive circle.

The 3.6 litre all-alloy engine was an advanced design with twin overhead camshafts per bank, and four valves per cylinder. Three years later a 4.2 litre version was introduced, with an output of 206kW (276bhp). Audi decided to give it four wheel drive, using a version of the system originally developed for the Quattro. It evolved with an epicyclic centre differential with electronically controlled friction plate limited slip and a Torsen rear differential. A Torsen centre differential was used in the manual gearbox version, retaining the original 50:50 torque division. The 3.6 used the five speed gearbox, while the 4.2 had a six speed.

Equipment was much in line with what was expected in a car of this class, and included air conditioning, alloy wheels, antilock braking system and power adjustment for the front seats.

BODY
Saloon; 4 doors; 5 seats; weight 1710kg (3762lb).

ENGINE
8 cylinders, in 90deg V; front; 81.0x86.4mm; 3562cc; compr 10.6:1; 184kW (250bhp) @ 5800rpm; 51.7kW/l (70.2bhp/l); 340Nm (34.7mkp) @ 4000rpm.

ENGINE STRUCTURE
Ohv; 4 valves per cylinder; 2 ohc per bank; 5 bearing crankshaft; chain and belt driven camshaft; aluminium alloy cylinder head; aluminium alloy cylinder block; Bosch Motronic M24; water cooled.

TRANSMISSION
4 wheel drive; 5 speed gearbox, optional 3 speed automatic; hypoid bevel final drive, 4.11:1; Torsen or epicyclic centre diff with electronic locking, Torsen rear diff.

CHASSIS DETAILS
Unitary construction; ifs, struts, coil springs; irs, trapezoidal struts, coil springs; anti-roll bar front and rear; telescopic shock absorbers; ventilated disc brakes; dual braking circuits; vacuum servo power assistance; ABS; rack and pinion PAS; 80l (17.6 Imp gal) (21.1 US gal) fuel tank; tyre size 215/60ZR15, rim width 7.5in.

DIMENSIONS
Wheelbase 270cm (104.6in), front track 151.5cm (59.4in), rear track 153cm (60.2in), ground clearance 9.5cm (3.7in), turning circle 12.9m (42.6ft), length 486cm (191.3in), width 181.5cm (71.5in), height 142cm (55.9in).

PERFORMANCE
Maximum speed 146mph (235kph); 24.0mph (38.7kph) @ 1000rpm; 0-100kph (62mph) 9.2sec; 9.3kg/kW (6.8kg/bhp); average fuel cons 22.9mpg (12.3l/100km) Euromix.

AUDI Coupe 2.3E; Coupe quattro 1989

Like the original Coupe, this model, launched at the 1988 Birmingham Motor Show was based on the current 80 saloon. From the screen pillars forward, the Coupe used the same pressings, with the distinctive Audi grille, and four interlocking rings, between deep rectangular headlamps. In contrast to the original, the new Coupe had an opening tailgate and split-fold rear seats, allowing the load space to be expanded, and making it much more practical. The Coupe had the same rear suspension as the saloon, with torsion beam, trailing arms and Panhard rod on the front-wheel drive 2.3E and V6-engined 2.6 models, and independent rear suspension with struts and wishbones on the quattro models.

Disc brakes, ventilated at the front were backed by Bosch ABS, while all models came with power steering as standard. A five-speed gearbox was standard, with a four-speed automatic offered as an option across the range.

BODY
Coupe; 3 doors; 5 seats; weight 1230kg (2706lb).

ENGINE
5 cylinders, in line; front; 82.5x86.4mm; 2309cc; compr 10.0:1; 98kW (133bhp) @ 5750rpm; 42.6kW/l (57.8bhp/l); 186Nm (19.9mkp) @ 4000rpm.

ENGINE STRUCTURE
Ohv; 2 valves per cylinder; ohc; 1 belt-driven camshaft, in cylinder head; aluminium alloy cylinder head; cast iron cylinder block; 6 bearing camshaft; electronic injection; water cooled.

TRANSMISSION
Front wheel drive; 5 speed gearbox, optional 4 speed automatic; hypoid bevel final drive; 4.111.

CHASSIS DETAILS
Unitary construction; independent front suspension, struts, coil springs; torsion beam rear suspension, trailing arms, Panhard rod, coil springs; anti-roll bar front and rear; telescopic dampers; disc brakes, ventilated at front, dual braking circuits; vacuum servo power assistance; ABS extra; rack and pinion steering; 70l (15.4 Imp gal) (18.4 US gal) fuel tank; tyre size 205/60VR15, rim width 6in.

DIMENSIONS
Wheelbase 255.5cm (100.6in), front track 144.5cm (56.9in), rear track 144.5 cm (56.9in), ground clearance 14cm (5.5in), turning circle 11.0m (36.1in), overall length 436.5cm (171.9in), overall width 171.5cm (67.5in), overall height 137.5cm (54.1in).

PERFORMANCE
Maximum speed 128mph (206kph), 35.5kph (22.1mph) @ 1000rpm; acceleration 0-100kph (62mph) 9.7sec; 12.6kg/kW (9.2kg/bhp); average fuel consumption 31.7mpg (8.9l/100km) Euromix.

AUDI Hybrid petrol-electric 1989

In an effort to combat traffic pollution many German towns and cities imposed 30km/h (19mph) speed limits, and introduced pedestrianised shopping areas. Audi's Duo Hybrid experimental car, could use the 100kW petrol engine out of town driving, but switch to the electric motor for urban use.

The Duo Hybrid had a standard five-cylinder 2.2-litre petrol engine driving the front wheels. At the rear, a 9.3kW DC electric motor gave a 50km/h (31mph) top speed from power supplied by a nickel/cadmium battery pack, weighing 181kg (398lb). This provided a range of around 30km (19 miles) in urban areas, and recharging took just 45min. A separate electric motor provided power for steering, brakes and the ABS system, while a small petrol-fed heater kept the engine's cooling system hot to provide interior heating.

The hybrid was long a goal of the celebrated Dr Porsche, some of whose earliest inventions were what he called "mixed drive."

Absence of petrol car bans in cities inhibited the Hybrid's development.

BODY
5 door estate car; 5 seats; weight 1,740kg (3828lb).

ENGINE
5 cylinders, in line; front; 82.5x 86.4mm, 2309cc; compr 10.0:1 100kW (136bhp) @ 5600rpm; 43.3kW/l (58.9bhp/l); 190Nm (19.4mkp) @ 4000rpm. Electric motor: 9.3kW (12.6bhp); 100Nm (10.2mkp).

ENGINE STRUCTURE
Ohv; 2 valves per cylinder; 1 belt driven ohc; aluminium alloy cylinder head, cast iron block; Bosch KE-Jetronic injection; water cooled.

TRANSMISSION
Petrol engine: front wheel drive; 5-speed gearbox; hypoid bevel final drive, 3.889; Electric motor; rear wheel drive, direct.

CHASSIS DETAILS
Steel unitary construction; independent front suspension, struts, coil springs; independent rear suspension, struts, coil springs; anti-roll bars front and rear; telescopic dampers; disc brakes, ventilated at front; dual braking circuits; vacuum servo; ABS; rack and pinion steering, PAS; 80.0l (17.6 Imp gal) (21.1 US gal) fuel tank; 205/60R15 tyres, 6.0in rim width.

DIMENSIONS
Wheelbase 268.5cm (107.7in), front track 147.0cm (57.9in), rear track 149.0cm (58.7in), overall length 479.5cm (188.8in), overall width 181.5cm (71.5in), overall height 142.0cm (55.9in).

PERFORMANCE
Maximum speed (petrol) 124mph (200 km/h); 31mph (50km/h); acceleration (petrol) 0-100km/h (62mph) 10.0sec, (electric): 0-30km/h (18.8mph) 8.0sec (petrol); 17.4kg/kW (12.7kg/bhp), electric 187.1kg/kW (138.1kg/bhp).

Above and right:
Front wheels: petrol drive
Rear wheels: electric drive
Petrol engine charged
rear-mounted batteries
of Audi Duo.

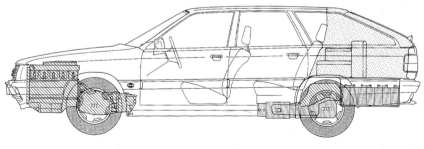

petrol engine   front drive   electric motor electric drive battery

AUDI 200; 200 Avant; 200 quattro 1989

Audi had traditionally separated its non-turbo and turbo medium-sized saloon and Avant estates as 100 and 200. With this model, however, the issue was confused a little with turbo 100 models. But in terms of trim and equipment, the 200 version was distinctly different.

The new 2226cc engine replaced the previous model's 2144cc five-cylinder unit with around 10 per cent more power and torque. Some of this increase was due to a more sophisticated electronic engine management and boost control systems. This was used to give a brief increase in turbocharger boost for faster and safer overtaking.

Inside the new 200 was a revised facia, zebrano wood veneer and on-board computer. The second Audi model range to be fitted with the Procon-ten safety system, as well as a fully galvanised body shell, the quattro version was fitted with the torque-sensing centre differential in place of the fixed 50:50 split differential of earlier models.

The launch of the V8 in September 1988 promised a tidying-up of the model range.

BODY
4 door saloon, 5 door estate; 5/7 seats; weight 1300kg (2860lb).

ENGINE
5 cylinders, in line; 81.0x86.4mm, 2226cc; compr 7.8:1; 147kW (200bhp) @ 5800rpm; 66kW/l (89.8bhp/l); 270Nm (27.5mkp) @ 3000rpm.

ENGINE STRUCTURE
Ohv; 2 valves per cylinder; belt driven ohc; aluminium cylinder head; cast iron; 6 bearing crankshaft; Bosch K-Jetronic injection, KKK turbocharger with intercooler.

TRANSMISSION
Front wheel drive; 5 speed gearbox; hypoid bevel final drive, 3.898; optional 3 speed automatic.

CHASSIS DETAILS
Steel unitary construction; independent front suspension, struts, coil springs; rear suspension torsion axle, trailing arms, Panhard rod, coil springs; anti-roll bars front and rear; telescopic dampers; disc brakes front and rear; dual braking circuits; hydraulic servo power assistance; ABS; rack and pinion; PAS; 80.0l (17.6 Imp gal) (21.1 US gal) fuel tank; 205/60VR15 tyres, 6.0in rim width.

DIMENSIONS
Wheelbase 268.5cm (105.7in), front track 147.0cm (57.9in), rear track 149.0cm 58.7in), ground clearance 11.0cm (4.3in), turning circle 11.6m (38.3ft), overall length 479.5cm (188.8in), overall width 181.5 (71.5in), overall height 142.0cm (55.9in).

PERFORMANCE
Max speed 143mph (231kph); acceleration 0-100kph (62mph) 7.5sec; 8.8kg/kW (6.5kg/bhp); 28.9mpg (9.8l/100km); average fuel consumption 21.4-40.9mpg (6.9-13.2l/100kph).

Audi was determined to retain the aerodynamic smoothness of the 100, although it compromised with the slightly raised front grille, first seen on the V8 and later adopted across the range. The 2.0 and 2.3 engines were carried over from the previous model, but in 1992 a new 2.5 litre direct injection turbocharged diesel was introduced, with 85kW and, a little later, a 110kW 2.6 litre V6.

On the new body the side windows were more upright, helping to reduce the interior heat generated in direct sunshine, but retaining the flush glazing which helped give the 100 such good aerodynamics. Although the boot lid opened down to bumper level, Audi kept the fixed rear seat, which meant that load space could not be expanded. However, a through-load facility, concealed by the rear seat folding armrest, allowed long items such as skis to be carried securely inside the car.

In 1994, when Audi adopted a new model designation system, the 100 became the A6, and was available with 2.3-litre 98kW, 2.6-litre V6 110kW, and 2.8-litre 128kW engines.

BODY
Saloon and estate; 4 doors (saloon), 5-7 (estate); 5 seats; weight 1325kg (2915lb) (saloon), 1375kg (3025lb) (estate).

ENGINE
4 cylinders, in line; front; 82.5x92.8mm; 1984cc; compr 9.2:1; 85kW/115bhp @ 5400rpm; 42.8kW/l (58.0bhp/l); 168Nm/17.1mkp @ 3200rpm.

ENGINE STRUCTURE
Ohv; 2 valves per cylinder; ohc; 1 belt-driven camshaft, in cylinder head; aluminium alloy cylinder head; cast iron cylinder block; 5 bearing crankshaft; electronic injection; water cooled.

TRANSMISSION
Front wheel drive; 5 speed gearbox; hypoid bevel final drive, 4.111; optional automatic.

CHASSIS DETAILS
Unitary construction; independent front suspension, struts, coil springs; semi- independent rear suspension, twisting beam, Panhard rod, coil springs; anti-roll bar front and rear; telescopic dampers; disc brakes front, drum rear, dual braking circuits; vacuum servo power assistance; rack and pinion steering, PAS; 80l (17.6 Imp gal) (21.1 US gal) fuel tank; tyres 195/65HR15, 6.0in rim width.

DIMENSIONS
Wheelbase 268.5cm (105.7in), front track 152.6cm (60.1in), rear track 152.5cm (60.0in), ground clearance 13.0cm (5.1in), turning circle 11.4m (37.0ft), overall length 479cm (188.6), overall width 177.5cm (69.9in), overall height 143cm (56.3in).

PERFORMANCE
Maximum speed 119mph (191kph); 21.0mph (33.8kph) @ 1000rpm; 0-100kph (62mph) 11.0sec; 15.6kg/kW, 11.5kg/bhp; av. fuel consumption 32.0mpg (8.8l/100km) Euromix.

AUDI Coupe S2 2.2 litre turbo quattro 1990

When the original Coupe was on the drawing board in the late 1970s, the permanent four wheel drive quattro idea was not even being considered. As a result, a new floorpan and rear suspension had to be developed. The S2 version of the new Coupe was planned from the start as the natural successor to the first Quattro.

The 2.2 litre turbocharged five-cylinder engine had twin overhead camshafts and four valves per cylinder. To make maximum use of the engine's power range, the S2 was one of a handful of production cars to feature a close-ratio six speed gearbox. The classic quattro-type rear suspension was retained, using lower wishbones and struts. Instead of the conventional diff between the gearbox and propeller shaft, which restricted the torque split to 50:50, the S2 had a Torsen diff, which adapted the torque output to front or rear. In normal operation, the torque split was 50:50, but the Torsen diff could vary this from 75:25 to 25:75 if one axle had more grip than the other. For icy conditions, the rear diff could still be locked manually.

A convertible version of the Coupe was launched at the Geneva motor show of 1991.

BODY
Coupe; 2 door; 5 seats; weight 1525kg (3355lb).

ENGINE
5 cylinders, in line; front; 81.0x86.4mm; 2226cc; compr 9.3:1; 162kW (220bhp) @ 5900rpm; 72.8 kW/l (98.8bhp/l); 309Nm (31.5mkp).

ENGINE STRUCTURE
Ohv; 4 valves per cylinder; ohv; 2 belt-driven overhead camshafts; aluminium alloy cylinder head; cast iron cylinder block; 6 bearing crankshaft; Bosch Motronic 2.3, KKK turbocharger, intercooler; water cooled.

TRANSMISSION
4wd, permanent; 6 speed gearbox; hypoid bevel final drive; 4.111; Torsen centre diff, lockable rear diff.

CHASSIS DETAILS
Unitary construction; ifs, struts, coil springs; irs, struts, coil springs; anti-roll bar front and rear; telescopic dampers; disc brakes, ventilated at front; dual braking circuits; hydraulic servo power assistance; ABS; rack and pinion steering, PAS; 70l (15.4 Imp gal) (18.5 US gal) fuel tank; tyre size 205/55ZR15, 7in rim width.

DIMENSIONS
Wheelbase 255cm (100.3in), front track 145cm (57.1in), rear track 147.5cm (58.1in), ground clearance 10cm (3.9in), turning circle 11.2m (37ft), overall length 440cm (173.2in), overall width 171.5cm (67.5in), overall height 137.5cm (54.1in).

PERFORMANCE
Maximum speed 154mph (248kph); 24.6mph (39.6kph) @ 1000rpm; acceleration 0-100kph (62mph) 5.9sec; 20.6kg/kW (14.7kg/bhp); average fuel consumption 27.4mpg (10.3l/100km).

Audi V8 Lang 4.2 1990

Long wheelbase limousines may not have a major share of the market, but they do make an impression, which is why Audi chose to add the Lang (long) version of the V8 to its range. To the back of the rear doors, the Lang was essentially the same as the standard V8, but an extra 32cm was added to the wheelbase behind the rear door opening, to make the Lang an imposing sight. The stretch meant redesigning the rear wings and roof panel and enlarging the rear quarter lights. The rear seat was moved back to provide a great deal more legroom, while headroom was scarcely affected. The boot remained the same size.

It was available with either the 184kW 3.6 24-valve V8 or the 206kW 4.2 version. Most long wheelbase rivals were rear wheel drive only; Audi V8 Lang customers enjoyed the advantages of four wheel drive to help them to the executive ski-slope or outpace pursuing kidnappers. Four-speed automatic versions had an electronically-controlled torque sensor in place of the manual cars' Torsen mechanical centre differential. The standard manual gearbox had five speeds, but a six-speed box could be specified.

BODY
Limousine; 4 doors; 5 seats; weight 1770kg (3894lb).

ENGINE
8 cylinders in 90 degree V; front, longitudinal; 84.5 x 93.0mm; 4172cc; compr 10.6:1; 206kW (280bhp) @ 5800rpm; 49.4kW/l (67.1bhp/l); 400Nm (40.0 mkp) @ 4000rpm.

ENGINE STRUCTURE
Ohv; 2 valves per cylinder; 2 ohc per bank; chain driven; aluminium cylinder head and block; 5 bearing crankshaft; Bosch Motronic M24 fuel injection; electronic ignition; water cooled.

TRANSMISSION
4wd, permanent; 5/6 speed, 4 speed auto; hypoid bevel final drive, 4.111:1; Torsen or epicyclic centre diff with electronic locking, Torsen rear diff.

CHASSIS DETAILS
Steel unitary construction; ifs, struts, coil springs; irs, lower wishbones, struts, coil springs; anti-roll bars front and rear, telescopic dampers; ventilated disc brakes, vacuum servo; dual braking circuits; rack and pinion PAS; 80l (17.6 Imp gal) (21.1 US gal) fuel tank; 215/60ZR15 tyres, 7.5in rim width.

DIMENSIONS
Wheelbase 302.0cm (118.9in), front track 151.5cm (59.4in), rear track 153.0cm (60.2in), ground clearance 9.5cm (3.7in), turning circle 12.9ft (42.6ft), length 519cm (204.3in), width 181.5cm (71.5in), height 142cm (55.9in).

PERFORMANCE
Maximum speed 154mph (249kph); 25.6mph (41.2kph) @ 1000rpm in top gear; 0-100kph (62mph) 6.8sec; 8.6kg/kW (13.9kg/bhp); average fuel consumption 22.5mpg (12.6l/100km).

German Touring Car Champion 1990; quattro 20-valve 1990

The first time Audi entered the German Touring Car Championship with the V8 quattro, Hans-Joachim Stuck won seven races and Walter Röhrl clinched the title with an eighth. Frank Biela won the championship in 1991. Audi's competition heritage included victory in the 1988 Trans-Am championship in America and seven wins in the 1989 IMSA-GTO series, and its attention was focussed on the German series which had been contested between BMW and Mercedes-Benz to boost sales in Europe.

BODY

4 door saloon, 1 seat; 1250kg (2750lb).

ENGINE

8 cyli in 90deg V; front; 81.0 x 86.4 mm, 3562cc; 345.6kW (470bhp) @ 9500rpm; 97.0kW/l (131.9bhp/l); 380Nm (38.8mkp) @ 7000rpm.

ENGINE STRUCTURE

Ohv; 4 valves per cyl; 2 chain and belt driven overhead camshafts per bank; aluminium alloy cyl heads and block; 5 bearing crank; Bosch fuel injection; water cooled.

TRANSMISSION

4 wheel drive; 6 speed gearbox; hypoid bevel final drive.

CHASSIS DETAILS

Steel unitary construction; ifs, struts, coil springs; irs, double wishbones, coil springs; ventilated disc brakes, double hydraulic circuits; rack and pinion PAS; 265x675 R19 tyres.

DIMENSIONS

Wheelbase 270.3cm (81.6in), front track 150.5cm (59.3in), rear 154.2cm 60.7in); length 487.4cm (192in); width 181.4cm (71.4in); height 133.5cm (52.6in).

PERFORMANCE

3.6kg/kW (2.7kg/bhp).

Far left: There were rumours that production of the original quattro would end in 1989. Demand for it to continue persuaded Audi not only to extend production until March 1991, but also to introduce the 20V engine, raising power output to 164kW (220bhp). Maximum torque was 309Nm (31.5mkp) at only 1950rpm. Maximum speed was 232kph (144mph) and 0-100kph acceleration took only 6.3sec. The quattro 20V had twin catalysts as standard.

Right: The last race
of a dramatic and
exciting 1990 season
at Hockenheim with
five drivers still in
the running for the
title. Stuck won both
heats ahead of
Frank Jelinski
and Walter Röhrl.

AUDI 100 Avant 2.0E 1990

The original 100 Avant seemed to fall halfway between a hatchback and an estate car, but there was no question of what the new Avant was setting out to be. The slightly raked tailgate gave it a far more practical load carrying ability. To allow space for the rear differential and drive line on quattro models, the load platform was higher than expected, so that on front-drive versions there was more storage space beneath it, yet it was clearly an estate car.

The engine range included the 98kW five-cylinder 2.3 litre and the 128kW 2.8 litre V8. The 2.3 litre 60kW diesel was quickly overshadowed by the turbocharged 2.5 litre TDi. With direct injection, this produced 85kW, and later appeared with 103kW, plus the option of a six speed gearbox.

As with all Audi's model range, the Avant had the Procon-ten safety system and fully-galvanised bodyshell.

Estate cars with a third row of seats were becoming scarce in 1990, and multi-purpose vehicles (MPVs) were still rare, so the provision of a pair of rearward facing seats in the back was a popular option.

BODY
5 door estate; 5/7 seats; weight 1360kg (2992lb).

ENGINE
4 cylinders, in line; front; 82.5x92.8mm, 1984cc; compr 10.3:1; 85kW (115bhp) @ 5400rpm; 42.8kW/l (58bhp/l); 168Nm (17.1mkp) @ 3200rpm.

ENGINE STRUCTURE
ohv; 2 valves per cylinder;1 belt driven ohc; aluminium cylinder head; cast iron block; 5 bearing crankshaft; Bosch injection; water cooled.

TRANSMISSION
Front wheel drive; 5-speed gearbox; hypoid bevel final drive, 4.111; optional 4-speed automatic.

CHASSIS DETAILS
Steel integral construction; independent front suspension, struts, coil springs; rear, twist beam, Panhard rod, coil springs; anti-roll bars front and rear;
telescopic shock absorbers; disc front brakes, rear drums; dual braking circuits; vacuum servo power assistance; ABS; rack and pinion steering; PAS; 80.0l (17.6 Imp gal) (21.1US gal) fuel tank; 195/65HR15 tyres, 6.0in rim width.

DIMENSIONS
Wheelbase 268.5cm (105.7in), front track 152.5cm (60.0in), rear track 152.5 (60.0in), ground clearance 13cm (5.1in), turning circle 11.4m (37.6ft), overall length 479.0cm (188.6in), overall width 177.5cm(69.9in), overall height 143.0cm (56.3in).

PERFORMANCE
Maximum speed 114mph (184kph); 33.8kph (21.0mph); acceleration 0-100kph (62mph) 11.0sec; 15.6kg/kW (11.5kg/ bhp); average fuel consumption 35.2mpg (8.0l/100km).

AUDI Quattro Spyder 1991

The Quattro Spyder was turned down by the marketing department as impractical. For years Audi had been winning rallies and races, broken records, and even set an all-time best in the Pikes Peak hill-climb in Colorado. It was determined to show an Audi that would be a style and technical landmark.

Audi's first mid-engined design used the production 2.8 V6 from the 100 range, with an adapted version of the quattro permanent four wheel drive system. The tubular steel chassis was clad in a smooth all-aluminium body, with conventionally-hinged doors. Fixed window frames provided torsional stiffness to the structure, allowing the Targa-type roof panels to be removed. Double wishbones were used at the front, while the rear saw the first use of Audi's trapezoidal link system, later used on the A4 two- and four-wheel drive models. Low profile 205/55ZR18 tyres were carried on five-spoke alloy wheels with 7.0in rims.

The Quattro Spyder was a little shorter than the production Coupe, stood a little over 46in high, and made a favourable impression on press and public at the 1991 Frankfurt motor show.

BODY
2 door convertible; 2 seats; weight 1100kg (2420lb).

ENGINE
6 cylinders in 90deg V; mid; 82.5x86.4mm, 2771cc; compr 10.3:1; 128kW (174bhp) @ 5500rpm; 46.2kw/l (62.8bhp/l); 245Nm (25.0mkp) @ 3000rpm.

ENGINE STRUCTURE
Ohv; 2 valves per cylinder; 1 belt driven ohc per bank; aluminium cylinder head; cast iron block; 4 bearing crankshaft; Bosch injection; water cooled.

TRANSMISSION
4 wheel drive; 5 speed gearbox; hypoid bevel final drives, 4.111; rear diff lock.

CHASSIS DETAILS
Tubular chassis; aluminium bodywork; independent front suspension, double wishbones, coil springs; independent rear suspension, four trapezoid links; coil springs; telescopic shock absorbers; disc brakes, ventilated at front; dual braking circuits; vacuum servo power assistance; ABS; rack and pinion steering; 70.0l (15.4 Imp gal) (18.5 US gal) fuel tank; 205/55ZR19 tyres, 7.0in rim width.

DIMENSIONS
Wheelbase 254.0cm (100.0in), front track 154.5cm (60.8in), rear track 158.0cm (66.2in), ground clearance 12cm (4.7in), turning circle 11.5m (38.0ft), overall length 421.5cm (165.9in), overall width 177.0cm (69.7in), overall height 117.5cm (46.3in).

PERFORMANCE
Maximum speed155mph (250kph); 0-100kph (62mph) 6.0sec; 8.6kg/kW (6.3kg/bhp); average fuel consumption 35.3mpg (8.0l/100km) estimated fig.

AUDI S4 2.2 20v Turbo 1991

Audi expanded its high-performance S-series in May 1991 with the launch of the S4, based on the 100 saloon and Avant estate. A notable feature of the 2.2 litre turbocharged engine was its amazing torque curve, which rose almost vertically to peak at just 1950rpm, resulting in extraordinary tractability. The standard car used a five-speed gearbox, with a closer-ratio six-speed transmission offered as an option for ultimate performance.

The S4 used the quattro four-wheel drive system, with a Torsen centre differential and manual locking for the rear differential when conditions were very slippery. Later the S4 was available with the 4.2-litre 32-valve V8 engine from from the V8, which gave an output of 206kW against the five cylinder's 169kW.

Body modifications were restricted to flared wheelarches to accommodate the fatter tyres, integrated front foglamps and a full-width rear light cluster.

BODY
4 door saloon, 5 door estate; 5 seats, weight 1610kg (3542lb).

ENGINE
5 cylinders, in line; front; 81.0x86.4mm, 2226cc; compr 9.3:1; 169kW (230bhp) @ 5900rpm; 72.8kW/l (103bhp/l); 350Nm (34.5mkp) @ 1950rpm.

ENGINE STRUCTURE
Ohv; 4 valves per cylinder; 2 overhead belt driven camshafts; aluminium alloy cylinder head, cast iron block; 6 bearing crankshaft; Bosch Motronic injection, KKK turbocharger; water cooled.

TRANSMISSION
4-wheel drive; 5 speed gearbox; hypoid bevel final drives, 4.111.

CHASSIS DETAILS
Steel unitary construction; independent front suspension, struts, coil springs; independent rear suspension, lower wishbones, coil springs; anti-roll bars front and rear; telescopic dampers; ventilated disc brakes; dual circuit circuits; vacuum servo power assistance; ABS; rack and pinion steering; PAS; 80.0l (17.6 Imp gal) (21.1US gal) fuel tank; 215/60ZR15 tyres, 7.5in rim.

DIMENSIONS
Wheelbase 268.5cm (105.7in); front track 152.6cm (60.1in), rear track 152.5cm (60.0in), ground clearance 13.0cm (5.1in), turning circle 11.4m (37.0ft), overall length 479cm (188.6), overall width 177.5cm (69.9in), overall height 143cm (56.3in).

PERFORMANCE
Maximum speed 151mph (243kph); 24.2mph (39.0kph); acceleration 0-100km/h (62mph) 6.8sec; 9.9kg/kW (7.0kg/kW); average fuel consumption 26.0mpg (7.3 l/100km) Euromix.

AUDI Cabriolet 1991

Image counts for a great deal among buyers of cabriolets, so Audi took a great deal of trouble getting its right. By careful strengthening of the open-topped bodyshell, a stiffening roll-over bar above the front seats was avoided, but to ensure that occupants would be protected in the event of an accident, the windscreen frame was reinforced to be able to take the car's weight. As a result of all this added strength, the cabriolet weighed around 180kg more than the Coupe with which it shared the same floorpan and front.

The hood was exceptionally easy to use. In place of the usual two catches on the screen rail, the Audi had a single T-bar in the centre. As this was released, the windows dropped by 15cm to free the top, which folded into a space behind the rear seats, covered by a steel closing panel. A light on the facia indicated that it was properly secured. The space needed for the folded hood did mean that rear seat space was restricted, but the boot remained sensibly large, thanks in part to the vertical fuel tank.

The cabriolet was available with 2.3/85kW, 2.6 V6/110kW and 2.8 V6/128kW engines.

BODY
Cabriolet; 2 doors; 4 seats; weight 1370kg (3014lb).

ENGINE
5 cylinders, front; 82.5x86.4mm; 2309cc; compr 10.0:1; 98kW (133bhp) @ 5500rpm; 42.6kW/l (57.6bhp/l); 186Nm (19mkp) @ 4000rpm.

ENGINE STRUCTURE
Ohv; 2 valves per cylinder; ohc; one overhead belt-driven camshaft; aluminium alloy cylinder head; cast iron cylinder block; 6 bearing crankshaft; Bosch KE-Jetronic, water cooled.

TRANSMISSION
Front wheel drive; 5 speed gearbox; hypoid bevel final drive; 3.889; optional 4 speed automatic.

CHASSIS DETAILS
Unitary construction; independent front suspension, struts, coil springs; torsion beam rear suspension, trailing arms, Panhard rod, coil springs; anti-roll bar front and rear; telescopic shock absorbers; disc brakes front and rear; dual braking circuits; vacuum servo power assistance; ABS extra; rack and pinion steering; PAS; 70l (15.4 Imp gal) (18.5 US gal) fuel tank; tyres 195/65VR15, 6in rim width.

DIMENSIONS
Wheelbase 255.5cm (100.6in); front track 145.5cm (57.3in); rear track 144.5cm (56.9in); ground clearance 12.5cm (4.9in); turning circle 11.1m (36.6ft); overall length 436.5cm (171.9in); overall width 171.5cm (67.5in); overall height 136cm (53.5in).

PERFORMANCE
Maximum 123mph (198kph); 22.1mph (35.6kph) @ 1000rpm; 0-100kph (62mph) 10.8sec; 14.0kg/kW (10.3kg/bhp); average consumption 30.5mpg (8.6 l/100km) Euromix.

One major criticism aimed at the previous 80 model was that it was simply too compact, especially when it came to luggage space. Audi answered most of its critics with the new 80. Not only was the boot larger, but for the first time the rear seats could be folded to expand load space. On the downside, the larger boot did mean that rear seat passengers did find legroom a little restricted.

As with the previous model, this 80 had the Procon Ten safety system fitted. A cable system linked the in-line engine with the steering column, so that in the event of a head-on accident, the column was pulled away from the driver, minimising injury risk. It was dropped when the driver's airbag became standard in June 1994.

This 80 was the second car in the Audi range to appear with what was to become the corporate grille, the first being the big V8. It was available with 2.0E/85kW, 2.3E/98kW, 2.6 V6/110kW, 2.8 V6/128kW and 1.9TDi/66kW engines. In the UK only the 2.8 V6 was available with quattro four wheel drive.

BODY
Saloon; 4 doors; 5 seats; weight 1230kg (2706lb).

ENGINE
4 cylinders, in line; front; 82.5x92.8mm; 1984cc; compr 10.4:1; 85kW (115bhp) @ 5400rpm; 42.8kW/l (58.0bhp/l); 165Nm (16.9mkp) @ 3200rpm.

ENGINE STRUCTURE
Ohv; 2 valves per cylinder; ohc; one overhead camshaft; aluminium alloy cylinder head; cast iron cylinder block; 5 bearing camshaft; electronic injection; water cooled.

TRANSMISSION
Front wheel drive; 5 speed gearbox; hypoid level final drive; 4.111; optional 4 speed automatic.

CHASSIS DETAILS
Unitary construction; independent front suspension independent, struts, coil springs; rear suspension, semi trailing arms, twisting beam, coil springs; anti-roll bar front and rear; telescopic shock absorbers; disc brakes, ventilated at front; dual braking circuits; vacuum servo power assistance; ABS extra; rack and pinion steering; 66l (14.5 Imp gal) (17.4 US gal fuel tank); tyre size 196/65HR15, rim 6in.

DIMENSIONS
Wheelbase 261.0cm (102.7in), front track 145cm (57.1in) 49. rear track 147cm (57.9in), ground clearance 13.5cm (5.3in), turning circle 11.2m (36.9ft), overall length 448cm (176.4in), overall width 169.5cm (66.7in), overall height 141cm (55.5in).

PERFORMANCE
Maximum speed 118mph (190kph); 20.9mph (33.7kph) @ 1000rpm; 0-100kph (62mph) 11.8sec; 14.5kg/kW (10.6kg/bhp); average fuel consumption 36.9mpg (10.4 1/100km).

AUDI 100 quattro 1991

It did not take Audi long to adapt the quattro four wheel drive system for uses other than in its high performance models. Give a normal front drive car four wheel drive, and its traction in all but the very worst conditions of ice and snow will be vastly improved. Accordingly Audi added quattro versions to many of its more mundane models, the 100 being a typical example.

From the drawing board stage a revised rear end of the floorpan was designed to accommodate the wishbone and struts needed for the quattro system. The Torsen torque-sensing centre drive automatically adjusted the amount of torque split front to rear, depending on road and driving conditions. In normal operation the split was 50:50, but the Torsen diff could vary this from 75:25 to 25:75 if one axle had more grip than the other. For the worst conditions, the rear drive could be locked manually, splitting the torque equally and preventing one rear wheel spinning while the other remained stationary. As with the two wheel drive 100 2.3E, disc brakes with ABS were standard. The 1991 100 quattro was available with 2.0/74 and 85kW, 2.6 and 2.8 V6, 110/128kW and 2.5 TDi/85kW engines.

BODY
Saloon; 4 doors; 5 seats; weight 1520kg (3344lb).

ENGINE
5 cylinders, in line; front; 82.5x86.4mm; 2309cc; compr 10.0:1; 98kW (133bhp) @ 5500rpm; 42.4kW/l (57.6bhp/l); 186Nm (19.9mkp) @ 4000rpm.

ENGINE STRUCTURE
Ohv; 2 valves per cylinder; ohc; one belt-driven camshaft; aluminium alloy cylinder head; cast iron cylinder block; 6 bearing crankshaft; Bosch KE-Jetronic; water cooled.

TRANSMISSION
4 wheel drive; 5 speed; hypoid bevel final drive; 4.111; optional 4 speed automatic; locking diff.

CHASSIS DETAILS
Unitary construction; independent front suspension, struts, coil springs; independent rear suspension, semi-trailing arms, lower wishbones, coil springs; anti-roll bar front and rear; telescopic shock absorbers; disc brakes, ventilated at front, dualbraking circuits; vacuum servo power assistance; ABS; rack and pinion steering; 80l (17.6 Imp gal) (21.1 US gal) fuel tank; tyres 205/60VR15, 6in rim width.

DIMENSIONS
Wheelbase 269cm (105.9in), front track 152.5cm (60in), rear track 152.5cm (60in), ground clearance 13cm (5.1in), turning circle 11.4m (37.4ft), overall length 479cm (188.58in), overall width 177.5cm (69.88in), overall height 143.0cm (56.3in).

PERFORMANCE
Maximum speed 125.8mph (202kph); 22.0mph (33.7kph) @ 1000rpm; 0-100kph (62mph) 10.4sec; 15.0kg/kW (11.1kg/bhp); average fuel consumption 28.1mpg (7.9 l/100km) Euromix.

AUDI Avus 6.0 litre W12 1992

In every way the Avus was one of the most spectacular design studies of its time, not only in its looks but in its engineering. The idea of using aluminium for both the tubular space frame chassis and bodywork had first been used by Audi on the mid-engined quattro Spyder (q.v.). On the larger Avus, also with a mid-engined layout, the looks were even more extreme. But it was the engine which attracted most attention.

In the motor industry in-line, horizontally-opposed 'boxer', V6, 8, 12 and even 16 cylinder engine layouts were accepted practice. But the idea of a W12 or 'broad arrow' layout, with three banks of four cylinders had never been used before in what could be, without stretching imagination too far, a production road car. The W12 layout had been used in the Napier Lion aero engine of the late 1920s and 1930s. A larger and supercharged version, developing 2350bhp, gave Sir Malcolm Campbell the world land speed record of over 246mph in 1931.

Twelve cylinders taking up the space normally occupied by four must have seemed a tempting proposition, and with the W12's short crankshaft

BODY
2 door coupe; 2 seats; weight 1250kg (2750lb).

ENGINE
12 cylinders in 2x60deg W; mid; 81.0x77.4mm, 5998cc; compr 10.5:1; 374kW (509bhp) @ 5800rpm; 64.4kW/l (84.9bhp/l); 540Nm (55.1mkp) @ 4000rpm.

ENGINE STRUCTURE
Ohv; 5 valves per cylinder; 2 chain driven ohc per bank; aluminium alloy cylinder head and block; 5 bearing crankshaft; Bosch injection; water cooled.

TRANSMISSION
4 wheel drive; 6 speed gearbox; hypoid bevel final drives; diff lock on rear axle.

CHASSIS DETAILS
Aluminium frame with aluminium bodypanels; independent front suspension, double wishbones, coil springs; independent rear suspension, double wishbones, coil springs;

telescopic shock absorbers; ventilated disc brakes; dual braking circuits; vacuum servo power assistance; ABS; rack and pinion steering; PAS; 225/60ZR20 tyres, 8.0in rim width.

DIMENSIONS
Wheelbase 280.0cm (110.2in), front track 170.0cm (66.9in), rear track 170.0cm (66.9in), length 442.5cm (174.2in),width 197.5cm (77.8in), height 117.5cm (46.3in).

PERFORMANCE
Maximum speed 211mph (340kph); acceleration 0-100kph (62mph) 3.0sec; 3.3kg/kW (2.5kg/bhp).

Right: Echoing 1930s Auto Unions racing on banked track at Berlin Avus circuit, with W12 engine seen in aluminium concept car, 1992 Avus showed Audi's technical mastery at Tokyo motor show.

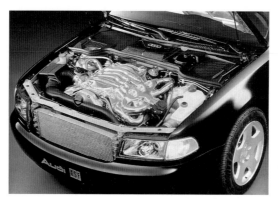

it promised smooth, almost turbine-like power. A W12 would also have been environmentally satisfactory. Engines over 4.5 litres need more than 10 cylinders to achieve the small dimensions necessary for ideal mixture burning, and the W12's 81 x 77.4 swept volume would have ensured good control of exhaust emissions. Alas the 6.0 litre, 60-valve W12 in the Avus named after the Berlin racetrack was only an engineering mock-up. However, tests on a prototype unit suggested a power output of around 374kW, giving the Avus a top speed in excess of 210mph.

Later Audi showed a new and smaller 4.8 litre of the W12 in the all-aluminium ASF prototype saloon, the forerunner of the V6 and V8-engined A8 models. This smaller engine had an output of 260kW, with a massive 480Nm torque, 425Nm of which was developed between 2700 and 5100rpm.

Like the mid-engined Avus, the front-engined ASF had quattro four-wheel drive and the Porsche developed manual-or-automatic Tiptronic transmission. The more powerful Avus had a projected 0-100kph time of around 3.0 sec, under half that of the ASF's 6.1sec.

AUDI 80 Avant 1992

In several ways the first small Audi estate car appeared to break the established rules. First, there was a step down into the load space, so that large, bulky objects could not easily be slid in or out. Also the deck at the rear was unusual in that it had a lot of hidden space underneath. The reason for this was that four wheel drive quattro versions were on the way, and the space was there to accommodate the rear diff and wishbone suspension.

Audi claimed estate car owners were typically younger and more intelligent than saloon car drivers, and aimed its sales pitch at active, married people in their thirties with enough disposable income. The Avant's load space was wider and more accommodating than the rival BMW Touring. The tailgate swung up high enough to avoid even the tallest drivers hitting the underside – and there was a handle on the inside to help close it.

The range included 1.6/74kW, 2.0 16V/101kW, 2.3/98kW and 1.9TD and TDi/55kW and 66kW engines, with quattro versions with the 2.6 V6/110kW, and 2.8 V6/128kW engines.

BODY
5 door estate; 5 seats; weight 1270kg (2794lb).

ENGINE
4 cylinders, in line; front; 82.5x92.8mm, 1984cc; compr 10.4:1; 86kW (115bhp) @ 5400rpm; 42.8kW/l (58.0bhp/l); 196Nm (16.8mkp) @ 3200rpm.

ENGINE STRUCTURE
Ohv; 2 valves per cylinder; one belt driven ohc; aluminium alloy cylinder head; cast iron cylinder block; 5 bearing crankshaft; electronic injection; water cooled.

TRANSMISSION
Front wheel drive; 5 speed gearbox, hypoid bevel final drive, 4.111; optional 4 speed automatic.

CHASSIS DETAILS
Unitary construction; independent front suspension, struts, coils; torsion beam rear suspension with trailing arms, coil springs; anti-roll bars front and rear; telescopic dampers, disc brakes, ventilated at front; dual braking circuits; vacuum servo power assistance, ABS; rack and pinion PAS; 66.0l (14.5 Imp gal) (17.4 US gal) fuel tank; 195/65HR15 tyres, 6in rim width.

DIMENSIONS
Wheelbase 261.0cm (102.8in), front track 145.0cm (57.1in), rear track 147.5cm (57.9in), ground clearance 13.3cm (5.2in), turning circle 11.2m (37.0ft), overall length 448.0cm (176.4in), overall width 169.5cm (66.5in), overall height 131.0cm (51.6).

PERFORMANCE
Maximum speed 115mph (186kph), 33.7kph (20.9mph) @ 1000rpm; 0-100kph (62mph) 12.2sec; 14.9kg/kW (11.0kg/bhp); average fuel consumption 32.8mpg (9.2 l/100km) Euromix.

AUDI Avant S4; 4.2 V8 1992

By 1992 a 4.2 litre version of the V8 engine brought a significant increase in performance. *Autocar* was not alone in concluding that if Audi's flagship had been launched with 4.2 litres and 206kW/280bhp instead of 3.6 litres and 184kW/250bhp it might have been more of a sales success. "The injection of steroids works wonders on a car that seems to have found performance and authority missing from the earlier version."

Audi built 6918 V8s in 1989, 4816 in 1990, but only 3000 or so in 1991, which was short of the expected 10,000 a year. Radical measures were required to stem the decline, and the quick way to more power was more engine capacity. This meant increasing the distance between the cylinder bores, which was crucial to the V8's economics. It went up from 88mm, which made it compatible with other engines in the group's inventory, to 90mm in the aluminium-silicon block. The stroke went up too, and the result was not only a more powerful engine but a smoother one right up to the electronically governed 150mph (250kph) which Germany's major car makers informally agreed was fast enough.

BODY
4 door saloon; 5 seats; weight 1710kg (3762lb).

ENGINE
V8 90deg; front, longitudinal; 84.5x93.0mm, 4172cc; compr 10.6:1; 206kW (280bhp) @ 5800rpm; 49kW/l (67bhp/l); 400Nm (40.8mkp) @ 4000rpm.

ENGINE STRUCTURE
Ohv; 4 valves per cylinder; 2 ohc per bank driven by belt and chain; aluminium cylinder heads; aluminium-silicon block; Bosch Motronic 2.4 fuel injection and electronic ignition; water cooled.

TRANSMISSION
4 wheel drive; 6 speed gearbox; optional 4 speed automatic; final drive; 3.78:1; electronic diff lock.

CHASSIS DETAILS
Unitary construction; i.f.s. by MacPherson struts, coil springs; i.r.s. struts trapezoidal links, anti-roll bars front and rear; telescopic dampers; ventilated discs brakes;

dual circuits; vacuum servos; ABS; rack and pinion PAS; 80.0l (17.6 Imp gal)(21.1 US gal) fuel tank; 215/60ZR15 tyres; 7.5in rims.

DIMENSIONS
Wheelbase 270.2cm (106.4in), front track 151.5cm (59.6in), rear 153.0cm (60.2in), ground clearance 19.5cm (7.7in), turning circle 11.5m (37.7ft), overall length 487.4cm (191.9in), width 181.4cm (71.4in), height 142.0cm (55.9in).

PERFORMANCE
Maximum speed 155mph (250kph), 41.2kph (25.6mph) @ 1000rpm; acceleration 0-100kph (62mph) 6.8sec (7.0sec automatic); 9.3kg/kW (14.9lb/bhp); average fuel cons. 20.8mpg (13.58 l/100km).

AUDI Avant S2 and RS2 1993

After being launched as a coupe in 1990, the turbocharged 169kW four wheel drive S2 had been joined by the Avant in 1992. The ultimate model was the RS2, developed jointly by Audi and Porsche. Based on the S2 Avant, the power of the 20-valve engine was increased to 232kW.

To handle this extra power Porsche engineering gave the RS2 the brakes from the 968 Club Sport, as well as the dampers, 17in cup alloy wheels and door mirrors. The transmission was similar to the S2, with a six-speed gearbox and a Torsen centre differential which automatically apportioned power between front and rear axles, depending on traction and road conditions.

The RS2 had the distinction of accelerating to 30mph in 1.5sec, 0.3sec less than the time taken by a McLaren F1. All RS models were built at Porsche's factory at Zuffenhausen near Stuttgart, because of the specialist work required. One result of the Porsche connection was that the RS2 remained exempt from the German manufacturers' agreement to limit top speed to 250kph.

RS2:

BODY
5 door estate; 5 seats; 1595kg (3509lb).

ENGINE
5 cylinders, in line; front; 81.0x86.4mm, 2226cc; compr 9.3:1; 232kW (315bhp) @ 6500rpm; 104kW/l (139bhp/l); 410Nm (40.8mpk) @ 2800-4900rpm.

ENGINE STRUCTURE
Ohv; 4 valves per cylinder; 2 belt driven ohc; aluminium cylinder head; cast iron block, 6 bearing crankshaft; Bosch Motronic 2.3 injection; KKK tubocharger with intercooler; water cooled.

TRANSMISSION
4 wheel drive; 6-speed gearbox; hypoid bevel final drives, 4.11; rear diff lock.

CHASSIS DETAILS
Steel unitary construction; independent front suspension, struts, coil springs; independent rear suspension, double wishbones; coil springs; anti-rolls bars front and rear; telescopic shock absorbers; disc brakes, ventilated at front; dual braking circuits, vacuum servo powered assistance; ABS; rack and pinion PAS; 64.0l (14.1 Imp gal) (16.9 US gal) fuel tank; 245/40ZR17 tyres, 7.0in rim width.

DIMENSIONS
Wheelbase 259.5cm (102.2in), front track 145.0cm (57.0in) rear track 147.5cm (58.1in), ground clearance 11.0cm (4.3in), turning circle 11.2m (37.0ft), overall length 451.0cm (177.6in), overall width 169.5cm (66.7in), overall height 137.5cm (54.1in).

PERFORMANCE
Maximum 163mph (262kph); 24.6mph (39.4kph) @ 1000rpm; acceleration 0-100kph (62mph) 5.8sec; 6.7kg/kW (4.9kg/bhp); average fuel consumption 25.9 mpg (10.9l/100km) Euromix.

AUDI S6 2.2 turbo 1994

Audi had been concentrating its high performance image on the smaller, more compact models such as the 80 and Coupe, distinguishing them with the initial S, with the 100 and its successor, the A6, left for the mainstream market – until the S6 was launched. A similar formula which had been used on the other S-range cars was repeated.

The 2226cc engine was a larger version of the classic 2144cc five-cylinder, but now with twin overhead camshafts, four valves per cylinder and the ubiquitous turbocharger, operating with an intercooler. A new rear suspension layout was used, with trapezoid links and MacPherson struts in place of the original quattro's lower wishbones layout. The drive through the quattro system was either by a six-speed manual gearbox or Audi's new four-speed automatic. This featured five automatically-selected drive programmes, adapting the shift pattern to the way in which the car was being driven. In addition, the S6 also had a traction control system. To complement the extra performance, the S6 had lowered suspension as well as super low-profile 225/50-section tyres on 7.5in Avus alloy rims.

BODY
4 door saloon, 5 door estate; 5 seats; 1650kg (3630lb).

ENGINE
5 cylinders, in line; front; 81.0x86.4mm, 2226cc; compr 9.3:1; 169kW (230bhp) @ 5900rpm; 75.9kW/l (103bhp/l); 350Nm (35.7mkp)@ 1950rpm.

ENGINE STRUCTURE
Ohv; 4 valves per cylinder; 2 belt driven ohc; aluminium alloy cylinder head; cast iron block; 6 bearing crankshaft; Bosch Motronic fuel injection, KKK turbocharger with intercooler; water cooled.

TRANSMISSION
Four wheel drive; 6 speed gearbox, 4 speed automatic with variable programme extra; Torsen centre diff, lockable rear diffs; hypoid bevel final drives, 4.111.

CHASSIS DETAILS
Steel unitary construction; independent front suspension, struts, coil springs; independent rear suspension, trapezium arm rear axle, struts; front anti-roll bar; ventilated discs front and rear; dual braking circuits; vacuum servo power assistance; ABS; rack and pinion; PAS; 80.0l (17.6 Imp gal) (21.1 US gal) fuel tank; 225/50ZR15 tyres, 7.5in rim width.

DIMENSIONS
Wheelbase 269.2 (106.0in), front track 156.3cm (61.5in), rear track 152.8cm (60.1in), 9.2cm (3.6in), overall length 479.7cm (188.9in); overall width180.4cm (71.0in), height 143.0cm (5.6in).

PERFORMANCE
Maximum speed 150mph (241kph); 24.0mph (38.6kph) @ 1000rpm; acceleration 0-100kph (62mph) 6.7sec; 9.8kg/kW (7.2kg/bhp); average fuel consumption 26.0mpg (10.9l/100km) Euromix.

AUDI A8 2.8 V6 1994

With light weight in mind, aluminium had long been used for bodies and major mechanical components. But its disadvantages were that it was more expensive and could not be easily pressed and welded into complex integral structures in the same way as sheet steel. Audi managed to solve this problem by developing a 'skeleton' in forged aluminium for the new A8, and then cladding it with relatively easily formed aluminium body panels. The result was a structure in which the framework took the strain.

The skeleton frame beneath the panels carried suspension loads, and because it was separate from the body, it also helped insulate occupants from road noise. This was important, because the aluminium body had less sound-deadening mass than one made in steel. The A8's low weight, just 1500kg, made it around 300kg less than its immediate rivals in the luxury car class, which helped compensate for the lower power output of the 2.8-litre V6 engine. The front-drive system was retained, but with a new suspension layout. By using a four-link layout, with the trapezoidal rear suspension redesigned, both ride and stability were improved.

BODY
4 door saloon; 5 seats, weight 1500kg (3300lb).

ENGINE
6 cylinders, in 90deg V; front; 82.5x86.4mm, 2771cc; compr 10.3:1; 128kW (174bhp) @ 5500rpm; 46.2kW/l (62.7bhp/l); 250Nm (22.5mkp) @ 3000rpm.

ENGINE STRUCTURE
Ohv; 2 valves per cylinder, 1 belt driven ohc per bank; aluminium alloy cylinder heads; cast iron block; 4 bearing crankshaft; Bosch Motronic injection; water cooled.

TRANSMISSION
Front wheel drive; 4 speed variable programme automatic; hypoid bevel final drive, 4.33; diff lock; traction control.

CHASSIS DETAILS
Aluminium subframes and bodywork; independent front suspension, four link, coil springs; independent rear suspension, trapezoid links, coil springs; dual braking circuits; vacuum servo power assistance; ABS; rack and pinion steering, PAS; 80.0l (17.6m Imp gal) (21.1 US gal) fuel tank; 225/60WR16 tyres; 7.5in rim width.

DIMENSIONS
Wheelbase 288.0cm (113.4in), front track159.1cm (62.6in), rear track 158.0cm (62.2in), ground clearance 15.6cm (6.1in), turning circle 12.3m (40.4ft), overall length 503.4cm (198.2in), overall width 197.3cm (77.7in), overall height 143.6cm (5.65in).

PERFORMANCE
Maximum speed 140mph (225kph); 23.6mph (38.0kph) @ 1000rpm; acceleration 0-100kph (62mph) 10.2sec; 11.7kg/kW (8.6kg/bhp); average fuel consumption 37.3mpg (7.6l/100km).

![Audi rings logo]

AUDI A8 2.8 V6 1994 (2)

The V6 iron-block engine from the 100 range was used, but in this version was only available with the four-speed automatic transmission, with the Dynamic Shift Program, which automatically adjusted the change pattern to suit the way the car was being driven. To back the transmission, the A8 had an electronically controlled diff lock and traction control.

The A8 was launched at the 1994 Geneva motor show to an audience that was on the whole respectful but cautious. There was a general expectation that the 2.8 litre option would be more popular than the 4.2. The aluminium technology received an unexpected accolade at the British motor show with an award for innovation presented by British Steel.

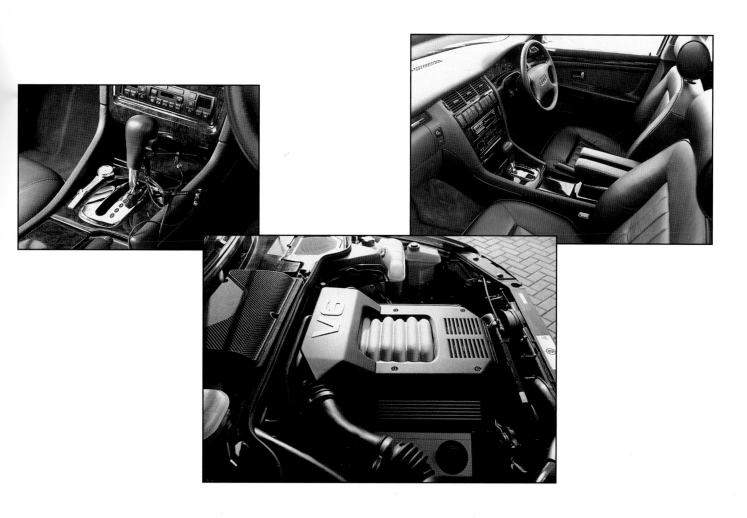

AUDI A8 4.2 V8 quattro 1994

The A8 made use of the V8 and driveline package in the a new all-aluminium body. The aluminium space frame, clad in aluminium, weighed about 40 per cent less than a steel body shell.

Unlike the front-drive A8 2.8 which had a four-speed automatic-only transmission, the 4.2 used the Porsche-designed Tiptronic system. This could be switched between manual gear changing, with just a flick forward or back for changing up or down, to fully automatic operation.

Refinements included double glazing and a heating system which responded to the direction and intensity of the sun. Despite its size and wide-section tyres, the A8 4.2 had a drag coefficient figure of just 0.29Cd. Included in the 4.2's standard specification was ABS with Electronic Brake-Force distribution control (EBV) which provided optimum braking to the wheel that needed it most.

Astonishingly, despite its technical innovations, the A8 failed to make Car of the Year in 1994, the vote going to the Ford Mondeo, VW Polo, and Vauxhall Omega, to the chagrin of many jurors.

BODY
4 door saloon; 5 seats; weight 1750kg (3856lb).

ENGINE
8 cylinders in 90deg V; front; 84.5x93.0mm, 4172cc; compr 10.8:1; 220kW (300bhp) @ 6000rpm; 52.7kW/l (71.9bhp/l); 400Nm (40.9mkp) @ 3300rpm.

ENGINE STRUCTURE
Ohv; 4 valves per cylinder; 2 belt and chain driven ohc per bank; aluminium alloy cylinder heads and block; 4 bearing crankshaft; Bosch Motronic injection; water cooled.

TRANSMISSION
4 wheel drive; 5 speed Tiptronic manual/automatic gearbox; diff lock, traction control; hypoid bevel final drive, 3.79.

CHASSIS DETAILS
Aluminium space frame; aluminium panels; independent front suspension, four links, coil springs; indendent rear suspension, trapezoid links, coil springs; anti-roll bars front and rear; telescopic shock absorbers; ventilated discs front and rear; dual braking circuits; vacuum servo power assistance, ABS; rack and pinion PAS; 90.0l (19.8 Imp gal) (23.8 US gal) fuel tank; 225/60WR16 tyres, 7.5in rim width.

DIMENSIONS
Wheelbase 288.0cm (113.4in), front track 159.1cm (62.6in), rear track 158.0cm (62.2in), ground clearance 15.6cm (6.1in), turning circle12.3m (40.4ft), overall length 503.4cm (198.2in), overall width 197.3cm (77.7in), overall height 143.6cm (5.7in).

PERFORMANCE
Maximum speed155mph (250kph); 27.5mph (44.3kph) @ 1000rpm; 0-100kph (62mph) 7.3sec; 7.6kg/kW (5.8kg/bhp); fuel consumption 24.1mpg (11.7l/100km) Euromix.

AUDI A4 1.6-litre; 1.8-litre, 1.8 turbo; V6; TDI 1994

In October 1994 the Audi range was renamed, 80 and 100 being dropped and replaced with A4 and A6. The A4 comprised 1.6, 1.8, 1.8 Turbo, 2.6 and 2.8 V6, and a 1.9TDI. The 1.8 petrol engine had five valves per cylinder; three inlets and two exhausts, with electronics managing the fuel injection and ignition. Knock sensors monitored the combustion process, and the solid-state high-tension ignition had no mechanical wearing parts.

There was not enough space for the five cylinder engine, so a turbocharger was provided for the 1.8, and a V6 offered as an alternative. The faster versions were provided with firmer dampers to make the handling more precise without becoming taut or uncomfortable. Audi's commitment to refinement was unwavering.

The turbo performance was swift and smooth. Its pulling power of 155lb ft was developed with great consistency between 1750rpm and 4600rpm. The 2.6 litre V6 also developed 150bhp at 5,500rpm, 200rpm short of the turbo and its torque peaked at 3500rpm. There was little difference in top speed but the more expensive V6 was smoother.

BODY
4 door saloon; 5 seats; weight 1235kg (2772lb), Turbo, 1285kg (2833lb) 2.6 V6.

ENGINE
4 cylinders, in line; front; 81 x 86.4mm, 1781cc; comp 9.5:1; 110kW (150bhp) @ 5700rpm; 61.7kW/l (84bhp/l); 210Nm (21.4mkp) @ 1750rpm;

ENGINE STRUCTURE
Ohv; 5 valves per cylinder; 2 belt driven ohc; aluminium cylinder head; cast iron block; 5 bearing crankshaft; Bosch multipoint injection; KKK-03 turbo 1.56bar; water cooled.

TRANSMISSION
Front wheel drive; 5 speed gearbox, 4 speed automatic option (V6 5 speed); quattro option; hypoid bevel final drive, 3.7, (V6 3.29).

CHASSIS DETAILS
Galvanised steel unitary construction; ifs, struts, four links, coil springs; rear torsion beam suspension with trailing arms, coil springs; anti-roll bars front and rear; telescopic dampers; disc brakes; dual braking circuits; vacuum servo power assistance, ABS; rack and pinion PAS; 62.0l (13.6 Imp gal) (16.3 US gal) fuel tank; 205/60R15W tyres; 6Jx15 wheels (7J alloy 2.8SE).

DIMENSIONS
Wheelbase 261.7cm (104.7in), front track 149.9cm (56.6in), rear track 147.9cm (59.2in), ground clearance 10.6cm (4.2in), turning circle 11.1m (36.4ft), length 447.9cm (179.2in), width 17.3.3cm (69.3in), height 141.5cm (56.6in).

PERFORMANCE
Maximum 127mph (220kph); 23.1mph (37.2kph); 0-100kph (62mph) 8.3sec; 11.2kg/kW (8.2kg/bhp); fuel consumption 30.1mpg (9.4l/100km).

AUDI A4 TDI, and TDI Avant 1995; A4 quattro Supertouring Champion 1996

The A4 was the first car to use a new 110bhp version of the VW group's 1.9 litre four cylinder direct injection diesel. Its important innovation was a variable geometry turbocharger which was quieter, faster, and more economical than its predecessor. The TDI appeared on the UK market in March 1996 in both saloon and Avant form. A testimony to the engine's flexibility was its imposing 166lb ft of torque between 1700 and 3000rpm which was the same as the impressive 2.6-litre petrol V6.

The Avant's detailing was praiseworthy with both an external release for the tailgate and an internal grab handle for pulling it shut. Audi was anxious to display its engineering competence even with small items such as the luggage space cover, and the tastefully chromed tie-down loops on the load-space floor. The capacity of the wide luggage space was 440 litres (14.8 cu ft).

A 90bhp TDI A4 was also available with a top speed of 114 mph (182kph). It took 13.3sec to reach 62mph on a 3.89:1 final drive ratio. Its power to weight ratio was 18.8kg/kW (13.8kg/bhp) against the 110bhp car's 16.1kg/kW (11.7 kg/bhp) and its average fuel consumption was some 2-3mpg worse than the 110.

A4 TDI:
BODY
4 door saloon/estate; 5 seats; weight 1240kg (2734lb).
ENGINE
4 cylinders; in line; front, longitudinal; 79.5 x 95.5mm, 1896cc; comp 19.5:1; 81kW (110bhp) @ 4150rpm; 42.7kW/l (58.1bhp/l); 225Nm (22.9mkp) @ 1700rpm; diesel.
ENGINE STRUCTURE
Ohv; 2 valves per cylinder; 1 belt driven ohc; aluminium cylinder head; cast iron block; 5 bearing crankshaft; Bosch VE injection; turbocharger, intercooler; electronic turbine management; water cooled.
TRANSMISSION
Front wheel drive; 5 speed gearbox, automatic option; hypoid bevel final drive, 3.889.
CHASSIS DETAILS
Galvanised steel unitary construction; ifs, struts, four links, coil springs; rear suspension, torsion beam, trailing arms, coil springs; anti-roll bars front and rear; double tube gas filled dampers; disc brakes; dual circuits; vacuum servo power assistance, ABS; rack and pinion PAS; 62.0l (13.6 Imp gal) (16.3 US gal) fuel tank; 195/65R15T tyres; 6J x 15 wheels (7J alloy TDI SE).
DIMENSIONS
Wheelbase 261.7cm (104.7in), front track 149.9cm (56.6in), rear track 147.9cm (59.2in), ground clearance 10.6cm (4.2in), turning circle 11.1m (36.4ft), length 447.9cm (179.2in), width 17.3.3cm (69.3in), height 141.5cm (56.6in).
PERFORMANCE
Maximum 122mph (196kph); 28.5mph (45.9kph); 0-100kph (62mph)11.3sec; 15.3kg/kW (11.3kg/bhp); 52.3mpg (5.4l/100km).

The metamorphosis of the 100 of 1982 into the 100 of 1990 and A6 of 1994 kept the main executive-class Audi near the top of the segment. It had a wide range of engines and transmissions, and both saloon and estate bodies survived with detail changes. Build quality and good paint finish ensured agreeable residual values, and by the mid-1990s Audi had recaptured both the romantic vision of August Horch and the excitement of Ferdinand Porsche's Auto Unions. The growing reputation of the four-ringed symbol on the world's most dramatic motor show concept cars, and confidence in the A8 as among the most technically advanced passenger cars ever, was at last turning Audi into a symbol of great prestige.

By 1995 the A6 was something of a veteran, even though still a car to aspire to. It was roomy, even if the gloomy interior failed to live up to the glamorous Audi image. It scored well for practicality, but its age showed up in a ride quality that had not kept pace with newer rivals. Perfectly adequate on smooth roads, it felt turbulent and wallowy over bumps and its lifeless steering was rated something less than best.

BODY
Saloon; 4 doors; 5 seats; weight 1420kg (3130lb).

ENGINE
4 cyl, in line; front; longitudinal; 81 x.86.4mm, 1781cc; compr 10.3:1; 92kW (125bhp) @ 5800rpm; 51.6kW/l (70.2bhp/l); 168Nm (17.1mkp) @ 3500rpm.

ENGINE STRUCTURE
Ohv; 5 valves per cylinder; 2 ohc; toothed belt driven; aluminium cylinder head; cast iron block; 5 bearing crankshaft; electronic multi-point fuel injection, overrun cutoff; electronic ignition; water cooled.

TRANSMISSION
Front wheel drive; 5 speed gearbox; optional electronic differential lock (std on SE); hypoid bevel final drive, 4.11:1.

CHASSIS DETAILS
Galvanised steel unitary construction; independent strut front suspension, coil springs, tubular anti-roll bar, double tube gas filled dampers; rear suspension torsion beam with trailing arms, Panhard rod, coil springs; anti-roll bar; disc brakes; servo and brake pressure regulator; rack & pinion PAS; 80l (17.6 Imp gal) (21.1 US gal) fuel tank; 195/65R15V tyres, 6Jx15 steel wheels, 7Jx15 alloy SE.

DIMENSIONS
Wheelbase 268.7cm (105.9in), front track 152.0cm (59.9in), rear track 152.4cm (60.0in), ground clearance 126cm (5in), turning circle 11.1m (36.4ft), overall length 479.7cm (189.0in), overall width 178.3cm (70.6in), overall height 142.0cm (55.9in).

PERFORMANCE
Maximum 122mph (198kph); 20.9mph (33.7kph) @ 1000rpm in top gear; 0-100kph (62mph) 11.3sec; 16kW/kg (11.8kg/bhp); average fuel consumption 30.4mpg (9.3l/100km).

AUDI A6 Saloon, Estate 2.6, 2.6SE, quattro 1995

Modern Audis never had space for a straight-six engine, but entry to the exclusive executive-car club demanded something better than a 4-cylinder. The result was Audi's long-standing devotion to the short 5-cylinder, followed by the development of a compact V6. The A6 embraced two versions of the V6, a 2.6 litre and 2.8 litre also used in the quattro four wheel drive variant.

The rationale behind a 90 degree V6 was obscure when it was introduced, since VW already had a narrow-angle 18 degree V6 for mounting transversely. Concern about uneven firing was settled with the first prototype in 1985. It had sufficient crankshaft stiffness, and by offsetting the big-end journals by 30 degrees a more regular firing sequence was accomplished. A better-balanced 60 degree V6 would have had smaller bearings with the 88mm bore spacings necessary to keep the engine compatible with others in the group. It could be built on the same production machinery as the V8, one of the practical reasons for the 90 degree angle. The crossflow aluminium cylinder heads were developed from the four-cylinder engines. The refined V6 had strong torque in the low and middle-speed ranges.

BODY
Saloon; 4 doors; 5 seats; 1450kg (3196lb).

ENGINE
6 cylinders, in Vee; front, longitudinal; 82.5 x 81.0, 2598cc; compr 10.0:1; 110kW (150bhp) @ 5750rpm; 42.3kW/l (57.6bhp/l); 225Nm (22.9mkp) @ 3500rpm.

ENGINE STRUCTURE
Ohv; 2 valves per cylinder; 1 ohc per bank; toothed belt driven; aluminium cylinder head; cast iron block; 4 bearing crankshaft; electronic multi-point fuel inj; electronic ignition with selective knock control; water cooled.

TRANSMISSION
Front wheel drive, permanent quattro option; 5 speed gearbox; hypoid bevel final drive, 3.889:1; automatic optional.

CHASSIS DETAILS
Galvanised steel unitary construction; i.f.s. using

MacPherson strut, coil springs, telescopic dampers; rear suspension, trapezium arm with transverse links, coil springs; telescopic dampers; disc brakes, servo and pressure regulator, ABS; rack and pinion PAS; 80l (17.6 Imp gal) (21.1 US gal) fuel tank; 205/60R15W tyres, 7J x 15 alloy wheels.

DIMENSIONS
Wheelbase 268.7cm (105.8in), front track 152.0cm (59.3in), rear track 152.4cm (59.4in), ground clearance 12.6cm (5.0in), turning circle 11.4m (37.4ft), length 479.7cm (187.1in), width 143.0cm (55.8in), height 152.0cm (59.3in).

PERFORMANCE
Max. speed 130mph (211kph); 22.00mph (35.4kph) @ 1000rpm in top gear; 0-100kph (62mph) 8.1sec; 13.1kW/kg (9.6kg/bhp); average fuel consumption 28.0mpg (10.08l/100km).

AUDI A6 Saloon, Estate 2.5TDI 140SE 1995

An Audi 100 (A6) diesel proved in a 1992 test run that at a constant 75mph it could cover 800 miles on a tankful of fuel. The combination of direct injection turbodiesel engine and six-speed gearbox gave outstanding economy of 64mpg (4.41l/100km) at 56mph (90kph).

Direct injection, in which the fuel was injected straight into a combustion chamber in the piston crowns, gave an Audi diesel up to 20 per cent better fuel economy than most contemporary engines. In an effort to reduce the harsh combustion noise of previous direct injection engines, Audi developed dual-spring injectors with five-hole nozzles to pump fuel progressively in two stages. This made the pressure increase less steep, reducing the characteristic diesel knock. Many owners could expect a fuel consumption of 40mpg (7.06l/100km) in everyday motoring, giving a touring range of over 700 miles between fill-ups from a car or roomy estate which rivalled many petrol-engined contemporaries for refinement and speed.

The TDI and V6 were introduced in 1992 and TDI 2.5 quattro in 1995.

BODY
Saloon; 4 doors; 5 seats; 1460kg (3219lb).

ENGINE
5 cylinders; in line; front, longitudinal; 81.0 x 95.5, 2461cc; compr 20.0:1; 103kW (140bhp) @ 4000rpm; 41.8kW/l (56.9bhp/l); 290Nm (29.6 mkp) @ 1900rpm.

ENGINE STRUCTURE
Ohv; 2 valves per cylinder; single ohc; toothed belt driven; aluminium cylinder head; cast iron block; 6 bearing crankshaft; diesel fuel injection, dual spring injectors, turbocharger with charge air cooler; water-cooled.

TRANSMISSION
Front wheel drive, quattro option; 6 speed gearbox; hypoid bevel final drive, 4.111:1; automatic optional.

CHASSIS DETAILS
Galvanised steel unitary construction; MacPherson strut, i.f.s., coil springs, telescopic dampers; rear suspension, trapezium arm with transverse links, coil springs, telescopic dampers; disc brakes, servo, pressure regulator and ABS; rack and pinion PAS; 80l (17.6 Imp gal) (21.1 US gal) fuel tank; 195/65R15V tyres, 6J x 15 alloy wheels (7JSE).

DIMENSIONS
Wheelbase 268.7cm (105.8in), front track 152.0cm (59.3in), rear track 152.4cm (59.4in), ground clearance 12.6cm (5.0in), turning circle 11.4m (37.4ft), length 479.7cm (187.1in), width 143.0cm (55.8in), height 152.0cm (59.3in).

PERFORMANCE
Max. speed 129mph (208kph); 32.97mph (53kph) @ 1000rpm in top gear; 0-100kph (62mph) 9.9sec; 14.2kW/kg (10.4kg/bhp); av. fuel cons. 40.9mpg (6.9l/100km).

2.5 five cylinder TDI

2,461 cc
85 kW (115 bhp at 4000rpm)
2x5 Nm at 1900rpm

Engine power kW		Engine Torque kW

Power
Torque
as per 80/1269 EG

Engine revs, rpm

The new hatchback was the first modern Audi with a transverse engine, and the first under a technical regime which required a reduction in the VW group's platforms from around 16 at the beginning of the 1990s to just four by the year 2000. Yet the directive for the A3 gave engineers plenty of scope, extending the concept of a *platform* beyond that of a mere chassis, making it more an abstract idea than a collection of components.

The A3 was designed to meet competition from the BMW Compact, effectively a truncated 3-series car, but this approach was rejected by Martin Freudenhagen, technical co-ordinator of the A-class (A3 and VW Golf family) models. "We cut the back off an A4 and turned it into a three door hatchback," he said, "but rejected it. A smaller Audi needed to be a totally new car."

Audi finished the first design study in the autumn of 1992 and the car was passed for production in the spring of 1993. The A3 range was introduced with three trim levels and a choice of four engines, 1.6 101bhp, 1.8 125bhp, turbocharged 1.8T 150bhp, and a 110bhp Tdi imported to the UK in 1997. Among the trim options was Alcantara, a suede-like material.

BODY
Hatchback; 3 doors; 4 seats; 1090kg (2403lb).

ENGINE
4 cylinders, in line; front, transverse; 81.0 x 77.4mm, 1595cc; compr 10.3:1; 74kW (101bhp) @ 5600rpm; 46.39kW/l (63.32bhp/l); 145Nm (14.5 mkp) @ 3800rpm.

ENGINE STRUCTURE
Ohv; 2 valves per cylinder; single ohc, toothed belt; hydraulic tappets; aluminium cylinder head; cast iron block; 5 bearing crankshaft; electronic multi-point fuel injection; electronic ignition with knock control; water-cooled;

TRANSMISSION
Fwd; 5 speed gearbox; final drive 4.250.

CHASSIS DETAILS
Galvanised steel unitary construction; ifs, Macpherson strut coil springs, bottom wishbones, tubular transverse anti-roll bar; torsion-beam rear axle and anti-roll bar; disc brakes front and rear with servo, brake pressure regulator, and ABS; rack and pinion, PAS; 55.0 l (12.01 Imp gal) (14.51 US gal) fuel tank; 195/65 R15V tyres, 6Jx15 alloy wheels.

DIMENSIONS
Wheelbase 251.2cm (98.9in), front track 151.3cm (59.5in), rear track 149.5cm (58.8in), ground clearance 13.0cm (5.1in), turning circle 10.9ft (35.8ft), length 415.2cm (163.4in), width 173.5cm (68.3in), height 142.3cm (56.0in).

PERFORMANCE
Maximum speed 116mph (188kph), 19.9 mph (31.9kph) @ 1000rpm in top gear; 0-100kph (62mph) 11.3sec; 14.7kg/kW (23.7lb/bhp); average fuel consumption 37.2mpg (7.59l/100km).

AUDI A3 1.8, 1.8 Sport, 1.8SE 1996

Five-valve technology and the transverse mounting of the engine were among the A3's innovations. A redesign of the iron cylinder block reduced its weight by 13kg and its width by 30mm. Turning it through 90 degrees entailed redesigning the inlet manifold and incorporating it in a new Audi nose-cone. Crash-protection measures provided comparable occupant safety with larger Audis.

The A3 had plenty of storage spaces and a lighter, airier appearance than either of its chief rivals, the BMW Compact and the Volkswagen Golf GTi. The 2.0 litre Golf was faster off the mark than the mid-range 1.8 but needed high revs to get the best out of it. The rear-drive 1.9 BMW was more powerful, but the Audi gained the vote of road testers on account of its superior handling and smooth ride. It earnt criticism for meagre legroom in the back.

The Sport and SE designations were largely matters of trim and equipment, not speed. The three variants were known as Attraction, Ambition, and Ambiente, each with their own style of alloy wheels and distinctive colours. Five valve technology (opposite) shows triple inlet valves, two exhausts.

BODY
Hatchback; 3 doors; 4 seats; 1140kg (2513lb).

ENGINE
4 cylinders, in line; front, transverse; 81.0 x.86.4, 1781cc; compr 10.3:1; 92kW (125bhp) @ 6000rpm; 51.65W/l (69.28bhp/l); 173.0Nm (17.6 mkp) @ 4100rpm.

ENGINE STRUCTURE
Ohv; 5 valves per cylinder 3 inlet 2 exhaust; 2ohc; toothed belt, linked by chain; hydraulic tappets; aluminium cylinder head; cast iron block; 5 bearing crankshaft; electronic multi-point fuel injection, overrun cut-off; electronic ignition with knock control; water cooled; three-way catalytic converter.

TRANSMISSION
Fwd; 5 speed gearbox; 0.837 fifth; 4.235:1 final drive.

CHASSIS DETAILS
Galvanised steel unitary construction; i.f.s., Macpherson strut coil springs, bottom wishbones, tubular anti-roll bar; torsion-beam rear axle and anti-roll bar; disc brakes with servo, brake pressure regulator, and ABS standard; rack and pinion PAS; 55.0 l (12.01 Imp gal) (14.51 US gal) fuel tank; 195/65 R15V tyres, 6J x 15 alloy wheels.

DIMENSIONS
Wheelbase 251.2cm (98.9in), front track 151.3cm (59.5in), rear track 149.5cm (58.8in), ground clearance 13.0cm (5.1in), turning circle 10.9m (35.8ft), length 415.2cm (163.4in), width 173.5cm (68.3in), height 142.3cm (56.0in).

PERFORMANCE
Max speed 126mph (202kph); 23.3mph (37.45kph) @ 1,000rpm; 0-100kph (62mph) 10.1sec; 12kg/kw (20lb/bhp); average fuel consumption 37.6mpg (7.51l/100km).

Above: Five-valve
technology shows
triple inlet valves,
two exhausts.

AUDI A3 1.8T Sport 1996

The turbo version of the A3 was hailed as evidence that Audi had not forgotten its heritage of exciting and dynamic cars. The prospect of a four wheel drive version to come convinced reviewers that the turbocharged A3 would be a satisfactory platform on which to build. The A3 seemed well-conceived from the outset and not so much trimmed down to a budget as built up to an ideal.

The A3 1.8T Sport had the same turbocharged 20-valve 110kw engine as the A4 1.8T, and since the A3 was smaller and lighter, its agile performance was not unexpected. The only other manufacturer with five valves per cylinder in a production engine was Ferrari with the F355, with the same aim of providing a large valve area with small camshaft loads and high specific power output. The turbo furnished the engine with a long flat torque curve as opposed to a steep increase in power. Body styling for the A3 featured Audi's customary high waistline, burly C-pillars, and large body-coloured bumpers. The 1.8T's Sport lowered and stiffened suspension was available as an option throughout the A3 range.

BODY
Hatchback; 3 doors; 4 seats; 1145kg (2524lb).

ENGINE
4 cylinders, in line; front; transverse; 81.0 x.86.4, 1781cc; compr 9.5:1; 110kW (150bhp) @ 5700rpm; 61.76kW/l (84.22bhp/l); 210Nm (21.4 mkp) @ 1750-4600rpm.

ENGINE STRUCTURE
Ohv; 5 valves per cylinder, 3 inlet 2 exhaust; 2ohc, toothed belt linked by chain, hydraulic tappets; aluminium cylinder head; cast iron block; 5 bearing crankshaft; electronic multi-point fuel injection, overrun cut-off; turbocharger; electronic ignition with knock control; water cooled; three-way catalytic converter.

TRANSMISSION
Fwd; 5 speed gearbox; 0.837 fifth; 3.684:1 final drive.

CHASSIS DETAILS
Galvanised steel unitary construction; i.f.s., Macpherson strut coil springs, bottom wishbones, tubular anti-roll bar; torsion-beam rear axle and anti-roll bar; disc brakes with servo, brake pressure regulator, and ABS standard; rack and pinion PAS; 55.0 l (12.01 Imp gal) (14.51 US gal) fuel tank; 205/55 R15W tyres, 7Jx16 alloy wheels.

DIMENSIONS
Wheelbase 251.2cm (98.9in); front track 151.3cm (59.5in), rear track 149.5cm (58.8in), ground clearance 13.0cm (5.1in), turning circle 10.9m (35.8ft), length 415.2cm (163.4in), width 173.5cm (68.3in), height 142.3cm (56.0in).

PERFORMANCE
Max.speed 135mph (217kph); 23.7mph (38.1kph) @ 1000rpm; 0-100kph (62mph) 8.1sec; 10.4kg/kw (16.8lb/bhp); average fuel consumption 36.7mpg (7.7l/100km).

AUDI S6 4.2 V8 (290bhp and 326bhp) 1996

The sporting A6 with the 2.2 litre 5 cylinder turbocharged engine launched in 1991, was augmented in November 1992 by a V8. It was redesignated and enhanced in 1994, and in 1995 became available with either a 213kW (290bhp) or 240kW (325bhp) version of the 32-valve engine.

Wide tyres, lowered suspension, and external cosmetic differences such as the flared wheel arches and 6-spoke alloy wheels, made the S6 a worthy competitor for the fastest autobahn traffic. Yet it could cruise at 80mph with the engine running at a leisurely 3250rpm. The car's quietness and refinement were sullied slightly by a level of wind noise that, by the middle 1990s, was thought loud.

The other main shortcoming of the A6 was the turbulent ride, a result of the lowered and stiffened suspension, and wide low-profile tyres. Yet it was a small penalty to pay for the immense cornering capacity and matchless traction which gave the S6 the performance and handling of a racing car along with the air-conditioned and leather-upholstered comfort of a classy executive saloon or estate car.

BODY
4 door saloon, 5 seats; weight 1695kg (Avant 1745kg).

ENGINE
8 cylinder, 90 degree V; front, longitudinal; 84.5mm x 93mm; 4172cc; comp 10.8:1; 213kW (290bhp) 5800rpm, 51kW/l (69.4bhp/l); 400Nm (40.8mkp) at 4000rpm.

ENGINE STRUCTURE
Ohv; twin ohc per bank; 4 valves per cylinder; Camshafts driven by belt and linked by chain; aluminium heads and block; 5 bearing crankshaft; electronic fuel injection; engine management by Bosch M5 4.1; water cooled.

TRANSMISSION
Permanent quattro 4 wheel drive, torsen centre differential, electronic traction control; 6 speed gearbox; 4.11 final drive; optional automatic, 3.78:1 final drive.

CHASSIS DETAILS
Galvanised steel unitary construction; ifs 4-link in sub-frame, upper & lower wishbones, anti-roll bar; torsion crank rear, anti-roll bar, gas-pressure dampers; disc brakes, ventilated at front; dual diagonal circuits, servo; R & P, PAS; 80l (17.59Imp gal) (21.11US gal)fuel tank; tyres 225/50ZR 16V; 7J rims.

DIMENSIONS
Wheelbase 269cm (105.9in); front track 156cm (61.4in); rear track 152.3cm (59.96in); ground clearance 10cm (4.0in); turning circle 11.4m (37.4ft); length 480cm (189in); width 180cm (70.9in); height 143cm (56.3)in.

PERFORMANCE
Max speed 154.7mph (249 kph); 25.6mph (41.2kph) @ 1000rpm in 6th gear; 0-62mph 5.9secs; 8kg/kW (5.8kg/bhp); fuel consumption 10.8/22.5l/100km (26.1/12.5mpg).

AUDI S8 1997

Meeting a demand for a swifter version of the A8, the S8 of February 1996 enabled Audi drivers to go even faster on the autobahn. The gains were not great – 1.8sec off the 0 to 60mph time – and the maximum speed agreed by industry-wide diktat was unchanged at 250kph. But acceleration in sixth was swifter, and by dropping down to fifth or fourth gear this substantial saloon could keep up with almost anything without losing its quietness or refinement.

The additional power was achieved by raising the compression ratio from 10.8 to 11.6:1, an inlet camshaft giving high and longer valve lift, uprating the exhaust systems, and revising the engine management system. UK market cars (Audi expected to sell around 60 a year) equipped with Tiptronic five-speed gearboxes were slightly slower than the German six-speeders. Ride height was 20mm lower, springs and torsion bars stiffer, making the already firm ride more resolute than ever.

Identification features included 18in Avus style six-spoke aluminium wheels, polished-aluminium wing mirrors and a different grille with stronger vertical bars. Technical sophistication was matched by high price.

BODY
Saloon; 4 doors; 5 seats; weight 1720kg (3784lb).

ENGINE
V8; 90 deg; front, longitudinal; 84.5mm x 93mm; 4172cc; compr 11.6:1; 250kW (340bhp) at 6600rpm; 59.9kW/l (81.5bhp/l): 410Nm (41.8mkp) at 3500rpm.

ENGINE STRUCTURE
Ohv; twin ohc per bank; 4 valves per cylinder; Camshafts driven by belt and linked by chain; aluminium heads and block; 5 bearing crankshaft; electronic fuel injection; engine management by Bosch M5 4.1; water cooled.

TRANSMISSION
Quattro permanent four wheel drive; central torsen diff; electronic wheelspin limiter; six speed manual gearbox; final drive 4.11:1

CHASSIS DETAILS
Aluminium space frame; aluminium panels; independent front suspension, four links, coil springs; independent rear suspension, trapezoid links, coil springs; anti-roll bars front and rear; dual circuits, vacuum servo power assistance, ABS; PAS rack and pinion; 90.0l (19.8 Imp gal)(23.8 US gal) fuel tank; 245/45ZR18 tyres on 8J rims.

DIMENSIONS
Wheelbase 288cm (113.4in); front track 159.1cm (62.6in), rear track 158cm (62.2in); ground clearance 15.6cm (6.1in); turning circle 12.3m (40.4ft); length 503.4cm (198.2in), width 197.3cm (77.7in), height 142cm (55.9in).

PERFORMANCE
Max speed 155mph (250kph); 25.6mph (41.2kph) @ 1000rpm; 0-100kph (62mph) 5.5sec; 6.9kg/kW (5.1kg/bhp); fuel cons 10.5/20.8 l/100km (27/13.6mpg).

Introduced in 1991 with a 5 cylinder engine, the Cabriolet was offered the following year with the 174bhp 2.8 V6 and by 1997 was also available with a four cylinder 1.8 litre 5-valve engine from the A4. The choice then extended to the 2.6 litre V6 (24bhp less than the 2.8), and a 1.9 litre 90bhp turbodiesel.

The manual hood was easy to operate. A T-handle lowered the electric windows slightly, then the driver pushed the front of the hood upwards, automatically tilting up the spring-loaded section at the back. A button released the metal cover of the rear compartment into which the hood folded itself neatly.

The compartment reduced the width and depth of the rear seat, and also invaded the luggage space. Airflow over the open four-seater was smooth, the sloping windscreen directing the draught over the front occupants' heads, although there was some turbulence in the rear. Leak proof and draught proof, with negligible wind roar, the Audi's soft-top was well insulated.

The car's principal competitors were Saab and BMW, and from 1993 it was equipped with an electric hood which opened or closed inside 30 seconds.

BODY
Open convertible; 2 doors; 4 seats; weight 1455kg (3201lb).

ENGINE
V6; 90deg; front, longitudinal; 82.5mm x 81mm; 2598cc; compr 10:1; 110kW (150bhp) @ 5500rpm; 42.3kW/l (57.6bhp/l); 225Nm (22.9mkp) at 3500rpm.

ENGINE STRUCTURE
1 ohc per bank, belt driven; 2 valves per cylinder; aluminium cylinder head; cast iron block; 4 bearing crankshaft; electronic fuel injection; Bosch Motronic ignition; water cooled.

TRANSMISSION
Front wheel drive; 5 speed manual gearbox; 3.889:1 final drive; optional automatic 4.29:1.

CHASSIS DETAILS
Galvanised steel unitary construction, reinforced; independent front suspension by struts, coil springs; rear suspension torsion beam axle, struts, coil springs, transverse stabiliser; anti-roll bars front and back; telescopic dampers; disc brakes front and rear, dual circuits, vacuum servo power assistance, ABS, PAS rack and pinion; 70l (15.4 Imp gal) (18.5US gal) fuel tank; tyres 205/60 VR 15 tyres on 7J rims.

DIMENSIONS
Wheelbase 255.5cm (100.6in), front track 145.5cm (57.3in), rear track 144.5cm (56.9in), ground clearance 14cm (5.5in); turning circle 11.1m (36.6ft); overall length 436.5cm (171.9in), overall width 171.5cm (67.5in), overall height 138cm (54.3in).

PERFORMANCE
Maximum speed 130mph (209kph); 22.0mph (35.4kph) @ 1000rpm; 0-100kph (62mph) 10.2sec; 13.2kg/kW (9.7kg/bhp); average fuel consumption 35.3/19mpg (8/14.9 l/100km).

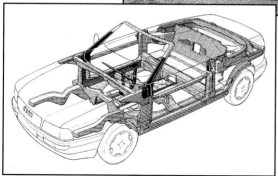

AUDI A6 1.8T 20v and 1.8T quattro 1997

The new A6, revealed at the Geneva motor show in the spring of 1997, showed an evolutionary mid-range Audi within the group's declared policy of basing cars on common concepts uninhibited by the old constraints of conventional 'platform' technology. The emphasis of the new range of cars was strongly on individuality, the distinctive nature of the Audi brand-name, and its strong sporting character. It was also aimed squarely at the BMW 5-series.

Four power units were available, a turbocharged 1.8 litre, 4 cylinder 110kW/150bhp, two V6s with 5-valve heads (2.4 litre 121kW/165bhp and 2.8 litre 142kW/193bhp) and a 1.9 litre direct-injection diesel with a VTG turbocharger. The traditional longitudinal engine location and front wheel drive were retained, and manual, automatic, or quattro transmissions.

The smooth A6 body style continued the elliptical arch style of the A4. The new A6 was 73mm longer between the wheels compared with the car it replaced, and it had shorter front and rear overhangs and wider tracks, demonstrating in effect that it was not merely a re-jigged version of the new VW Passat.

BODY
Saloon; 4 door; 5 seat; weight 1355kg (2987lb), 1450kg (3197lb) 4wd quattro.

ENGINE
4 cylinder; in-line, front, longitudinal; 81.0 x 86.4mm; 1781cc; compr 9.5:1; 110kW (150bhp) @ 5700rpm; 61.7kW/l (84bhp/l); 210Nm (21.4mkp) @ 1750-4600rpm.

ENGINE STRUCTURE
2ohc; belt-driven; hydraulic tappets; 5 valves; aluminium head; 5 bearing crankshaft; turbocharger, with intercooler; Bosch Motronic; individual ignition coils; knock, boost-pressure control; water cooled.

TRANSMISSION
Fwd; 5 speed gearbox; 3.7:1 final drive; optional automatic; optional quattro four wheel drive with torsen centre diff 3.889:1.

CHASSIS DETAILS
Galvanised steel unitary construction; i.f.s., 4-link in sub-frame, upper and lower wishbones, anti-roll bar; torsion crank rear, anti-roll bar, gas-pressure dampers; disc brakes, ventilated at front; dual diagonal circuits, servo; rack and pinion PAS; 70l (15.4 Imp gal) (18.5 US gal) fuel tank; tyres 195/65 R15V tyres, 6in rims.

DIMENSIONS
Wheelbase 276cm (108.6in), 275.9cm quattro (108.62in); front track 154cm (60.6in); rear track 156.9cm (61.77in); clearance 12cm (4.72in); turning circle 11.7m (38.39ft); length 479.6cm (188.8in); width 181cm (71.26in); height 145.3cm (57.2in).

PERFORMANCE
Maximum 135mph (217kph); 23.1mph (37.2kph) @ 1000rpm in top gear; 0-100kph (62mph) 9.4sec; 12.3kg/kW (9.0kg/bhp); fuel cons 6.6-10.7l/100km (26-42mpg).

AUDI A6 2.4 and 2.8 V-6 1997

The carefully-engineered A6 evolved from many of the A4's initiatives. It used the A4's ingenious multi-link front suspension and a torsion beam rear axle with coil spring and damper struts.

One of the A6's important innovations was to mount the suspension on sound-absorbing sub-frames, an elegantly detailed way of ensuring the refinement that customers in the executive sector increasingly demanded.

2.4:

BODY

Saloon; 4 door; 5 seat; 1400kg (3086lb), 1450kg (3197lb) auto, 1495kg (3296lb) quattro, 1555kg (3428lb) auto quattro.

ENGINE

6-cylinders, in V; front, longitudinal; 81mm x 77.4mm; 2393cc; compr 10:1; 121kW (165bhp) @ 6000rpm; 50.6kW/l (68.7bhp/l); 230Nm (23.4mkp)@ 3200rpm.

ENGINE STRUCTURE

2ohc per bank, belt and chain-driven; hydraulic tappets; 5 valves; aluminium head; 4 bearing crank; Bosch Motronic; individual ignition coils; knock control; water cooled.

TRANSMISSION

Fwd; 5 speed gearbox; 3.889:1 final drive; optional ZF 5-speed automatic 2.727:1; optional quattro with torsen centre diff, 4.1113:1; automatic quattro 3.3:1

CHASSIS DETAILS

Galvanised steel; ifs 4-link in sub-frame, upper and lower wishbones, anti-roll bar; torsion crank rear, anti-roll bar, gas-pressure dampers; disc brakes, ventilated at front; dual diagonal circuits, servo; rack and pinion PAS; 70l (15.4 Imp gal) (18.5 US gal) fuel tank; tyres 195/65 R 15V, 6in rims.

DIMENSIONS

Wheelbase 276cm (108.6in), 275.9cm quattro (108.6in); front track 154cm (60.6in); rear track 156.9cm (61.77in); ground clearance 12cm (4.72in); turning circle 11.7m (38.4ft); length 479.6cm (188.8in); width 181cm (71.3in); height 145.3cm (57.2in).

PERFORMANCE

Max 138mph (222kph); 22.5mph (36.2kph) @ 1000rpm; 0-100kph (62mph) 9.1sec; 11.6kg/kW (8.5kg/bhp); 7.4-13.7l/100km (20.6-38.2mpg).

There were quattro versions throughout the range, with rear suspension by double wishbones, a smaller boot owing to the space it took up, and an increase in weight. The quattro transmission shaved about 1mph off the front-drive car's top speed and added 0.2sec to the time taken to reach 62mph. The 2.8 engine measured 82.5mm bore x 86.4mm stroke

giving a swept volume of 2771cc. It was slightly heavier at 1420kg (3130lb), had a top speed of 146mph (236kph), and reached 62mph in 8.1sec.

The years since the introduction of the ground-breaking Audi 100 of 1982 with its 0.30 coefficient of drag saw its rivals catch up, and Audi scarcely improving its position, the A6 achieving a satisfactory and quiet 0.28.

Cutaway drawings show
(p404) safety systems
in the doors and (p406)
airbags and bumper
structures.
Right: 5-valve
technology in the
2.4-litre V6 engine.

AUDI A6 1.9 turbodiesel direct injection 1997

The A6 turbodiesel showed that it was possible to obtain 61mpg (4.6l/100km) in town and nearly 50mpg (5.7l/100lm) overall fuel consumption from an upper-segment executive car. With 81kW (110bhp) and satisfactory pulling power, a modern turbocharged diesel engine was capable of providing a roomy, well equipped saloon with a perfectly respectable performance.

Audi described its graphical display of engine pull as being like a table mountain, rising steeply at low engine speeds to provide swift acceleration where it was needed most, at between 60 to 120kph (37 to 75mph) which it covered in 16.5sec. A development of many years of diesel technology produced a turbocharger with variable turbine geometry (VTG) which adjusted the turbo boost from 2,000rpm, providing one of the world's most refined and quiet diesel cars.

The A6, like the A3, broke new ground in offering three trim levels, Advance (natural wood, warm and soft fabrics), Ambition (expressive of lifestyle, structured materials and muted colours), and Ambiente (Mediterranean, supple materials, exclusive and elegant), all equal in quality and price.

BODY
Estate; 5 door; 5 seat; weight 1430kg (3152lb).

ENGINE
4 cylinder; in-line, front, longitudinal; 79.5 x 95.5mm; 1896cc; compr 19.5:1; 81kW (110bhp) @ 4150rpm; 42.7kW/l (58bhp/l); 235Nm (24mkp) @ 1900rpm.

ENGINE STRUCTURE
Single ohc; toothed-belt-driven; 2 valves per cylinder; aluminium cylinder head; 5 bearing crankshaft; turbocharger with intercooler; Bosch VP37 electronic distributor pump, direct injection VTG turbocharger with intercooler; water-cooled.

TRANSMISSION
Front wheel drive; 5-speed gearbox; 3.7:1 final drive; optional automatic; 3.39:1.

CHASSIS DETAILS
Galvanised steel unitary construction; ifs, 4-link in sub-frame, upper and lower wishbones, anti-roll bar; torsion crank rear, anti-roll bar, gas-pressure dampers; disc brakes, ventilated at front; dual diagonal circuits, servo; rack and pinion PAS; 70l (15.4 Imp gal) (18.5 US gal) fuel tank; tyres 195/65 R 15V, 6in rims.

DIMENSIONS
Wheelbase 276cm (108.6in); front track 154cm (60.6in); rear track 156.9cm (61.77in); ground clearance 12cm (4.72in); turning circle 11.7m (38.39ft); length 479.6cm (188.8in); width 181cm (71.26in); height 145.3cm (57.2in).

PERFORMANCE
Max speed 120mph (194kph); 28.5mph (45.9kph) @ 1000rpm in top gear; 0-100kph (62mph) 12.3sec; 17.7kg/kW (13kg/bhp); fuel consumption 5.2-8.5l/100km (33.2-54.3mpg).

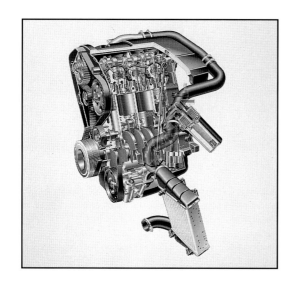

Right: Direct injection (left) sprays fine mist of fuel into inlet tract with air. Swirl chamber of indirect injection (right) pre-mixes fuel and air before combustion.

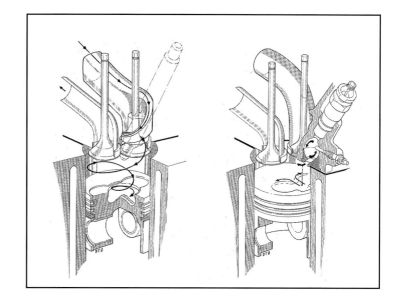

The AUDI TT and TTS Coupe and Roadster 1998

Audi revived the names of NSU's TT and TTS of the 1960s for the title of a new series of sports cars introduced as concepts at the Frankfurt and Tokyo motor shows of 1995, based on the floor-pan of the A3 with an uprated 1.8 turbo engine transversely mounted. By the time production plans were announced for Hungary, the order book was over-subscribed.

The radical appearance of the TT and TTS led to some caution at Audi. The severe geometric ellipses, the designers alleged, were a product of the Bauhaus, the great 1930s' school of art and style headed by Walter Gropius. Yet they also had the air of an Auto Union racing car from the free-flowing hand of Ferdinand Porsche. They even managed a tribute to the original rally Quattro and German sports cars of the 1950s with their sparse interiors.

Production TTs had the latest safety equipment including two airbags. Few alterations were made to the radical shape conceived in Audi's Californian design studio by Freeman Thomas. A choice of 1.8 litre engines was given; 225bhp with two intercoolers giving a top speed of 243kph, or 180bhp giving 225kph.

BODY
Sports coupe; 2 doors; 2 seats; weight 1220kg (2684lb).

ENGINE
4 cyl, in line; front; transverse; 81.0 x.86.4mm, 1781cc; compr 9.5:1; 168kW (225bhp) [134kW (180bhp)] @ 5700rpm; 94.3kW/l (126bhp/l) [75.4kW/l (102bhp/l)]; 280Nm (28.6mkp) @ 2220-5500rpm [235Nm (24mkp) @ 1950/4700rpm].

ENGINE STRUCTURE
Ohv; 5 valves per cyl, 3 inlet 2 exhaust; 2 toothed belt ohc linked by chain, hydraulic tappets; aluminium cyl head, cast iron block; 5 bearing crank; electronic multi-point fuel inj; turbocharger, 2 intercoolers; electronic ignition; 3-way catalytic converter.

TRANSMISSION
4wd, permanent; 6 speed; multi-plate clutch; electr tract control.

CHASSIS DETAILS
Galvanised steel unitary structure, aluminium lids, doors; ifs, Macpherson strut coil spring, bottom wishbones, tubular anti-roll bar; irs with parallelogram links, coil springs; anti-roll bar; disc brakes with servo, rear ventilated discs, electronic brake distribution EBD, ABS; 2 circuits, rack and pinion PAS; 66l (13 Imp gal) (14.5 US gal) fuel tank; 225/45 ZR17 tyres, 7.5J x 17 alloy wheels.

DIMENSIONS
Wheelbase 251.2cm (98.9in), front track 151.3cm (59.5in), rear 149.5cm (58.8in), ground clearance 13cm (5.1in), turning circle 10.9m (35.8ft), length 404cm (160in), width 186cm (73.2in), height 135cm (53in).

PERFORMANCE
Max 243kph (151mph) [225kph (140mph)]; 0-100kph (62mph) 6.4 [7.4]sec; 7.3kg/kW (5.4kg/bhp) [9.1kg/kW (6.8kg/bhp)]; 34mpg (8.3l/100km).

AUDI Al$_2$ design study 1997

Once the A8 was safely on the road, Audi set about determining how the Audi Space Frame (ASF) could be applied to a small car built in large numbers. The result was Al$_2$; Al the chemical symbol for Aluminium, 2 representing the second generation of the ASF principle. Two designs were studied, one with a fixed roof and 5 doors for the 1997 Frankfurt motor show, and one with 3 doors and a removable rear hatch, for the Tokyo motor show two months later.

Compact and upright, providing minimum space for four seated adults, one of Al$_2$'s aims was to show it could bring 3l/100km (94mpg) within sight. Its target weight was around 750kg (1653lb), 30% less than an Audi A3 and 15% less than a VW Polo. Large areas of heavy glass were avoided, and the engine was an ingenious 3-cylinder version of the A3, equipped with a 5-valve cylinder head and direct petrol injection (FDI for Fuel Direct Injection). FDI challenged the established strict stoichiometric 14.7:1 air/fuel ratios of conventional catalytic engines, injecting fuel at pressures of 100bar instead of the customary 3-4bar and varying the mixture according to speed and load.

BODY
Saloon; 3/5 doors; 4 seats; 810kg (1786lb).

ENGINE
3 cylinders; in line; front, transverse; 81.0 x 77.4, 1196cc; compr 11.5:1; 55kW (75bhp) @ 5500rpm; 46kW/l (62.7bhp/l); 115Nm (11.7mkg) @ 3000rpm.

ENGINE STRUCTURE
5 valves per cylinder; aluminium cylinder crankcase; Fuel Direct Injection FDI; water-cooled.

TRANSMISSION
Front wheel drive; automated 5 speed gearbox; hydraulically operated single dry plate clutch.

CHASSIS DETAILS
Aluminium Audi Space Frame: ASF; MacPherson spring-strut front suspension in aluminium; torsion beam rear suspension; front disc brakes, aluminium brake callipers, rear aluminium alloy drum brakes; ABS/EDL diagonally-split dual circuits; rack and pinion PAS; 175/55 R 16 tyres, 6J x 16 wheels.

DIMENSIONS
Wheelbase 240.6cm (94.7in), front track 143.0cm (56.3in), rear track 142.6cm (56.1in); length 376.5cm (148.2in), width 162.0cm (63.8in), height 155.7cm (61.3in).

PERFORMANCE
Maximum speed in excess of 170kph (106kph); 0-100kph (62mph) less than 12sec; 32.1kg/kW (23.6kg/bhp); average fuel consumption 65.7mpg (4.3l/100km).

AUDI S4 quattro; S4 quattro Avant 1997

20 years after the first tentative quattro made its way from design into production, the Biturbo 30-valve V-6 S4 introduced at Frankfurt in 1997 represented the apotheosis of the fast four wheel drive road car. On the basis of the A4 saloon and Avant estate car, the S4, like the original quattro, had an understated appearance except for additional intakes to gulp air into the two intercooled turbochargers running at up to 180,000rpm. The engine was the world's first production V6 with five valves per cylinder and two turbos, and combined enormous reserves of power and torque with the docile behaviour of a shopping car.

The S4's performance could be compared to the cars that won 7 saloon car-racing championships in 1996 with engines producing 290bhp (216kw). Despite being heavier than the stripped-out racers, the S4's 261bhp (195kw) gave near-track performance, even with top speed limited to 155mph (250kph). The S4 had air conditioning, front and side airbags, and upholstery in Alcantara or leather. S4 and S4 quattro were series-built on the Ingolstadt assembly lines, not hand-made in limited numbers by Porsche like previous RS2 Audis.

BODY

4 door saloon; 5 door estate; 5 seats; 1510kg (3329lb), estate 1540kg (3395lb).

ENGINE

6 cylinders in 90deg V; front; 81mm x 86.4mm; 2671cc, compr 9.3:1; 195kW (261bhp) @ 5800rpm; 73kW/l (97.9bhp/l); 400Nm (40.8mkp) @ 1850rpm.

ENGINE STRUCTURE

Overhead valves; 2 overhead cam; 5 valves per cyl; aluminium cyl head and block; 4 bearing crank; electronic fuel injection, two KKK turbochargers with intercoolers; water cooled.

TRANSMISSION

Permanent four wheel drive; central Torsen differential; 6 speed; synchromesh; electronic traction control; 4.11 final drive.

CHASSIS DETAILS

Monocoque steel structure; independent four-link front suspension; independent rear suspension by double wishbones; coil springs, telescopic dampers; disc brakes 30mm ventilated at front, 25mm rear; twin piston calipers; ABS and electronic brake distribution (EBS) standard; PAS; 62l (13.6 Imp gal) gal (16.3 US gal) fuel tank; 225/45R17W tyres, 7.5J x 17in 6-spoke Avus alloy wheels.

DIMENSIONS

Wheelbase 261cm (102.3in), front track 150cm (59.1in), rear 149cm (58.7in), ground clearance 11cm (4.3in), turning circle 11.4m (37.4ft), length 448cm (176.4in), width 173cm (68.1in), height 140cm (55.1in).

PERFORMANCE

Max speed 155mph (250kph); 25.8mph (41.4kph) @ 1000rpm; 0-100kph (62mph) 5.6sec (Avant 5.7sec); 7.7kg/kW (5.8kg/bhp), estate 7.9kg/kW (5.9kg/bhp); average fuel consumption 17.9-32.5mpg (8.7l-15.8l/100km).

AUDI A6 Avant 1998

True to tradition, once the A6 saloons were established, an Avant version was not far behind. Mechanically much the same as the saloons, the estate counterpart had the same three five-valve petrol engines and two diesels. These were a 1.8 litre turbocharged 4-cylinder, a 2.4 litre V6, and a 2.8-litre 144kw (193bhp) also being available with quattro four wheel drive. The diesels were a 1.9 litre TDI and a 2.5 litre four-valve TDI also available with quattro four wheel drive and an identical sports specification to the petrol A6 quattro Avant.

Compared to its predecessor of the same length, the 1998 Avant had more space and was only some 50kg (110lb) heavier. It had a luggage capacity of 1590 litres with the back seat folded and loaded to the roof. Luggage volume to the lower edges of the windows was 455 litres. The maximum payload was 580kg (1279lb), yet fuel consumption remained much the same as the saloon. The Avant featured the fully galvanised construction of the A6 saloon which was the first Audi to combine galvanised steel with aluminium for the bonnet and door frames, allowing the body warranty to be extended from 10 to 12 years.

2.4:
BODY
Saloon; 4 door; 5 seat; 1400kg (3086lb), 1450kg (3197lb) auto, 1495kg (3296lb) quattro, 1555kg (3428lb) auto quattro.

ENGINE
6-cylinders, in V; front, longitudinal; 81mm x 77.4mm; 2393cc; compr 10:1; 121kW (165bhp) @ 6000rpm; 50.6kW/l (68.7bhp/l); 230Nm (23.4mkp)@ 3200rpm.

ENGINE STRUCTURE
2ohc per bank, belt and chain-driven; hydraulic tappets; 5 valves; aluminium head; 4 bearing crank; Bosch Motronic; individual ignition coils; knock control; water cooled.

TRANSMISSION
Fwd; 5 speed gearbox; 3.889:1 final drive; optional ZF 5-speed automatic 2.727:1; optional quattro with torsen centre diff, 4.1113:1; automatic quattro 3.3:1

CHASSIS DETAILS
Galvanised steel; ifs 4-link in sub-frame, upper and lower wishbones, anti-roll bar; torsion crank rear, anti-roll bar; gas-pressure dampers; disc brakes, ventilated at front; dual diagonal circuits, servo; rack and pinion PAS; 70l (15.4 Imp gal) (18.5 US gal) fuel tank; tyres 195/65 R 15V, 6in rims.

DIMENSIONS
Wheelbase 276cm (108.6in), 275.9cm quattro (108.6in); front track 154cm (60.6in); rear track 156.9cm (61.77in); ground clearance 12cm (4.72in); turning circle 11.7m (38.4ft); length 479.6cm (188.8in); width 181cm (71.3in); height 145.3cm (57.2in).

PERFORMANCE
Max 138mph (222kph); 22.5mph (36.2kph) @ 1000rpm; 0-100kph (62mph) 9.1sec; 11.6kg/kW (8.5kg/bhp); 7.4-13.7l/100km (20.6-38.2mpg).

R71 PWL

Audi Press Office 0181

The A6 Avant was the basis of the Audi allroad quattro shown at the Detroit motor show in January 1998 (see facing page). Essentially an inflated A6 Avant, with wide Kevlar wheel-arches to accommodate wide wheels and tyres, it drew on Audi's rally experience to draw up a plan for a new sort of dual-purpose all-activity car. Its aim was to carry five occupants in great luxury on and off-road with the speed and agility of a rally car and the cross-country qualities of an agricultural vehicle.

The essential ingredient the A6 lacked was generous ground clearance. Audi's answer was air springs, which could raise or lower the body as required. At its lowest, the allroad quattro sat at about the level of the ordinary A6 with a clearance of 14.5cm (5.7in) to the ground. On the driver's command it could be raised to 19.5cm (7.6in), a match for many off-road leisure vehicles. Among the refinements built into the system was an arrangement for raising and lowering the car to ease access for passengers or loading. If the ground clearance still proved inadequate, the allroad quattro had a stout ribbed aluminium undershield. Tyres were fat Michelins, hand-cut on the prototype, on 17in wheels with two dual sets of alloy spokes. Kevlar was also used for the roof panel, making it strong enough to withstand carrying the stuff 4x4 owners seem to need; small boats, bikes, storage bins, shooting or fishing tackle, hampers, or camping gear. In customary Audi fashion, no detail was overlooked.

AUDI – Car of the Year

1968	Winner	Ro80
1973	Winner	Audi 80
1975	Third	Audi 50
1977	Second	Audi 100
1979	Third	Audi 80
1983	Winner	Audi 100
1987	Second	Audi 80
1996	Third	Audi A4

Acknowledgments and Bibliography

Research has been carried out with the co-operation of Audi, and the publishers would like to thank Len Hunt, former Director of Audi UK, for making this book possible, and to Richard Ide, MD Volkswagen Group United Kingdom Ltd, for encouraging the idea in the first place.

Thanks go to Audi press relations manager Natalie Dinsdale, press officer Janet Mills and press assistants Andrea Baker and Paula Gillard, and in Ingolstadt Judith Nitsch, Lothar Franz and Thomas Erdmann, for photographs and other assistance, as well as to Ralph Plagman for providing NSU information and pictures. We are indebted to Peter Noad, specialist in Audi, Volkswagen, NSU, Auto Union and DKW for carrying out painstaking revisions, and our thanks also go Martin Lewis for research, to Clive Richardson for help and advice, and to Neill Bruce, Julian Mackie and the National Motor Museum who helped supply photographs.

Particular thanks go to David Bann, Andrew Barron, Diane Lappage, Gordon Rennie, and to family and friends, for their support and assistance.

'A History of Progress' Audi AG PR Ingolstadt, 1992; 'Porsche, Excellence was Expected' Karl Ludvigsen, Princeton Publishing, 1977; 'Cars are my Life' Ferry Porsche and Günther Molter, PSL, 1989; 'Complete Encyclopedia of Motorcars' ed G N Georgano, Ebury 1982; 'Encyclopaedia of Motor Sport' ed G N Georgano, Ebury and Michael Joseph 1971; 'Classic Car Profiles', ed Anthony Harding, Profile Publications 1960s; 'Alle Horch Automobile 1900-1945' Werner Oswald, Motorbuch Verlag 1979; 'Complete History of the German Car' Jan P Norbye, Portland House, 1987; 'The Motor Year Books' Temple Press, 1949-1957; 'Automobile Revue Catalogue to 1998' Hallwag Automobile Year 1954-1998, JR Editions; 'The Grand Prix Car' Laurence Pomeroy, Motor Racing Publications 1955-1956; 'Quicksilver, Development of German Grand Prix racing cars' Cameron Earl 1948, 1996 HMSO. Among magazines: part work *On The Road,* and *The Motor, The Autocar, Autosport,* and *Motor Sport, Classic car, Classic & Sportscar,* and *Veteran & Vintage,* to whose proprietors' motoring historians we owe continuing thanks.

Index